TOURISM
IN
HISTORY

TOURISM IN HISTORY

From Imperial Rome to the Present

Maxine Feifer

STEIN AND DAY / *Publishers* / New York

First published in the United States of America in 1986
Copyright © 1985 by Maxine Feifer
All rights reserved, Stein and Day, Incorporated
Printed in the United States of America
STEIN AND DAY/ *Publishers*
Scarborough House
Briarcliff Manor, N.Y. 10510

Library of Congress Cataloging-in-Publication Data

Feifer, Maxine, 1947-
  Tourism in history.

  Previously published in Great Britain under title:
Going places.
  Bibliography: p.
  Includes index.
  1. Tourism trade—History.   I. Title.
G155.A1F36   1986   380.1'459104   85-40968
ISBN 0-8128-3087-3

For my parents.

Contents

Introduction

The idea of writing this book came to me first at the Hôtel Mère Poulard at Mont St Michel in Normandy. In the midst of dinner one evening, the guests rose as one and adjourned to the hearth in the foyer. There they stood watching a young man with a wire whisk who was preparing omelettes. He looked, as far as I could see, like anybody else would look preparing omelettes. But the hotel's namesake, Mère Poulard, was famous for her omelettes' creamy consistency; they're now a gastronomic speciality of the town. So even though there's nothing to *see* in their preparation, people stand and watch. The event has become mystified by the curious process that tourism brings into play: set up by the travel writer and framed by the camera, other people's ordinary lives are transformed into exotic entertainment, history into myth. There was also something singularly *modern* about it: who but "alienated" twentieth-century urbanites would be mystified by somebody whisking eggs (a kind of reversal of the savage astounded by a cigarette lighter)?

Mont St Michel itself is visited for its famous monastery, standing on a granite outcrop in the sea where the tide whips in at phenomenal speeds. It is a consummate piece of architecture, showing every style from early Romanesque to late Gothic, and the site of a particularly dramatic pilgrimage, where pilgrims wade out into the swirling waters to reach the craggy tip of the peninsula. Now, though, the point can be reached by a causeway. And all along the narrow, twisting street that leads to the top there are crêperies, Coca Cola stands, and tourist boutiques selling gimcrack souvenirs. The street is so choked with tourists that one can hardly get to the top. More modern blight: overcrowding, voyeurism, destruction of the delicate tissue of the past. The tourist has come all this way to see something venerable, beautiful, and above all different – and what he finds, principally, is an atmosphere of other tourists: the modern plight.

So it came as a particular surprise to learn that Mont St Michel has been mobbed with tourists and choked with souvenir and "fast-food" stands for nearly a thousand years. The tourists have been complaining about each other all that time. It casts a different light on the twentieth-century tourist, and a different light on the venerable past, too.

The Shorter Oxford English Dictionary defines the tourist as "one who travels for pleasure or culture, visiting a number of places". More and more people are tourists. Tourism is one of the biggest growth industries in the modern industrial world and has enjoyed that status for over twenty years. Yet nobody wants to be called a tourist.

"Traveller" is the preferred appellation, connoting independence, *savoir-faire*. A traveller may be a loner or an explorer, but a tourist is following a programme. He's using one culture's set of instructions for sampling the delights of another culture. To be a traveller is, in the broad sense, an occupation; but the tourist is on holiday from his normal life. He wants to be taken out of himself, to get at the exotically foreign (thus the history of the tourist is a history of exotica, too). But, as the word "tour" derives from "tower", the trip is circular: he ends up back where he started.

As an exponent of leisure and mobility, the tourist seems pre-eminently modern. But ours is not the first society to have produced tourists. The word "tourist" itself was coined by Stendhal in the early nineteenth century, and there were numerous tourists among the ancient Romans, complete with guidebooks, cheap souvenirs, tourist traps, garrulous touts, and bikini beaches; tourists have reappeared periodically ever since (in a continuous and broadening stream for the last hundred years), variously seeking culture and pleasure according to the lights of their time. Thus what is sacred in one era becomes a curiosity in another; and later, it turns into art. The tourist's itinerary throughout the ages also describes what one society makes of another, comparative culture. And it provides information on ordinary life at home, by detailing what the tourist must seek elsewhere. Following the tourist through history makes a kind of package tour of the past, with all the delectations laid out in sequence, and all the paradoxes that have always attended on trying for the best of both worlds.

The dictionary definition of a tourist is a broad one; what the name "tourist" *suggests* has a narrower sense. But my aim hasn't been to produce an academic study, nor an encyclopaedia of tourism. What has interested me has been to trace the ancestry of the present-day Western Anglo-Saxon tourist – that is to say, most readers of this book – to see where his habits and tastes began historically and how they've moved through time: the book is intended as a history of style, a thematic history, but especially as an entertainment. So there's been no attempt to include everything germane to the tourist – but, rather, to get a "line".

There were a number of tourists from the Arab world in the Middle Ages, who went about seeing the sights of Asia with travelling harems in caravans, stopping in the shade for a mint julep when they wanted a break. In China and Japan, there were tourists well back into antiquity, who went especially to visit scenes of natural beauty, sometimes travelling hundreds of miles to stand before a waterfall or a cherry tree, whereas nature tourism did not appear in the West until the nineteenth century. But these traditions have been independent of Europe; and among Europeans, the present book has been drawn most strongly from the touristic annals of the English. The choice was not altogether determined by circumstance, though: for centuries England has produced most interesting and "representative" tourists.

Since my aim was to write an entertainment, my method has been to create a prototypical tourist for each epoch and to follow him on a "typical" tour composed of what real-life tourists did and saw. So each tour is, strictly speaking, a fiction (except the last one, where I speak for myself). But all the elements, the socio-geographic details as well as the opinions and reactions, have been drawn from factual research, not from invention.

In order to stay as close as possible to the tourist, I have written the tourist's story in the third person singular. While it is true that males have been tourists in every touristic epoch, and women have not, nonetheless my reason for referring to the tourist as "he", except in some special cases, has been for the sake of formal simplicity. So I hope that no reader's feminist allegiances will be affronted on that score.

The tourist of the past could not have known what twentieth-

4

century social scientists were going to say about him. So it seemed inappropriate to interrupt my narrative with analytical quotes from modern writers. But I must acknowledge an enormous conceptual debt to particular writers whose names do not appear in the text: E. S. Bates, Fernand Braudel, Lionel Casson, Francine du Plessix Gray, Clare Howard, Earle Dean MacCannel, Peter Quennel, Susan Sontag, Jonathan Sumption, Edmund Swinglehurst, and Louis Turner and John Ashe. And I am spiritually indebted to Mic Cheetham, Jo Lynch, Alan Samson, Cherryl Searle, and especially my parents, without whom I'd have lost faith and called off the tour.

TOURISM
IN
HISTORY

CHAPTER ONE

The Imperial Roman

The year is AD 130. The place is Thebes, in Egypt, by the colossal broken stone statue of Pharaoh Amenhotep III. The hour is shortly after dawn. Even though it's early, a crowd of souvenir merchants is pressing forward. They proffer the usual mementoes: little flasks of Nile water, terracotta replicas of the statue. But the merchants are elbowed aside to make way for a royal party: Emperor Hadrian, his queen Sabina, and assorted companions, attendants and guards. The Roman visitors have sailed all the way up the Nile to see Egypt's most talked-about sight, the speaking statue. Every morning at this time, since the earthquake of 27 BC when its top fell off, the statue has emitted a cry, something like the snapping of a lute string. It must be the gods talking, or at least a freak of nature – either way, not to be missed.

The party makes its way up to the statue's enormous feet, which are covered in graffiti left by previous visitors, most of them chiselled in neo-Homeric Greek verse. Then the priest-guide goes into his usual spiel. Any minute now, promises the priest, comforting words for his bereaved mother will be uttered by Memnon (formerly Amenhotep, now renamed according to Roman mythology).

Those among the visitors of a sentimental bent are charmed by the notion. Empress Sabina's attendant poetess, Julia Balbilla, even goes one better than the legend with the suggestion that today Memnon will be courting "that lovable beauty" Sabina herself. The better educated, though, regard the priest's fanciful interpretation with a tolerant smile. They've read the geographer Strabo's section on Memnon (Strabo suspected a hoax).

Everybody waits. Memnon keeps silent. At that juncture, Seneca's pronouncement on tourism must have seemed doubly appropriate: "Such long travels and so many changes of scene have not been able to shake off the gloom and heaviness of your mind." For already the blight of boredom was well known to plague sophisticated Roman travellers. In fact, Imperial Roman tourism had nearly all of the trappings of its late-twentieth-century counterpart, even to the final ironies.

(Next day, however, Memnon was more obliging and broke his silence. Julia Balbilla was sure his earlier dumb show was just a ruse to get Sabina to return alone, without Hadrian. The poetess set the whole incident in classic rhyme, and hired a local stonecutter to inscribe her verses in one of Memnon's feet.)

Strictly speaking, the Romans were not the first to "travel for pleasure or culture, visiting a number of places". Herodotus the Greek, who travelled in the fifth century BC, has often been called the first tourist because he went everywhere, just to gratify his curiosity. Herodotus saw everything, from the temple at Karnak, where his only aesthetic observation was that "it was large", to a birthday party in Persia – pickled duck and barley wine were served, and the host circulated with the replica of a corpse, to encourage his guests to reflect upon mortality. However, Herodotus was a unique phenomenon, part of no larger social movement. Nobody else travelled in that manner, just to have a look around, until many hundreds of years later.

Also in the centuries just before Christ's birth there was wide travel among the Greeks across their own land, to the sacred games. But that didn't constitute genuine tourism either. It was on their home ground, it rarely included stops for sightseeing and, most important, it had not the quality of escape, for the traveller remained within his own culture and within the culture's sacred context – a context from which there would have been no wish to escape, from all that is known of the golden age. The first culture genuinely to produce mass tourism, in both the letter and the spirit of the term, was Imperial Rome. In the second century AD, it was at its peak.

Second-century Rome teemed. There were narrow streets, tall apartment buildings, a continual din of commerce and contention. The rich lived on the upper storeys with central heating and plumbing, but the poor were crowded into low tenements with no "mod cons", and the stench of their streets was notorious. At night the city was rife with mugging and rape. Often the perpetrators were young aristocrats who went slumming in gangs, disguised in thugs' caps. Clandestine violent crime had been a favourite pastime of the Emperor Nero, who hurled his stabbed victims into the sewers, and once opened a market stall stocked entirely with items he had stolen. Rome was just the sort of place to drive one out of town for a vacation.

Then, too, the Romans had a distinct concept of leisure and amusement – unlike their predecessors, for whom celebration had a sacred aspect. They were avid party-givers and great gourmands. They talked endlessly and passionately about food, and staged banquets featuring such delicacies as sausage smoked over pomegranate and damson, beef stuffed with live quails, and dormouse with poppyseed and honey; to be sure of maintaining an appetite, one disposed of previous courses in the *vomitorium*; and for after-dinner entertainment there were acrobats practising archery with their feet, tumblers, mimes, wanton buffoons, and naked Spanish ladies with castanets dancing on the tables.

Diversions were not only lavish, they were frequent. In some years, more than a third of the days were marked off on the calendar as holidays. Then the populace flocked to the games where, besides chariot races and shows of skill, they might see the whole arena flooded with saltwater, stocked with sea creatures and a flotilla of battleships, and a thunderstorm simulated for a naval battle (most ships would be sunk); Orpheus in a man-made moving forest, mangled to death by a bear (not an enactment, but the real thing – the actor was a condemned criminal); or a safari with giraffes, ostriches, lions, and other exotic beasts from Africa in a reconstructed jungle; while in between main events men tore each other apart with their bare hands, or slavewomen wrestled grotesquely with dwarfs.

Predictably, the sensibilities grew jaded. No wonder, reasoned Seneca, that tourism developed. He opined, "Men travel widely to different sorts of places seeking different distractions because they are fickle, tired of soft living, and always seek after something which eludes them."

The mood was ripe. But also optimum for the development of tourism was the Pax Romanus: two hundred years of peace, unprecedented in the world's history, all subsumed under the Roman Empire. It meant one could travel from Hadrian's Wall to the Euphrates without crossing a hostile border. Often the way was easy, for there was an extensive system of wide, well-marked, well-paved roads – a carriage ride was frequently smoother in the second century than in the eighteenth. Lines of communication were open throughout the Empire. Inns accommodated the many travelling functionaries and traders. In short, the "touristic infrastructure" was excellent. The obelisks of Egypt, the statuary of Greece, spoils of the conquests of Alexander the Great, stood on display along the boulevards and in the circuses all over Rome, whetting the prospective tourist's appetite to go to the source.

Still, travel was slow, and few were permitted long periods away from work. So tourism to faraway cultural attractions usually had to be combined with other purposes – mainly military, though wives and children were allowed to go along. But there was ample opportunity for shorter pleasure jaunts when the Senate had its spring recess and again during the government closure in autumn – ideal weather for a vacation. Then the vast population of bureaucrats and officials, solvent, urbane, and not tied to the land, was free to go off for several weeks of sightseeing and relaxation.

Beyond that minimal demographic profile, the Imperial Roman tourist cannot be known directly, since there are almost no surviving reports (travel diaries, letters) of his daily activities on tour. His character can only be inferred, from the writings of the great social commentators of his age, on the one hand; and from the artefacts and structures of his daily social usage, on the other. By those traces, the family-style Roman tourist of the imperial age, eating oysters on the Bay of Naples, may be imagined as having much in common with his remote descendant the late-twentieth-century package tourist, the one who saw the whole world as his oyster. After his long confinement in the "office", the Roman was determined to pack as much pleasure and diversion as possible into his time off. For while he did not question the superiority of Roman methods and the urban lifestyle, still the sense of having everything down pat must have had its portion of emptiness: he was dying for something different to divert him. He also expected the machinery of the world to run smoothly: his diversions and pleasures had to be promptly delivered. Though he was on holiday to escape being serious, he was serious about getting what he wanted, and impatient when he didn't.

The Latin word for the holiday excursion was *peregrinatio*, and the popular destination was the Bay of Naples, the Italian Riviera. Just over a hundred miles from Rome, it was four days' journey down the Via Domitiana to something quite different: bikini beach parties at Baiae, cosmopolitan harbour life at Puteoli, and Grecian high culture at Naples.

Preparations were elaborate. Since vehicles were banned from Rome, the tourist had to hire one at the city gates, or have his own brought round. There were carriages to suit every purse: the modest two-wheeled *birota* for one or two travellers, the light gig called a *cisium* for a small middle-class party, or the simple, square, open *raeda* for larger groups. And by adding ornamental canopy supports and silk curtains, one could turn one's *raeda* into a luxury *carpentum*. Further amenities could be added, like swivel seats and milometers. But all carriages gave a bumpy ride, with their wooden wheels and iron tyres. So the "best people" had themselves transported in a litter; each litter was carried by eight slaves and featured detachable straps in case a laggard slave required an impromptu thrashing.

Such inns as there were could not be suffered by tourists of the upper echelon. Some bought little rest lodges called *diversoria*, spaced at intervals along the way – not much more than shacks, but at least they were exclusive. Others camped out in truly noble fashion. The entire household of servants came along to create a "home away from home": maids, valets, chefs, costumed slaves, love-boy pages with masks to protect their delicate complexion. There were silken tents, bedding and commodes, complete cook-ware, gold platters and crystal goblets – the more fragile pieces were carried individually by slaves, a procession of precious plate and glassware. As in later epochs, the vacation was an occasion for the most opulent "conspicuous consumption". (Privately, the tourist raged to his wife that he might have to sell himself into gladiatorial servitude because of what it had cost just *getting* to the coast.)

If necessary, the tourist and his family could always find some kind of public accommodation, with the government system of modest inns all along the major roads (another important feature of "secondary touristic infrastructure"). With an *itinerarium* – a kind of prototypical Michelin map – the party knew in advance what amenities each inn offered: a square within a square (symbolizing a courtyard) signified a first-class inn, supplying grooms, porters, cartwrights, even veterinarians; two triangles surmounting a rect-angle (a country house) was less fancy; a triangle atop a square was most rudimentary – just a shelter and water. Even at the best country inns, though, there was no luxury. Room décor featured a bed and a candelabra; one's own servants generally did the cooking; and for entertainment there was only the complaisant chambermaid (if the tourist was a man on his own).

Still, it was not for the pleasures of the roadside that the Roman tourist went on *peregrinatio*. While he found changing scenery agreeable, it was a mild sort of enjoyment. But by the sea the pleasures were rich and varied. It was maritime cities, warned Cicero, that posed the greatest moral danger, precisely because they had so much charm.

Most dangerously charming of all the Riviera towns was Baiae, the "golden shore of Venus", in Martial's slogan. (The tourist was pleased to quote Martial's line for his wife as their *carpentum* approached the city.) Baiae was notorious as the resort of "impure and pure delights" for the rich and dissolute. Besides the "beautiful people", Baiae attracted crowds of others, who came to stare at them and partake of the other seaside pleasures, much like Riviera resorts of the present day. Wide-eyed, the middle-class tourists dismounted from their *cisia* and set out to find a boarding-house – not an inn, though the town had plenty of both; as a haunt of gamblers and prostitutes, the inn was no place to go for a family vacation. Not even at the boarding-house, unfortunately, could the tourist escape the bedbugs. However, to experience Baiae in the fullness of its sybaritic reputation, one really had to stay at a villa. All the "best people" owned them, or at least had friends to invite them down for a spring vacation.

Vacation villas first appeared on the Bay of Naples two hundred years before the birth of Christ, and by the second century AD development was at its peak. The dry, scrubby shores had been painstakingly transformed into verdant tiers and covered with many-porticoed white stone houses facing the sea. They dotted the higher slopes and clustered close up against each other on the prime sites at the water's edge, as dense as the hotels of Miami or Torremolinos now. In some places the underwater surface was black from landfilling.

Inside, the villas were cool, dark and restful, with small windows to keep out the sun. But one spent as much time outdoors as possible and that was where wealth and luxury were best displayed. After an effusive welcome, the tourist and his wife would be shown about: they would stroll admiringly down tree-lined avenues and formal gardens – sometimes irrigated with wine instead of water – stopping to exclaim over the glassed-in baths, ball courts, fancy fountains, and heated swimming pools. Most spectacular of all were the fishponds. It was by the attentions he lavished on his fish that the scion of a villa let his neighbours know what stuff he was made of. The Lady Antonia adorned her fish with gold jewellery. Domitian had a famous pet fish that swam up to be caressed. Horace displayed his great sensibility by weeping when one of his fish was eaten, although it was common practice to raise fish for the table. And one Vedius Pollo made the ultimate gesture towards his eels by feeding them a live human slave. The tourists looked and listened, patted the favoured dolphin on the head, and made their host glad he had invited them.

Next day, the typical round began, a series of effortless delectations. If the tourist's bedroom was one of those built out over the sea, he might start his morning with a spot of fishing before he even got out of bed – all he had to do was extend a fishing pole out of the window. Next, perhaps, he would go out for a dip. There was a particular *frisson* in watching the rough ocean waves while one swam in a heated pool. Soon it would be time for lunch, a prolonged affair if there were guests from another house-party. The ladies were delightful in silks from the island of Kos – the height of seaside chic – and, crowned with a garland of roses, one could spend all afternoon drinking under the plane trees.

Other days, the litter-bearers carried the visitors into town for a promenade around the Lucrine Lake, or along the beach, or perhaps up to see someone else's famous fishpond (the more elaborate ones were popular attractions, open to the public). Or there might be a sail on a friend's yacht, under silken, fringed canopies that kept off sun and flies (the middle classes rented rowing boats). Every tourist at Baiae also visited the great sulphur hot springs. They were housed in an enormous marble complex of fountains, basins, terraces, stairways and avenues, and crowded with itinerant jugglers, food-sellers, masseurs, beauty experts, and hordes of holiday bathers – despite Seneca's admonition that "perspiration should flow only after toil".

The wealthy tourist wouldn't eat at a restaurant, though Baiae was crowded with them, little places where one sat at the counter for sausage or plain roast meat, a hunk of bread, and a cup of watered wine. But nobody failed to sample the famous oysters from the Lucrine Lake beds, bred by a special saltwater process (developed by

Sergius Orata, an early real-estate speculator who also invented the shower-bath). And as a final commemoration of a day by the shore at Baiae, the tourist might buy his wife a little glass phial with a schematic picture of the lighthouse, pools, parks, and oyster beds: hardly art, but amusing.

At night, after the family-style tourists went to bed, Baiae really proved its reputation. That was the time for moonlight sailing parties on the lake, with drinking bouts, wild music, nude swimming, sex with strangers. When Nero came to Baiae, he ordered a series of floating brothels stocked with noblewomen to be set in the water for the occasion. But any time during the season there were plenty of naughty ladies – and naughty boys made up to look like ladies – cruising around Baiae. Seneca had the last word:

I make the best of Baiae. I left it the day after I arrived. . . . Can you imagine that Cato would ever have lived in a bijou villa just to keep tally of the unfaithful wives sailing by, of the gaily painted craft . . . of the roses bobbing on every ripple of the lagoon, and listen to the nocturnal caterwauling of those who were moved to song?

Fortunately for those of more sober tastes, Puteoli, most urbane of the Riviera towns, was just along the coast. The tourist came into Puteoli when he felt like a day in the city, much as a twentieth-century beach vacationer might. There he could do his banking and take care of business affairs. He could enjoy the cosmopolitan atmosphere of the dockyards, admiring boats from all over the Mediterranean, watching the unloading of cargo, mixing with the crowds that always gathered when the ships came in. There was also an arena where he and his wife might see some gladiatorial combat (women attended the blood sports as avidly as men). Announcements of coming attractions were painted on the arena's outside wall, but real *aficionados* kept well informed of where their favourite gladiators would be performing and often scheduled a tour to coincide with one they especially wanted to see. Puteoli arena was not big enough to be flooded for a naval battle, but there were plenty of gory spectacles, and the celebrities appeared there regularly. The agreeably scandalized tourist and his wife might also catch sight of a few audacious noblewomen, scathingly called *gladiatrixes*, who travelled with the team to be near one of the combatants. Oblivious of their reputation, the gladiatrixes writhed in their seats and called out to their favourites in the ring. Since the show was continuous and there was plenty of food for sale, the tourists would make a day of it.

Then, on to the east was Naples, the cultural resort, a bit of ancient Greece, the "Old World". The virile, if not brutal, Roman civilization was one that looked backwards for high culture to the golden age of Greece. There reposed sacredness, art, grace of living – safely over and done with, revered with a touch of melancholy nostalgia. Greek culture for the Romans was "precious", in both the positive and the pejorative senses of the word. The Greeks, after all, were a conquered people, Roman subjects. The generals and businessmen of Rome looked on the artists and philosophers of Greece with a combination of respect and contempt; they took their wives to the theatre, but they snorted at the "effeminate Greek". It was a double view most favourable to tourism, encouraging the desire to sample another culture, but not too seriously.

Naples had been founded by Greeks, and still had a sizeable Greek population; most of them happened to be corn merchants, but the imagination could easily transform them into something more quaint. There, the tourist lived *à la grecque*: speaking Greek and dressing in the Greek-casual mode of household tunic and *chlamys* (long shawl) instead of the usual toga. At villa house-parties, the poetry dinner (recitations of verse between courses) was particularly appropriate. Naples had a Greek-style gymnasium (athletics were also part of the Greek heritage) and a Greek theatre where dance and music festivals were held. It was there that the Emperor Nero, a great *philhellene* who dreamed passionately of the heroic past, had given his first musical performance, a trial run before he went on stage in Greece itself. Dressed in a long green robe and plucking the strings of a harp, he made sure his aria received the proper reception by placing a claque of 1500 "Augustals" in the audience. They were trained to respond in an apparently spontaneous manner that was in fact carefully orchestrated with applause, murmurs, exclamations and castanets at the appropriate junctures.

A thriving literary colony was in residence at Naples, the city of Virgil; and a large retirement community, especially for elderly scholars. For the tourist, Naples provided an ideal journey into the golden past – and one could be back in Rome in just a few days.

If the Roman citizen could ever afford a longer trip, it was the same golden past that especially beckoned: to classical Greece, Homeric Troy, and ancient Mother Egypt. As the decadence of

Rome deepened, the age of heroes and gods was more and more exalted in the Roman imagination. The tourist wanted to stand on the great historic sites – and the mythological sites, too, for he drew no clear distinction between them – and then to see the great artistic representations of myth and history by the old masters.

The Roman cultural tourist was literate; he knew something beforehand about what he was going to see. He had already read Herodotus, part of a cultured person's required reading in any case. But after its publication towards the end of the second century, the *Guide to Greece*, by Pausanias, was the definitive guidebook. Painstaking in method, prosaic in style, conservative in taste (for Pausanias, the finest Greek art came from the fifth century BC), soberly questioning the myths but with a deep sentimental appreciation of mythology, Pausanias told the philhellenic Roman tourist what he particularly wanted to know. Every important architectural feature and work of art was described, every significant inscription was copied (nineteenth-century travellers still found Pausanias unsurpassed): if not entertaining, eminently useful.

His reading done – it had to be done ahead of time, because the big leather-bound papyrus volumes were too heavy and too valuable to carry along – the tourist prepared to book passage abroad. Nearest to home and richest in treasures was Greece – the pantheon of gods and heroes was prodigious, and each was commemorated many times over in landmarks and works of art. From Rome to the Gulf of Corinth the journey took from one to two weeks, depending on how the wind blew.

Passenger ships were not to appear until the nineteenth century; the tourist had to travel by cargo boat. He found a ship by wandering about the docks at Ostia (near Rome) or Puteoli, enquiring for vessels bound in his direction. The official sailing season was from mid-March until mid-November, though few boats left before May. Around the time of departure the tourist and his entourage would book into a harbour inn, to be within hearing of the ship's herald when the moment to leave was cried in port. Sailing dates were imprecise, always subject to changes in the wind. Then, barring last-minute bad omens – a passenger sneezing on the gangplank, a crow in the rigging, a crew member dreaming of big black goats – a sheep or bull would be sacrificed and the ship would set sail.

The tourist boarded a wooden vessel powered by a large square mainsail, capacious but slow. Since there was no passenger accommodation, he would bring his own wine, food, and cookware, plus servants to prepare meals; he also took along a small sleeping-tent, which a servant erected each night on deck. There was little to worry about on the journey: thanks to the Pax Romanus, the seas were free of pirates – another essential element of good touristic infrastructure. The only peril was from storms. The Romans considered seasickness beneficial to the health, so the tourist was braced to bear that discomfort stoically.

The first attraction came into view as the ship sailed through the Straits of Messina, alongside Sicily: the live volcano of Mount Etna, one of the few natural wonders on the tourist's itinerary. The smoking crater, full of fire and brimstone, had to be an entranceway to Hell – a freak of nature and a glimpse of the spirit world, fascinating on two counts. So, if he could, the tourist stopped and climbed up for a closer look.

Climbing Etna was exceptional; the urbane Roman was no mountaineer. Unlike tourists of later epochs who have sought out the difficult to prove their mettle, the Roman took it easy when he could. Nor did he find mountains beautiful – Roman taste in landscape favoured *amoenitas*: gentle, decorous "charm", symmetrical and mild. Hadrian was most atypical; he climbed Etna because he wanted to see the sunrise. (On another occasion when Hadrian climbed a mountain for the sunrise it was put about that he would have served Rome better by staying at home with a book of philosophy.) The dreaded Emperor Caligula was so scared by Etna's rumbling that he sailed straight past without stopping at all.

Everyone, however, stopped at Delphi, the first major visit on the Grecian tour. Delphi was the sanctuary of Apollo, and in the second century AD it was still thriving, attracting visitors from all over the Empire. On arrival, the tourist made a ritual sacrifice to the god and then had the oracle tell his fortune. He didn't receive the message in the reverent meditative spirit of his Grecian predecessors – he was, rather, more like a twentieth-century follower of newspaper horoscopes – but he was still very curious, and his wife was especially so.

His devotions done, the visitor would turn next to a general tour of the temples and grounds. With centuries' accumulation of precious offerings, Delphi was like a vast museum; even Pausanias admitted that nobody could possibly take in all of it. There were countless statues displayed outdoors – victorious kings commissioned whole series at a time to give thanks for their triumphs in war. Shields hung on architraves and friezes, and one colonnade was studded with mastheads taken by Athens in the Peloponnese. Inside the temples were more fragile and valuable items. There were mytho-historic curiosities, like the iron chair of the poet Pindar and a necklace of Helen of Troy. There were famous paintings, and there was sheer loot: the most philistine of tourists could not have failed to admire a gold lion weighing 375 pounds, nearly a ton of gold bowls, and the gold throne that once belonged to the fabled King Midas. Sacred objects, *objets d'art*, oddities, wealth: the distinctions were unclear, but the Roman's taste embraced all of it.

He might have liked to meditate on the treasury in a vague, poetic way, for he enjoyed sentiment. But he never had a quiet moment to do it, because Delphi was mobbed with guides. One couldn't escape them. Without being asked, they spouted historical fact and mythological conjecture nonstop. They even described invisible attractions, like the empty spot where, supposedly, a famous courtesan had once dedicated an outdoor barbecue. The satirist Lucian, however, thought the tourist had it coming; he declared, "Abolish fabulous tales from Greece and the guides there would all die of starvation, since no tourist wants to hear the true facts, even for nothing." Etiquette required tipping the guide, and it was also the most effective way of getting him to be quiet.

After Delphi, the next important stop was Athens. By the second century AD Athens had been a famous place to visit for over six hundred years. It was written in the fifth century BC:

> If you've never seen Athens, your brain's a morass.
> If you've seen it and weren't entranced, you're an ass.
> If you left it without regrets, your head's solid brass.

The Roman tourist couldn't fail to rise to the occasion.

The city tour started with a walk up the hill of the Acropolis, with a pause to stand where the mythological King Aegeas leapt to his death in the sea (henceforth called the Aegean), a truly "immortal" feat, since the distance spanned several miles. The view was staggeringly beautiful, too, but the visitor was less inspired by that. Like the mountaintop, it was too grand and imposing, not the kind of sweet scenery he favoured. And since the gods, too, were thought to prefer intimate settings, there was nothing "divine" about sweeping vistas

– they just conveyed emptiness. So, not wanting to linger over "nothing", the tourist continued on to the Parthenon, great repository of the art of antiquity. He stood looking at it, in its fullness of culture, "his" heritage, and felt he had arrived.

The temples and statues of Greece didn't always have the pristine, classical simplicity so admired by visitors. Originally the temples were painted many colours and gilded profusely, and statues often had glass or gemstone eyes, real clothes, gold beards, and marble wigs. Like all religiously inspired art, they were meant to invoke the real thing: the vivid presence and literal power of the gods. But the Imperial Roman tourist, already somewhat lapsed in his faith, found Greek art most artistic when it was refined with a patina of old age, romantically dim and distant. Arrived at the Parthenon, he asked especially where he could find the Praxiteles, the Myrons, the Appeles, the Phidias, all at least five centuries old.

He sighed agreeably over their quality of faded remoteness. Still, he wanted the *content* to seem believable: the tourist was by no means so cut off from his past as to view it all as fanciful nonsense. Pausanias, while deeply admiring what he saw on the Acropolis, still found himself disturbed by the unrealistic subject matter. Why did the painting of Ditriphus show him shot full of arrows when the ancient Greeks never used arrows? Where exactly could one meet a real satyr? He asked the guides but, while rarely at a loss for words, they were disinclined to interrupt their prepared speeches and consider such questions. To get the explanations he wanted, the tourist usually had to track down a priest (but few, besides Pausanias, ever bothered).

Nevertheless, what the Roman visitor to Athens lost in simple faith he made up for with detached aesthetic pleasure, and then with the simple pleasure of having arrived. He was not disappointed by the Acropolis. As a souvenir of his visit, the serious – or wealthy – art lover bought a miniature replica of Phidias' "Athena", emblem of Athens. Or, for a simple memento, it is believed that there were quick-sketch artists on the site to depict the tourist against a backdrop of Grecian pillars: the prototype of a holiday snap.

More than artistic representations of great men and events, the tourist wanted to experience great presence itself, or its lingering aura. Most esteemed of all Athens' attractions were the graves and dwellings of the heroes, places imbued with the noble or the divine. From history, the tourist visited the houses of Socrates,

Demosthenes, Alcibiades. Then he paid homage to the many graves of mythological figures, pre-eminently that of Odysseus. As Atticus put it, "My darling Athens attracts me not so much for her Greek buildings and monuments of ancient art as for her great men, where they dwelled, sat, talked, and lie buried." Standing where the great had stood, the Imperial Roman considered the barbarians, who were even then trampling his golden past into oblivion. He felt a shiver of poignant gratitude that he'd been able to see it before it all disappeared.

From that high point, the tourist wandered down over the peninsula to the other great cities of classical Greece. Some of the way he might take a carriage; elsewhere the narrow, rocky paths obliged him to travel on foot. He dressed for all weather: a wide-brimmed leather hat, good boots or sandals, and over his tunic a light cape or in case of rain a leather, knee-length, hooded *paenula* (the woman's version reached her ankles).

For accommodation, there was the usual choice between rough country inns and camping out (the servants carried equipment), unless one was lucky enough to have friends-of-friends in the villages one was passing. In that case, one would surely be offered a fine dinner and the guest room, for the ancient code absolutely required extending hospitality to worthy strangers. It was this requirement which brought on the first instance of a town ruined by tourism: on the beach at Hippo Diarrhytus, in Tunisia, a tame dolphin appeared that allowed a schoolboy to ride on its back. The dolphin attracted many visitors, and the townspeople were obliged to put them up and feed them, at great expense. "Finally," wrote Pliny the Younger, "the place was losing its character of peace and quiet. It was then decided that the object of the public's interest should be quietly destroyed."

The scenery was generally splendid, albeit of secondary interest. However, with Pausanias one could identify more certifiable attractions in the countryside, evocatively abandoned amidst the foliage: a broken statue in a meadow of flowering yarrow, a marble bust in a field of sheep – the perfect setting, to the nostalgic Roman sensibility. In places like Olympia and Epidaurus the treasures were thickly massed, and the sacred presence was most powerful.

Unique on the itinerary was Sparta. Sparta, too, boasted art and curios from the fabulous past: suspended from the roof of one temple was the giant hatched egg of Leda the swan, fertilized by Zeus, whence Helen of Troy had emerged – so went the orthodox legend, though sceptics suggested it must have been an ostrich egg. But the chief attraction of Sparta was a bizarre contemporary spectacle, the festival of Artemis. That was blood sport with a difference. After the preliminary sacrifice of a wild boar to predict the outcome of the competition, and of several puppies to appease the gods of war, the first event was the Feast of Naked Boys, where the flower of Spartan youth danced. Then, in a sportsground surrounded by moats, the fight took place, with biting, kicking, gouging out of eyes. It was often known for boys to die during the trial by whipping. The fact that the boys were aristocrats, and that the sacred significance of the festival was still intact for the Spartans, must have added an extra edge to the Romans' cruel enjoyment. Then the tourist switched modes and put himself in a Homeric frame of mind for Troy, in Asia Minor, a short journey eastwards across the water.

More than any other artist, Homer was the one who gave shape to the heroic Greek past. Both in content and in style, the past lived in Homer's writings. No image was more satisfying, more exalting to the Roman imagination, than one from the *Odyssey* or the *Iliad*; Pausanias' highest words of praise were "just the way Homer describes it". Time merely enhanced the effect, and just to stand on the ground where the great events had transpired was well worth the trip, even if there wasn't much to see.

A wall-less town of mud huts, Troy became a major centre of tourism in the Imperial Age. It was actively promoted by the government: Julius Caesar, who reckoned he was directly of the lineage of the Trojan hero Aeneas, had granted Troy independence and tax exemption, as well as added territory; later, Claudius bestowed the ancient prototype of an "arts grant".

The tourist had to go on a guided tour to appreciate Troy, since little met the eye. Literate guides quoted chapter and verse from the *Iliad* to the parties as they visited the Greek landing beaches, the cave of Paris, the fig tree by the gates, the tombs of Ajax and Achilles, the place where Zeus carried off Ganymede, the stone where Cassandra was tied (milk, it was said, issued from the front, and blood from the back). The tourist murmured an appropriate quote – preferably in ancient Greek – in his wife's ear, and felt himself well in the spirit of the place.

There was plenty more to visit in Asia Minor, though of dubious authenticity. As the years went on, more and more obscure heroes from Homer came to light with a grave or a house in the region; and for each one, many guides appeared to tell visitors all about it. Otherwise the Roman tourist could proceed directly to the ultimate destination: Egypt. Egypt would take him as far back in time as he could get. The immense, ancient gods still presided over the landscape, full of mystery – Egyptian cults had an enthusiastic following among the Imperial Romans, especially the women. Hot, sunny, and dry, the Egyptian weather was ideal for holidaying; and, as a Roman colony, Egypt provided the ideal of exotica in safety.

It was just a short distance along the coast from Troy to Alexandria Troas, where boats left regularly for Alexandria in Egypt. Alternatively one could go direct to Alexandria from Rome. As the world's greatest port, Alexandria was renowned for its ships: splendid, swift, grand in scale, especially the grain ships. Lucian described one, 180 feet long and 45 feet wide, high masts surmounted with a gilded goosehead, the goddess Isis represented on the prow, and a bright red topsail. The cargo capacity was a thousand tons, and there was room for nearly a thousand passengers. The cruise was particularly recommended for those suffering from tuberculosis or headache. In two weeks, the tourist was in Egypt.

He had one of those quintessential "moments" when Alexandria was sighted: from thirty miles offshore the Lighthouse, one of the world's seven wonders, came into view, looming larger and larger as the ship pulled into harbour. It was not unlike a twentieth-century European visitor's first view of New York City; and the similarity did not stop there. Like New York in the present era, Alexandria was the ultimate cosmopolitan city. The tourist wandered amidst a mêlée of diverse nationalities: Greeks, Jews, Egyptians, Syrians, Indians, Ethiopians. In the teeming market, the tourist could buy gold dust, carved ivory, tortoiseshell, pearls, Chinese silks, and Arabian spices. At local eating places he could sample such ethnic specialities as smoked fish with garlic, snails, giblet stews, and barley beer. The natives had a reputation as sarcastic fast-talkers – "witty and ready in abuse", said Seneca. Alexandria had its "Times Square", a quarter with rough all-night drinking clubs, erotic shows, and a jazzy, syncopated music which became the vogue in Rome. Well-connected sophisticates might even attend the orgiastic rites at the temple of Serapis. The revels continued out of town along the Canopus waterway, where there were wild boating parties like the ones at

Baiae and luxury nightclubs featuring flute music and roast beef. At the same time, Alexandria was a Mecca of contemporary high culture, world famous for its university and musical concerts. The tourist took in a bit of everything. But, as New York is not "the real America", Alexandria was not "the real Egypt". To see that, the tourist had to travel inland, up the Nile.

He rented for the purpose a kind of cabin cruiser, built of sweet acantha wood planks, with papyrus sails and a little awninged shelter made of reeds. Drifting at his ease, he could enjoy attractive riverscapes of water lilies and bulrushes, swamp birds and hippo-potami, and in the background pink sands and camels (giving him decorative ideas for when he got home). He might also enjoy recalling the many literary associations and legends of the Nile – that was the essence of travel. The boat made many stops for spectacular riverside attractions.

First was Memphis, shrine of Ptah, where the sacred bull of Apis was kept. Through a small window of the stable the divine animal could be glimpsed, and when tourist parties showed up Apis was taken from his cell for a run in the temple courtyard. Then just to the west were the colossal emblems of ancient Egypt, the Pyramids and the Sphinx.

The Imperial Romans were by no means the first tourists to visit the Pyramids. Graffiti on the pyramid bases date back to the thirteenth century BC: in 1261 BC Ptah-Ewe wrote that he "came to contemplate the shadow of the Pyramids"; in 1244 it was scratched into stone that "Hadnakhte, scribe of the treasury, came to make an excursion and amuse himself on the west of Memphis". By the second century AD the paws of the Sphinx and the pyramid bases were densely covered with messages.

The Roman was impressed, and pleasantly baffled, by the Sphinx and the Pyramids. Like travellers of the romantic type in any epoch, he was stirred by mystery. The pyramid walls still bore their elegant finish, the hieroglyphics clear and sharp, but the symbol-writing was no longer intelligible to anyone. This didn't prevent the guides from improvising translations for romance-hungry visitors. The guides might embellish other facts about the Pyramids as well: Strabo was told that the little stones around the edifices were petrified lentils and rice grains. Aristides heard that the Pyramids extended as far underground as above. On days when the tourists were especially numerous or distinguished, men from the nearby village of Busiris would shinny up the smooth sides as an extra attraction.

On up the Nile was Arsinoe, shrine of the crocodile god Suchus. If the tourist brought roast meat or pastry and honeyed wine, he could watch the sacred animals eat; they must have been very fat, since the priests never refused to show a tourist a feeding. After their snack, to round off the performance, the priests brushed the crocodiles' teeth. More from amusement than religious reverence, the Roman visitor expressed his appreciation. The river trip climaxed with a visit to the Valley of the Kings and the talking statue of Memnon at Thebes, where Hadrian and his party arrived on an off-day.

Laden with souvenirs – he paid heavily when he passed through customs, for there was a twenty-five-per-cent duty on imported luxury items – the tourist made his way back to Rome in an expansive mood. He set out his best acquisitions in the "art room" of his villa, and perhaps had a dinner party to show them off. But if Seneca was right, the tour had been of moderate value at best. He wrote, "Travel will do you good by giving you a knowledge of people, shapes of mountains, plains extending to unknown lengths, valleys with eternal waters trickling through . . . but you will not become better or more sensible."

Seneca's counsel, as usual, was mostly honoured in the breach. In fact, in the later years of Empire, the appeal of tourism was enhanced: the barbarians were taking hold; civilization was falling apart; and the scenes of Rome's glorious heritage were more moving than ever. Soon, the tourist sensed – with a *frisson* of melancholy that stirred his weary sensibility – the "Old World" would disappear altogether. He felt he might be seeing it for the last time.

CHAPTER TWO

The Medieval Pilgrim

The year is AD 385, and the streets of Jerusalem are thronged. Among the native inhabitants are people from all over the Roman Empire, each distinct in garb and comportment. One party draws stares because of the unusual intensity of the central figure, a wealthy Roman widow in black. Obviously she is one of the Christians, those doom-ridden foreigners who increasingly come to Jerusalem. Besides her entourage of servants, a local guide is in attendance, halting the party with nearly every step to recall a moment from Biblical history: "Here" – for instance – "Rachel paused." The Roman lady, Paula, stoops to pick up a handful of pebbles, still perhaps imbued with Rachel's spirit. Another stop: the house of Simon the Pharisee. Here Paula opens her Bible to read aloud. With each pause, she grows more emotional. In the end she "threw herself down in adoration before the cross as if she could see the Lord himself hanging from it. And when she entered the tomb, she kissed the stone. . . . What tears she shed there," wrote St Jerome, "what sighs of grief, all Jerusalem knows" – nothing like the usual idle curiosity-seeker or nostalgic aesthete touring abroad from Rome. For Christianity was beginning to take root in the West, whereupon all "culture" stemmed from the Bible; all "pleasure" was subsumed under piety; and the emergent form of tourism was pilgrimage.

As the Dark Ages went on, the Christian influence spread in Europe. But in the half-dozen centuries after Paula's trip, only a handful of Europeans made the Jerusalem pilgrimage. It was a bad time for travel. Where the barbarians had passed, the roads, communication systems and inns that the Romans had built fell apart. The paved highways deteriorated into rutted, muddy tracks, fraught with violent danger: bears, wolves, marauders. The unified Roman world fragmented into small warring domains, defensive enclaves knowing little of each other – and nearly universally illiterate, so long-distance communications were barely operable. Innkeeping, especially out of town, was a most unpopular profession. Roving bandits sacked churches and burned libraries, so what tangible culture did exist in that fearful, contracted age was destroyed and dispersed over and over again. It was hazardous to travel and difficult to find what a tourist might have wanted to see.

Then came the year AD 1000, an immense round figure like a vast portent. Everyone thought the world would end; when it didn't, elation was high. The shadow of the Dark Ages seemed to lift. Light streamed over Europe, and the world became full of things to look at. The heathen invaders had been driven back, and with peace came prosperity. Wealth poured into the Church, whereupon the Church went on a building spree. The monk Radulphus Glaber wrote, "One would have thought the world was shaking itself to cast off its old age and was clothing itself everywhere in a white robe of churches", rich in sculpture and jewel-like stained glass, with wide aisles and towering naves for vast congregations, and splendid processions. Most splendid of all were the holy treasuries: chalices, tapestries and sainted relics in exquisitely crafted reliquaries of gold, silver and gemstones. Particularly in France, the new churches were major tourist attractions.

Wealth poured into the monasteries, too. In the enriched monastic libraries there were stories of early voyages to the Holy Land, and the monks began publishing new "promotional literature", letting the public know about miracles and holy relics, urging all to go on pilgrimage. The crowning example, published in the twelfth century, was the *Liber Sancti Jacobi* for pilgrims to Santiago de Compostela in Spain, the shrine of St James, the first martyred apostle. According to legend, only one week after James's beheading in Jerusalem his body miraculously travelled to the Bay of Padrón in Spain. Then in 834 St James performed another miracle, said the legend: his ghost appeared to lead the Spanish army against the Moorish infidels, and the saint by his own hand slew 70,000. The first four volumes of the *Liber Sancti Jacobi* contain liturgies, the legends and miracles of St James, and the archetypal pilgrimages of Charlemagne and Roland. But volume five describes Basque cuisine, Navarrais sexual mores, road and river conditions, and other particulars of the route to Compostela – a practical travel guide.

By the mid-thirteenth century, vast numbers of people were on the roads to share in the benefits of pilgrimage. It was widely believed that the best remedy for any ailment was to appeal to a saint – much more effective than visiting a doctor. With malnutrition and disease widespread, there were continual occasions to seek divine help. The Virgin Mary was the great healer, and her shrines at Soissons, Beauvais, Chartres and Paris were mobbed with sufferers on stretchers, shivering under blankets, delirious with fever, near collapse after days on the road, but in a state of high elation to have reached the holy place at last.

Pilgrimage was also used to correct moral infirmity. Often criminals were sentenced to a difficult journey – perhaps through the mountains in chains and on their knees. Thousands more sinners voluntarily chose pilgrimage as a means of expiation. Penitential pilgrimage became so popular that the Church made it into a system, by means of indulgences. A journey from Wales to Rome, for example, followed by 395 high masses, earned the penitent ninety-two years of pardon from his sins. The longer and more arduous the journey, the greater the remission.

By the thirteenth and fourteenth centuries, pilgrimage was a mass phenomenon, practicable and systematized, served by a growing industry of networks of charitable hospices and mass-produced indulgence handbooks. During the fifteenth century, the "decadent Gothic" period, its spirit shifted again. On the eve of the Protestant Reformation and of the Renaissance, pilgrimage was more popular than ever; but the pious motivation was now tinged with more worldly impulses: culture and pleasure – tourism in fact. The romance of faraway places came most especially alive with the emergence of a new literary genre: the travel book. The classic bestseller was Sir John Mandeville's *Travels*, published in 1357, soon translated into nine foreign languages, and imitated almost yearly for the next century and a half.

Mandeville went from western Europe all the way to Southeast Asia (he also described an optional side-trip to Eden, but admitted it was hearsay). With an extended stay in the Holy Land, this was strictly speaking a pilgrimage, but it evoked scenic beauties and curiosities, too, many tinged with the miraculous. There were rubies along the shore at Cyprus and air so pure on Mount Athos in

Greece that "philosophers wrote letters with their fingers and at the year's end they came again and found the letters still there". There were strange foods with mystical properties: at the Dead Sea, one that looked ripe but was really full of ashes, a sign of God's wrath; in Jerusalem, "long . . . apples of Paradise. And they be right sweet and of good savour, and though ye cut them in never so many gobbets . . . overthwart or endlong, evermore ye shall find in the midst the figure of the holy cross of Our Lord Jesus" – they were, in modern parlance, bananas. The farther from Christendom, the more fantastic the sights: two-headed geese, wool-bearing trees, eyeless men with mouths on their shoulders, mouthless men who sucked meat through a pipe, men with long hounds' ears, not to mention practitioners of sexual freedom and communism. At the same time there were tips for the tourist: high-quality balm can be bought in India, but test it to be sure it's not wax or turpentine. Speaking at once to the man of piety, the man of action, and the practical man, Mandeville was the leading travel writer of his age.

From the reverent to the worldly, everyone desired to make pilgrimage, and pilgrims came from all social classes – except the very poor, who were tied to the land. The royal aristocrats travelled gorgeously. The genteel might go in well-organized little groups: typical was the party of four German noblemen from Ulm in 1483, who engaged a barber-cum-musician, an esquire, a schoolmaster, a cook, a manciple-cum-steward, an interpreter, and a chaplain-cum-guide. The last, Friar Felix Faber, chronicled the journey, under the *nom de plume* Fabri, and his *Evagatorium* became a popular book. A vast number of pilgrims came from the middle class, like those in Chaucer's *Canterbury Tales*: some military men, a doctor, a lawyer, an estate agent, a scholar, a miller, a yeoman, some artisans, a prioress, an epicurean monk, a beggar, and a pardoner, although the last two really belonged to the class of professional travellers (pardoners made a living selling indulgences).

A notorious character from the *Canterbury Tales* was the Wife of Bath – women were by no means excluded from the ranks of the pilgrims, though not everyone approved. Austere churchmen like St Boniface adjudged women restless and fickle, responsible for the frivolous shifting in popularity between shrines. Women were also warned against pilgrimage because, especially at popular holy places, they might be crushed or trampled, the most dramatic form of medieval tourist blight. On the other hand, like Paula, emotionally receptive women could make exemplary pilgrims. When Friar Faber reached Jerusalem he encountered six European matrons aged over eighty; the friar expressed his heartiest admiration.

For most people, pilgrimage was the only legitimate excuse to leave home, the only escape from the relentless surveillance of the village, where many people considered it their business to keep their fellows on the righteous path. On pilgrimage, illegitimate lovers who "just happened" to leave at the same time could discreetly pursue their affair; pilgrimage offered lots of opportunities for casual sex, too. Adventurers and hustlers of all types found credulous provincials easy to exploit on foreign ground. Paradoxically, pilgrimage was a unique opportunity to break free of moral restraint, a motive not unknown to later generations of tourists.

There were no organized tours to the land of mouthless men in the fifteenth century. But by that time there were regular, all-in package tours from Venice to the Holy Land, fare to include passage, meals, inns, donkey rides and bribes for the infidel. Thousands of Europeans crossed the treacherous Alps to see Rome, city of popes and Christian martyrs. And there were mass sightseeing parties from England, France and Germany to Santiago de Compostela. These travellers had at their disposal guidebooks, accommodation bureaux, travel agencies, a range of inexpensive souvenirs and nearly all the accoutrements of present-day tourism.

Despite such amenities, preparations to go abroad were extensive. Foreign travel was an exceptional event. First there was the raising of funds. The rich, who travelled first class, required one year of their customary income for the Jerusalem journey; the bourgeois, travelling more modestly, spent one year of their lower income. Or if there was no wealth to spare, land could be sold. But the pilgrim could often get a kind of "travel grant", too: clergymen might be sponsored by their religious orders, and trade guilds subsidized their members. Otherwise the pilgrim might apply to his local monastery for a loan; or he could engage himself as a "palmer" to a wealthy patron: in exchange for paying the pilgrim's way, the patron received full spiritual benefit from the trip (the name derived from the palm frond, emblematic souvenir of Jerusalem). Finally, the pilgrim could often economize on food and lodging since many hospices provided those amenities free. He counted what he had, reckoned his possible savings, and prayed for the best.

Next, the pilgrim had to put his spiritual affairs in order – to leave under the onus of a misdeed would taint the virtue of the pilgrimage. Besides, the journey was dangerous: if he never returned, his sins would be forever unatoned. He made a will, a privilege accorded few in the medieval world. Then he made a full confession, and put things to rights with all wronged parties. The rich frequently offered a general farewell penance with a donation to the community, and the shrewd stipulated that it be restored to them should they return alive. The pilgrim's departure was at last announced from the pulpit, and his fellow parishioners invited to state their objections; creditors of all types came forward then for payment. If pilgrimage was a form of escapism, it still required the sanction of the world from which one was escaping.

Thus unburdened, the pilgrim fitted himself out for the voyage. High nobility maintained their customary level of opulence: the Duke of Saxony travelled to Rome in 1480 with two hundred retainers, each astride a horse with a jewelled halter; and the Duke of Brunswick's entourage included apothecaries, courtiers, physicians and twenty-seven personal servants. But this was hardly an appropriate mode for pilgrimage, intended as a chastening exercise. Observed the *Liber Sancti Jacobi* tartly, "If St Peter entered Rome with nothing but a crucifix, why do so many pilgrims come here with bulging purses and trunks of spare clothes, eating succulent food and drinking heady wine?"

As a rule, the pilgrim travelled light, at least if he were not going beyond Europe. It befitted his non-worldly purpose, and it left him with less to lose along the dangerous ways he'd be passing. His costume was distinctive and striking: the pilgrim stood out unmistakably, as surely as any camera-wreathed, sun-hatted, twentieth-century tourist in an Oriental medina. He wore a broad-brimmed hat, turned up in front, with a long scarf hanging off the back and wound round his waist. Over his long-sleeved mantle went a coarse russet tunic sewn with crosses, called a *sclavein*, and large rosary beads hung from one shoulder. To his waist he strapped a soft leather pouch, or *scrip*, which held his food, cookpot and bowl, and money (minimal, for both humility and safety). He carried a crooked, metal-tipped walking stick, or staff, useful to drive off dogs, wolves and demons. In this "outfit" the pilgrim was a true prototype: tourists have perennially marked the occasion of a trip with special new clothes, and the exigencies of travel have often generated fashions and artefacts that are practical, durable and streamlined. A final ritual of departure consisted in the blessing of scrip, staff and sclavein by the Church. Thus, all new, he was set to cross the world.

When the pilgrim was ready to leave, he asked at the local inn what travellers might be going his way. Though solitary pilgrimage was deemed most virtuous – maximum difficulty and minimum worldly distraction – hardly anyone was brave enough to face the dangers alone. Even if their group wasn't formally packaged, pilgrims tended to stick together, though not always with the same companions. So, on the appointed day, the pilgrim left home with his new brethren (and sisters) and set off on the first leg of the journey, towards the coast.

The most accessible – and so the most popular – destination for northern European pilgrims was Santiago de Compostela. From England, the Compostela trip made a perfect holiday excursion: round trip under three weeks. It was a four-day sail each way from Plymouth to La Coruña in Spain, and then a few hours' walk. By the fifteenth century, licensed boats plied the way regularly. The first English pilgrim-shipper's licence was issued in 1394; by 1428 there were 280 pilgrim ships to Spain from London, 200 from Bristol, 90 from Dartmouth, and so on – 925 in all. Often the ships combined piety with commerce, returning with wine.

The overland trip was much more interesting. It took longer: on foot, two months from Paris, at twenty miles per day (slower through the Pyrenees); on horseback, about thirty miles a day. But there was wonderful sightseeing, both sacred and secular. *En route* to the Channel crossing, the pilgrim made his first important stop at Reading Abbey, where there was a dazzling array of "forthcoming attractions", assembled, in fact, to encourage pilgrimage. Throughout the fifteenth century (it was destroyed with the Reformation) Reading Abbey was one of England's wealthiest, with a prodigious collection of sainted leavings. There were splinters from Aaron's rod, chips from the rock of Moses, and fragments of the True Cross; a robe worn by St Thomas and one from the wardrobe of the Virgin Mary; St Luke's tooth; St James's hand; and three relics of Jesus – a shoe, a phial of blood and the foreskin. (Sceptics looked askance at this last: if Jesus' holiness was not yet acknowledged at his birth, why would the foreskin have been saved? But then, few pilgrims were sceptical.)

Fixing his thoughts on such sanctified splendours as best he could, the pilgrim endured a short but painfully choppy Channel crossing;

alternatively, he could view his seasickness as a penance. Disembarking at Calais, he regained his level head, and started the trek southeastwards with the people he'd met on the boat.

The cavalcade of miraculous relics was not slow to present itself. After three days' walk, the pilgrim came to the first great stopping place on the itinerary, Amiens Cathedral, where the skull of John the Baptist was kept. He bought a brooch representing the venerated head and triumphantly pinned it to his hat.

A few days more brought the pilgrim to Paris, where the great attraction was Sainte Chapelle, whose reliquary held bits from the sponge, reed, and cloak used in Christ's walk to Calvary; the Crown of Thorns; breast milk and hair from the Virgin Mary; and more fragments of the True Cross. To the south was Orléans, with even more fragments of the True Cross. Later scholars reckoned that if all the fragments of the True Cross displayed in the fifteenth century were assembled, there would be enough wood to build three ocean liners. Not far beyond Orléans was St Jean d'Angely, where one hundred monks stood perpetual guard over the skull of. . . John the Baptist.

For those who had just recently been at Amiens, an explanation was in order. One curate used to tell the pilgrims that the first relic "must have been the skull of the saint as a young man". This was not the only duplicate relic the pilgrim would run into: no less than five shrines, for instance, claimed to possess the body of St Gilles. The *Liber Sancti Jacobi* declared indignantly,

Shame upon the Hungarians for claiming part of his body. Curses upon the monks of Chamalières who imagine that they have the whole body. The same to the people of St Seine who boast of his head, and to the Normans who actually display a body purporting to be his. For it is quite impossible that a single particle of the holy body could ever have left its hallowed tomb.

Both St Jean d'Angely and Amiens remained venerated shrines throughout the Middle Ages. Full of belief, the pilgrim made an ideal tourist.

Tourism was big business: innkeepers and souvenir manufacturers prospered, and the Church benefited most of all, by the spectacular offerings of wealthy pilgrims. Competition between shrines could be fierce. A case in point was Vézelay Cathedral in Burgundy, a celebrated attraction in the early centuries of pilgrimage, boasting the corpse of Mary Magdalene. In 1279, the monastery of St Maximin in Provence suddenly claimed that Mary Magdalene's remains were with them, substantiating their assertion by the "suave odour" emanating from the 1300-year-old sarcophagus, a sure sign of divinity. The Count of Provence sponsored a gala opening ceremony to display the relic, and Pope Boniface VIII further ensured its popularity by conferring a handsome indulgence on it. Soon Vézelay was stricken from the recommended itinerary and forgotten.

Besides these sanctified remains, the pilgrim was presented with the variegated sights of the road, and his eyes were opened wide. The travelling party shared the way with carters transporting hay, corn and oats in plank boxes, latticed wagons and barrows; with painted, gilded litters hung with embroidered curtains through which fine ladies with plucked eyebrows could be seen fondling miniature dogs; with mounted knights; and with herds of kine. On foot, the pilgrim was frequently spattered with mud; he was also exposed to French fashion, social usage, and agricultural methods, and, like all mass tourists, pilgrims attracted their own entourage. When pilgrim traffic was heavy, roadside "victuallers" appeared, selling from their tents wine, fruit, fish, meats, pasties, bread, and cake – the prototypical "fast-food" stand. Beggars stationed themselves at wayside crosses, singing and playing wooden clappers. Itinerant prostitutes joined the pilgrim parties, too; inevitably some of the faithful fell by the wayside. Village life would never be the same again.

The pilgrims also entertained themselves, with story telling and sing-alongs. Most unpopular were sticklers for piety like Margery Kempe of Norfolk, who persistently directed the conversation to the subject of divine love. When her fellow travellers reminded her that she was far from her tolerant husband in England, who might put up with her preaching, she replied that God's love was just as important on the Continent. At times like those, the musicians brought out their bagpipes, an instrument particularly recommended by Archbishop Arundel to solace, and drown out, the complaints of the pious – though the archbishop had in mind those suffering from sore feet.

The evening halt provided the pilgrim with some respite. The *Faubourg St Jacques* (St James's Quarter, for pilgrims *en route* to his shrine) was usually just outside the town gates, to accommodate late arrivals. There the pilgrim found all the necessities: a chapel for evening devotions, some inns, and usually a charitable hospice. Establishments catering to the pilgrim trade displayed the sign of the cockleshell, St James's emblem.

The inn was built around a courtyard, where animals could be lodged. Inside the main hall, the floors were strewn with rushes, and there were long communal tables with benches; only the most luxurious inns had wall hangings. A single brazier provided warmth, and there was dim lighting and a want of ventilation. But at least the inns were cheap: daily room and board cost approximately £2 a day, reckoning at the pound's value in 1980.

The pilgrim supplied his own tableware, a cup and a knife; forks were not yet in use. Instead of plates there were trenchers: thick slabs of old, hard bread. Later, the used trenchers, soaked with meat juice, might be donated to the poor. The fare was simple: meat and bread, occasionally with vegetables but always with lots of wine – inns were notorious for drunkenness, and the pilgrim was usually full of convivial spirit. There was little on the menu for Margery Kempe, vegetarian teetotaller.

After supper there was entertainment from *jongleurs* – travelling performers who sang or recited, accompanying themselves on lute or hurdy-gurdy. In the early days of pilgrimage, the jongleurs' story-songs, or *gestes*, had to do with the heroic deeds of devout men; most popular was the *Chanson de Roland*, about the holy warrior. But with the decline of faith, the gestes took on earthier tones. John Lackland complained, "Nowadays entertainment and minstrelsy is nothing but lewdness, flattery, and filthy stories." The pilgrim and his pals had a good guffaw. Sometimes, though, the jongleurs presented the most pious tourists with a moral dilemma. One evening, Friar Faber's party was well amused by jongleurs, but afterwards one refused to tip the players, deeming such expenditures unworthy of a pilgrim. Friar Faber was asked to judge the question: he pronounced in favour of tipping and later verified his judgement by looking the matter up in Jean Gerson's treatise *On Avarice*. Less morally equivocal, surely, was the question of engaging a prostitute for the night; nonetheless, virtually all inns supplied them.

Not even the virtuous spent the night alone, however. Inn guests slept a dozen to a room (more in the servants' room), and two or sometimes four to a bed. An *English Manual of French Conversation* translated the necessary exchange with one's bedmate: "William, undress and wash your legs, and then dry them with a cloth and rub

them well, for love of the fleas, that they may not leap on your legs."
More spartan still were the charitable hospices, though they did
provide free medical and burial services. For dinner there was
usually only bread and wine; for sleeping, only straw pallets on the
floor, with an even more virulent complement of vermin, including
rats. As one austere couplet expressed it,

> Bedding there is nothing fair,
> Many pilgrims it does appear.
> Tables use they none of to eat,
> But on the bare floor they make their seat.

Nonetheless, by the time night fell and the hospice opened its doors,
the stone bench outside was usually full of waiting pilgrims.

As the way to Compostela progressed, the well-favoured heart-
lands of central France gave way to strange, forsaken scenes. The
Bordeaux region, according to the *Liber Sancti Jacobi* (clearly a
Francophile guide) was almost the last civilized place the pilgrim
would see until he reached the shrine. Bordeaux was highly recommended for its fish and wine, plus two sainted relics. South of
Bordeaux, good things were left behind. The pilgrim's route led into
the Basque country, one of the sorriest regions known to humanity.
He was warned of its mosquitoes and quicksand, of the diet –
nothing but honey, millet, and pork for humans, and nothing at all
for horses, so riders were advised to stock fodder in advance – and
most of all, of the people.

The *Liber Sancti Jacobi* commented in disgust,

They eat with their hands, slobbering over the food like any dog or
pig. To hear them speaking, you would think they were a pack of
hounds barking. . . . They have dark, evil, ugly faces. They are
debauched, perverse, treacherous and disloyal, corrupt and sensual
drunkards. . . . They will kill you for a penny. Men and women
alike warm themselves by the fire, revealing those parts which are
better hidden. They fornicate unceasingly, and not only with
humans. . . . That is why they are held in contempt by all decent
folk.

The pilgrim had no romantic or ethnographic interest in the "primitive" or the "quaint" – the culturally prescribed response was simple
revulsion. Needless to say, xenophobic hostility ran high on both
sides. But tourists throughout the ages have endured "native

squalor" to glimpse the glorious past; so too did the pilgrim grit his teeth (not, it may be supposed, without an agreeable sense of superiority mixed with his distaste), huddle closer to his fellow travellers, and press on to Compostela.

There were other well-travelled pilgrim routes to Spain from northern Europe. German pilgrims – who spent the most money, and were robbed and cheated most frequently – came down through eastern France along the Rhône valley, and then headed west. Another stream of pilgrims originated in the Auvergne mountains of central France; though dangerous high country, it was very satisfactory to the penitential urge.

All roads converged on the Pyrenees. There, the going was slower. The pilgrim might not travel more than six miles a day, stopping at noon to consume the free ration of bacon, bread, and cheese he'd packed in his scrip at the last hospice that morning after an early mass. At the high point, he crossed the steep Col de Cize, following in the steps of Charlemagne. The mountaintop was thickly planted with crosses, left over the years by passing pilgrims to commemorate attainment of the spot. But at the other side of the Col, warned the *Liber Sancti Jacobi*, the pilgrim might be searched and beaten if he failed to pay the toll.

After that – for such is the caprice of worldly fortune – the pilgrim came to one of Europe's most luxurious hospices: Roncesvaux, sumptuously endowed by Spanish royalty currying favour with the French. On arrival, the pilgrim's feet were washed for him. Full meals were served, with fruit and almonds for dessert. At night there were real beds to sleep in. Spanish hospitality was not recommended in general, however. The *Liber Sancti Jacobi* warned the pilgrim off red meat, and the river fish was disgusting: "If anyone can eat their fish without feeling sick, then he must have a stronger constitution than most of us."

This was wild country, but the pilgrim had protection. Crimes against pilgrims were judged more severely than crimes against others; pilgrims were protected by both civil statute and an accepted code of chivalry. It was deemed exceptionally virtuous to give charity to pilgrims, especially in the form of roadworks. Among the eccentric religious hermits of northern Spain, several devoted themselves to that enterprise: St Dominic of the Causeway, for instance, built a cobbled road between Logroño and Burgos, a dangerous, swampy region; he attached a pilgrims' shelter to his own hut, and even erected a wooden bridge across the river Oja.

Compostela drew near, and the road grew increasingly crowded. Besides earnest seekers, the pilgrim met an assortment of professionals: pardoners selling indulgences, holy souvenir sellers with trinkets from other shrines, and merchants purveying more worldly goods. Most eye-catching and disturbing were the beggars, noisily singing out for alms; some painted false blood on their arms, or had themselves made up as lepers. As for the locals, they were described by a fifteenth-century German visitor as "fat as pigs and slothful at that, for they have no need to cultivate the soil when they can live off the pilgrims". The pilgrim's eyes grew wide, then narrow.

Still, he had techniques to screen out these incongruous elements, ceremonial acts to place him in the proper spiritual frame of mind. Just before he reached Compostela, he took a ritual bath in the Laventula River. Then he picked up a block of limestone and carried it to Triacastela, where it was received as a donation for Compostela building repairs. Clean and "paid in full", he was now ready to behold the shrine.

He entered the city from the northeast, by the Francigena (French) Gate, and followed a narrow street lined with inns and eating-places to the north cathedral door, pausing in the small church square with its fountain of spouting lions. There the pilgrim was tempted with every kind of salesman and inexpensive diversion. Itinerant musicians played horns, tambourines and zithers; jugglers and magicians displayed their tricks; all passed the hat. Foodsellers and prostitutes advertised their wares.

The souvenir trade was especially lively. James's emblem, the cockleshell, was the most popular and distinctive memento of the time, and instantaneously proclaimed the pilgrim's accomplishment. Originally it was mandatory that the pilgrim go down to the sea and find his own shell. By the beginning of the twelfth century, however, shells were sold in the cathedral square, and by the end of that century little lead shell-shaped badges had replaced the real thing. The pilgrim himself knew nothing of all that; he was just glad to have his badge.

Clutching his souvenir – and keeping a hand over his wallet, because pickpockets and cutpurses were everywhere – the pilgrim joined the crush inside the cathedral. The multilingual din was deafening; particularly distracting were the songs of drunkards. It must have been most uncomfortable for those who were ill: cripples limping on crutches, groaning madmen in chains. The stench could be as bad as the noise, and fainting was common.

Still, the pilgrim felt the spirit of Santiago de Compostela. Though he complained about the mob, especially the badly behaved ones, he never said the place was ruined by tourism. He was part of something larger, and if he performed correctly there was no question of the place not "working" for him. His first climactic moment came when he caught sight of St James's statue, resplendent in its gold cape. Next he made his way to the sculpted Portico de la Gloria, where St James perched above the tree of Jesse. The pilgrim elbowed his way through the crowd to put his fingers between the tree's twisted roots; a second climax.

Inside a column, the sculptor Maestro Mateo had placed a stone representation of himself, a kind of signature. So as a final devotion, the pilgrim touched his head to the head of the maestro, who came to be called the Saint of Skull Rappings. How many times, tramping through the Pyrenees, had he imagined the moment? That gesture, ceremoniously, completed the pilgrimage. It remained simply to hasten home.

If the pilgrim were a man of greater means – and, perhaps consequently, of greater intrepidity – he could venture farther, however. Compostela was Europe's most popular pilgrimage place, but Rome had most prestige. After the sack of Constantinople in 1204, Rome possessed more Christian relics than any other city, including the miraculous vernicle, Veronica's handkerchief, which bore the imprint of Christ's face. In the indulgences that could be earned there, Rome surpassed even Jerusalem. It was the site of the most sensational early Christian martyrdoms and remained the great cultural repository of antiquity. The difficult journey across the Alps added *cachet*. For the pilgrim tourist, Rome had "everything".

The height of the tourist season was Easter. Indulgences were more generous during Lent, there were grand papal celebrations, and the pilgrim bound for the Holy Land could then continue on to Venice in time for a May sailing. For the English or German traveller, this meant leaving home in February – dead winter. It took the average horseback rider seven weeks to travel the twelve hundred miles from London to Rome; twice that long for foot travellers; half as long if one rode express.

The quickest route was through France. If, however, the English pilgrim disembarked in the Low Countries, he would find a valuable

chapter in William Wey's popular practical guidebook. Arrived at
Bruges, the pilgrim read in Wey that it was a good place to engage
transport, because many types were on offer: "then may you ride
fast or soft, early or late, and the more privily, without much asking
after your ways, lodging places, or any other thing that you list". In
Flanders the pilgrim was cautioned to stay away from ditches. It was
imprudent to divulge personal information, or to be observably
drunk. Above all, warned Wey, "Do take care for yourself and
yours, for Englishmen have but little love in many parts, but if it be
for their money."

Either way, it was a gruelling journey because it meant crossing
the Alps. Usually, the pilgrim bought a horse (just under £600 at
1980's equivalent value) upon landing on the Continent, and sold it
at the journey's end. Or horses could be hired for stages of the trip.
Most pilgrims to Rome were sufficiently well heeled to have
servants, who were generally expected to run along on foot beside
their mounted masters. Surviving expense logs show that extra
horses were often bought in mid-journey; the servants couldn't keep
up the pace.

The usual itinerary took the English pilgrim from the Channel to
Paris, then east to Burgundy and south down the Rhône valley to
Avignon, especially in the fourteenth century, when Avignon was
the site of a rival papacy. For a hundred years the city teemed. Every
variety of sinner came to buy redemption, and the Church grew
fabulously wealthy. Its showplace was the Pope's Palace, a garish
agglomeration of Arabic windows, pyramidal chimneys, crenellated and machicolated battlements. Inside there were gilded walls,
star-spangled archways, terraces covered in exotic flowers, and
stables filled with pure white horses; ecclesiasts dined off gold plate
and slept on ermine-trimmed pillows. Beggars, peasants, merchants, and monks crowded the narrow streets, as well as couriers
with white wands, armoured knights, dandies with tight codpieces,
bells sewn on their sleeves and long pointed shoes, and prisoners in
fetters. Avignon had foodsellers, prostitutes, even freakshows –
visitors marvelled at a one-armed woman who could sew, spin, toss
a ball, and play dice with her toes. All amenities, both spiritual and
worldly, were on offer – including, for instance, over forty Italian
banking houses. However, it was hard to find room at an inn, and
sewage problems were monstrous. The pilgrim mingled with the
crowd.

From that hotbed the pilgrim had to turn to the barren east, to cross the horrible Alps. Praying, he rode into a zone of bitter skies and icy roads so narrow and treacherous that man and rider often plunged into deep fissures in the rocks. Fatal avalanches were frequent. Piety drove the pilgrim on. Adam of Usk went in an ox wagon, "half dead with cold . . . blindfolded so I could not see the dangers of the pass". Another medieval traveller described a stay in the Alpine village of St Remy,

In this place, as in the jaws of death, we remained huddled together day and night in peril of death. The village was crowded with a multitude of travellers. From the lofty rocky heights frequently fell masses of snow which swept all before them, burying nearby houses in which some travellers were quartered while some travellers sat at table; the victims were found sometimes suffocated, sometimes bruised and weak.

On the morning that the guides were persuaded, for a large sum, to clear a path, the travellers solemnly took the Holy Sacrament, fearing that they might not survive once they left. Many of the guides who preceded them, swathed in shaggy furs and shod in iron-pointed boots, were killed in an avalanche. As to the picturesque scenery that attracted later tourists so strongly, the medieval travel-ler hardly had time to appreciate it. For him the sheer, sharp geometries of that mineral kingdom, with its goitred human popu-lation, necks swollen and eyes bulging from the peculiar Alpine waters, suggested only the nether regions of Hell. The pilgrim stiffened and spurred his horse on. It was an unutterable relief to descend into the sunny hills of Tuscany, although there one faced another danger: the region was rife with German bandits.

When the weary pilgrim caught his first sight of Rome, it all seemed worthwhile. Master Gregory of England exclaimed over "innumerable palaces bristling with a cornfield of towers; I was overwhelmed, and imagined how Caesar would have seen it from that spot. . . . For even if Rome falls into complete ruin, yet nothing that is intact can be compared to it."

On coming closer, the pilgrim might change his mind; by the late Middle Ages the city had indeed fallen into ruin. The pilgrim saw rubble everywhere. Ancient monuments lay in casual decay, their stones disassembled to be used for new buildings; Rome's chief industry, besides tourism, was its limestone kilns. Much of the city was deserted, and to wander through its streets was to find oneself, alternately, first in congested enclaves of narrow alleys and balcony-encrusted slum dwellings, and then in stretches of road reverted to a rural state, overgrown with trees and vines amidst which goats and sheep grazed. Even the Forum housed oxen and pigs. At night, in the middle of the city, the pilgrim heard howling wolves.

At the same time, in the heart of Rome along the Tiber, the tourist industry thrived. There was accommodation to suit every purse, from charitable hospices to ultra-luxurious inns famous throughout Christendom. In the fifteenth century the city boasted over a thousand, including separate hostels for a dozen nationalities. As an Englishman, the pilgrim might head for two English national hostels: Holy Trinity and St Edmund, and Holy Trinity and St Thomas of Canterbury. Margery Kempe put up at the latter, but eventually her eccentric behaviour – she had given up her temperance lectures, but she was always describing her demonic visitations and wore an unconventional white costume – so unnerved her fellow guests that they demanded she leave the hostel.

Margery Kempe was, in one sense, the perfect medieval tourist – or rather, anti-tourist. She fixed her attention always inward, ignoring the things of this world (except when they reminded her of the other world; the sight of a young mother, for instance, could set Margery howling over the Virgin Mary). Most pilgrims, though, could not resist looking around Rome, where layer upon layer of artistic treasures from every age surrounded them.

The medieval pilgrim tourist did not believe in "art for art's sake", apart from its religious aspect. He did not relish the detached enjoyment of standing back from what he saw, of considering historical curios or alien forms of beauty. Such pursuits were decadent, they made too much of the world. But insofar as the secular world did grip his imagination, which it did more and more as the Middle Ages waned, Rome was the place to gratify that imagination, crowded with classical architecture and marble statuary in poignant ruins.

The great sourcework on antiquity was the *Mirabilia Urbis Romae* (*Wonders of Rome*), cataloguing

temples and palaces of emperors, consuls, senators, and prefects . . . in pagan times. . . . And we have tried as best we could to recall to the memory of man the beauty of these edifices in their gold and silver, bronze and ivory and precious stones.

44

By the Middle Ages the rare gems and gleaming metals had disappeared. Only a few elegant stone fragments remained, amidst great heaps of "building materials". With the *Mirabilia* in hand, or with a guide who had memorized it, the pilgrim could evoke the splendours that used to be: the Circus Maximus, "topped with arches all around, ceiled with glass and shining gold"; the Capitol surrounded with "molten images of all the Trojan kings"; the Pantheon "all covered with gilded brass, insomuch that from afar it seemed as it were a mountain of gold".

Not all evocations of the past were accurate. The guide said that Rome was founded not by Romulus but by Noah (more in keeping with the pilgrim's Biblical preferences). And many pilgrims attached Christian significance – even indulgence status – to pagan edifices: Master Gregory wrote disapprovingly that Julius Caesar's tomb, a porphyry pyramid, was

called by the pilgrims St Peter's needle, and with great effort they crawl under it where it is supported by four bronze lions. And they lyingly say that they are saved from sin and do genuine penance if they can crawl under the stone.

Most of all, Imperial Rome was remembered for its martyrdoms: burnings, boilings, impalings, gladiatorial sacrifices, mechanical tortures, grisly extravaganzas dreamed up by the likes of Caligula. Guides recounted each gory detail, and the pilgrims suffered vicarious agonies at every turn. Touring groups could be heard throughout the city, weeping and wailing. The underground catacombs, where the early martyrs were buried, were a great attraction: a dark, hellish maze, suggestive of endless night. But all of this was recreation. There was also serious sightseeing to be done: paying tribute to the great relics and collecting indulgences.

First on the pilgrim's list was St Peter's Cathedral, with a hundred altars displaying Judas Iscariot's hanging rope, the stone St Peter cried upon, many sainted limbs and, most sanctified of all, the vernicle. To stand before the vernicle conveyed Rome's largest indulgence, multiplied still further if one had come a long way: seven thousand years for Romans, ten thousand for Italians, and the English pilgrim, as a foreigner, earned fourteen thousand. The vernicle badge he bought afterwards became one of his most treasured souvenirs

Next came the Lateran basilica, displaying Aaron's rod, Moses' tablet, the Ark of the Covenant, John the Baptist's hair-shirt, the Virgin's tunic, the magical five loaves and two fishes, the grey-bearded head of St Peter, the red-bearded head of St Paul, and, in an oil-filled, gem-encrusted crucifix, the umbilical cord and foreskin of Christ. Besides Reading Abbey, mentioned earlier in this chapter, three French churches and one in Belgium also claimed to possess the foreskin, but the one at the Lateran was most generally credited with authenticity.

That was only the beginning. Rome had over a thousand recommended churches. The contemporary tourist who favours the system of starred attractions would have been delighted, because every grave, relic and sanctuary was quantified according to the heavenly pardon it conferred. Ratings were often clearly displayed: at St Lawrence's Church, the daily indulgence (seven thousand years) was posted on a billboard.

The pilgrim had to keep informed, since indulgence status was continually revised with the vagaries of ecclesiastical politics. This was excellent for the guidebook business: guidebooks were frequently reissued, updated with the latest indulgences and the most efficient routes through the city for seeing them. They were generally mass-produced pamphlets, light enough for the pilgrim to carry in his scrip as he walked. For easy recollection, the routes and indulgences were sometimes given in doggerel verse. The *Stations of Rome* intoned,

> At the church where St Julian liveth,
> Here is his chin, with his teeth,
> And other relics, many and dear.
> To them is granted eight thousand year.

The pamphlets were translated into several languages, and occasionally altered to appeal to foreign preferences: an English version described the relics of the apostle Thomas, on show at the Church of St Maria Maggiore, as relics of Thomas à Becket instead.

For "entertainment", the pilgrim could attend a passion play. Like their ancient predecessors, the medieval Romans were virtuosi of special effects and spared nothing in recreating on stage the death agonies of the martyrs: bags of blood were spilled, smoke belched from great vats, and actors realistically portrayed scourgings and crucifixions.

The ultimate living spectacles at Rome were the displays put on by the Popes, the high point of any visit. In the fifteenth century the processions were more splendid than ever, with finely wrought gold crowns, scarlet silk hats and cloaks, rich banners and vestments, gleaming swords, and pure white horses. The ecclesiastical calendar was liberally marked with celebrations: publication of a papal bull; blessing the poor (the Pope, all in white, bathed the foot of a beggar with water from a golden jug); Christmas, when the Emperor, as defender of the faith, received a sword, a churchman was knighted, and two exotic, bearded black monks were presented to the crowd. The major celebration of the year was Easter. There was a glorious procession throughout the city, and the passion play was put on in the Forum for a highly emotional audience. The climactic ceremonial moment came when the Pope drank communion wine through a golden tube. Then, there was a banquet where the Pope distributed free pepper and ginger. Distinguished foreign tourists often received a place of honour, even a chance to participate: on the Saturday after Easter, Adam of Usk had the honour of holding the Pope's tray of Agnus Dei wax cakes, and the Englishman was given the leftovers.

From Rome at Easter, the pilgrim could easily reach Venice for the late-spring sailing to the Holy Land, where the Scriptures became living reality. Less spoken of – but increasingly alluring – was the call of the exotic: sand dunes and date palms, silks and spices, the fabulous Orient.

Venice made an eminent departure point for the Jerusalem voyage. Parson Richard Torkington of Kent said,

The richness, the sumptuous building, the religious houses and the establishing of their justice and councils, with all other things that make a city glorious, surmounteth in Venice above all places that I ever saw. . . . for there was nothing that I desired to have but I had it directly.

The Venetian tourist industry was complete with publicity. Some promoters literally went too far: as Friar Faber's party approached Venice by river boat, another boat came to meet them carrying a hotel tout in fancy silks. The tout began reviling the inn where the Faber party had already booked, and got so excited in his protestations that he fell into the water.

The city offered a variety of accommodation: members of the cloth could stay at monasteries, merchants at their national trading posts, and for pilgrim tourists there were state-licensed inns catering to various nationalities. At least four of these, at the end of the fifteenth century, specialized in German clientele: the Black Eagle, the Mirror, the White Lion, and the Sign of the Flute. Faber's party chose the last, which was distinguished by a fierce dog that made all but Germans feel most unwelcome. Sightseeing amenities were excellent. Making his way to St Mark's Square, the pilgrim found government-licensed guides perpetually stationed there to serve as interpreters and also to help him change money and do his shopping. Though always wary of foreigners, the pilgrim was relieved to see them.

One of the pleasantest ways to see Venice was by rowing boat, via the canals. There was no lack of holy attractions: St Zacharias' open-mouthed head, St Catherine's hand, St Damian's arm, Constantine's thumb, and a breastbone from Mary Magdalene. The pilgrim appreciated them reverently. One may shudder, today, to imagine the dismemberment whereby these treasures were obtained, but by the medieval ethic to seize a sainted appendage showed deep devotion. St Hugh of England, for instance, distinguished himself as a very holy man when, after communion at Fécamp Abbey in France, he bit the finger off the bandaged arm of Mary Magdalene to add to his relic collection. St Hugh explained, "If a little while ago I handled the sacred body of the Lord with my fingers . . . and partook of it with my lips and teeth, why should I not treat the bones of the saints in the same way and without profanity acquire them whenever I can?"

The pilgrim was also impressed by the secular sights of sophisticated Venice. Foremost was the naval arsenal, with twelve powder mills, tackle factory, rope and sail works, armaments collection and, at the end of the visit, the government wine cellar, where the tourist was offered a complimentary drink. Also, as a port city, Venice displayed a prodigious quantity and variety of consumer goods: carpets, tapestries, brocades, silks, jewellery, spices, and especially food. Canon Pietro Casola of Milan, in Venice *en route* to the Holy Land in the late 1400s, was not much interested in the Venetian churches, but he wrote, "The baker's shops are countless and of incredible beauty; and there is bread the sight of which tempts even a man who is surfeited to eat again."

It was at a Venice sideshow that the pilgrim marvelled over his first elephant – a mere foretaste, he imagined, of the fabulous beasts beyond Europe. The Venetians themselves provoked stares: gorgeously clad men and shameless women wearing high heels, low-cut dresses, lots of jewellery, long curly wigs (which were sold in the markets, suspended from long poles), and heavy make-up which ran in the heat. The pilgrim, at least in his writings, disapproved. Canon Casola remarked acidly,

These Venetian women, specially the pretty ones, try as much as possible in public to show their chests – I mean the breasts and shoulders. . . . I marvelled that their clothes did not fall off their backs. . . . Perhaps this custom pleases others; it does not please me. I am a priest by way of the saints.

The pilgrim's most important business in Venice was arranging his Holy Land trip. He had to secure passage, change money, and do lots of shopping; scrip, staff, and sclavein no longer sufficed. The high nobility went to the Holy Land by private galley. Some travelled at the expense of the Venetian government, who deemed it "wise and prudent to oblige the princes of the world . . . having in view the facilities and favours which our merchants trading in those ports may receive". Henry Earl of Derby, later Henry IV, was treated to such a journey. Supplies alone (typical item: 100 lb of almonds) cost the equivalent, at 1980 values, of over £65,000. Another nobleman, Ferdinand of Aragon, hired a separate cargo boat just to carry horses and falcons for his amusement in Jerusalem.

Venice provided well-organized facilities for the middle-class pilgrim: there the all-in package tour had its inception. For one price, the pilgrim received round-trip transport – including a sleeping berth and two hot meals with wine daily, plus a morning aperitif – and guided travel throughout the Holy Land, including all fees, tolls and bribes – the last being essential to prevent confiscation of baggage, endless delays over red tape, or mischief from the camel drivers. Total cost of a ten-week trip in the late 1400s was sixty gold ducats, equivalent to £1650 in 1980.

Pilgrim tour operators sailing out of Venice had to comply with numerous government regulations. Boats were regularly inspected for seaworthiness; in wartime (the seas were often fraught with conflict with the Arabs) they had to bear arms; and the amount of freight they could carry was limited – lest the passengers find themselves crowded by boxes or overwhelmed by the odour of some particularly aromatic cargo. Sailors had to be at least eighteen years old and were required to swear to steal no more than five shillings (equivalent to approximately £40 today) from the passengers. The captain had to promise to protect the passengers from the rough, ill-bred galley slaves.

The leader in the Venice–Jerusalem package tour industry was Agostino Contarini, who had travel agents as far away as the Low Countries, but he was not without competition. Shortly before a sailing, Contarini and his rival Pietro Lando set up booking facilities in St Mark's Square, flying white banners marked with a red cross, the pilgrim's sign. Seeing prospective customers approach, each set about arguing his own merits while reviling the other. The pilgrims were invited to see for themselves: they visited both boats, conveniently moored in the Grand Canal.

The pilgrims admired a many-oared wooden boat, 250-ton cargo capacity, with an iron prow "made something like a dragon's head, with open mouth, wherewith to strike any ship which it may meet". There were high masts and elaborate rope fixtures; a tall poop deck; the captain's cabin and dining area; and a small outdoor kitchen adjacent to the food-animal pens. The pilgrims' cabin was below the rowers' deck; below that was the sand ballast, and below that the bilge water. These nether regions would prove less than savoury later on, but for the moment it all looked ship-shape.

After the boat tour, the captains treated their guests to a promotional snack of foreign delicacies: wine from Crete, sweetmeats from Egypt, sometimes a whole meal. Parson Torkington was most impressed with elaborate dishes made in the shape of castles and saints. Having chosen a galley and signed a contract, the party returned to the boat and each chalked his name on the berth space he wanted. William Wey strongly recommended upper-level berths, "for in the lowest it is right hot and stinking".

There still remained time for last-minute shopping – not too long, the pilgrim hoped, because Venice was expensive, but captains were reluctant to commit themselves to a sailing date. For bedding, Wey named a shop near St Mark's where mattress, linens and quilts could be resold at half price on the way home. One needed cool linen underwear for hot weather and an overcoat for chill; a chest with a lock; a laxative, a restorative, and plague pills; a basin in which to spit or be sick; and rose- or carnation-scented aromatics to dispel the general atmosphere. The German pilgrim Arnold von Harff also supplied himself with "a stately merchant's gown" for making an impression and "a heathenish dress with a blue veil" for going unnoticed.

Though meals were included, Wey advised the pilgrim to lay in food and drink, "for sometimes ye shall have feeble bread and feeble wine and stinking water so that many times ye will be right fain to eat of your own". Besides, most travellers got tired of Italian cooking. Minimal utensils and supplies included two barrels of wine (Paduan wine was recommended), one barrel of water (preferably drawn at St Nicholas), cheese, sausage, salted meat, biscuit, dried fruit, sugar, and a cage full of chickens (with a supply of chicken-feed). When he had spent what he must (about £150 today), the pilgrim was advised to change money, since Venetian ducats were universal currency and it was difficult beyond Europe to find foreign merchants willing to perform the exchange of other moneys.

The galley departed amidst great fanfare: multicoloured, embroidered silken banners flying, pilgrims singing holy songs, galley slaves shouting and trumpets blowing. From that auspicious beginning, things tended to decline – the month-long journey was hardly a pleasure voyage.

The pilgrim found the general tone to be one of boredom varied with intense discomfort. He had to make his own amusements: he might read (holy books, of course), converse, pray either silently or with his shipmates – sermonizing was the only organized recreation on shipboard. Casola's fellow traveller Francesco Trivulzio favoured his shipmates with sermons that went on for hours, literary flights on such topics as the allegorical significance of ships or the spiritual meaning of trade. Friar Faber also attempted to do some preaching, but he was silenced by rude giggling in the audience, which was, in any case, multinational and so lacked a common language. Von Harff, on the other hand, found much to interest him in the here-and-now, and spent his days measuring, estimating, and taking notes on all structures and functions he observed on the galley. Others sang or played music: bagpipes, clavichords, flutes, zithers. The French gambled, and what Friar Faber called "men of a low class" – Saxons and Flemings – got drunk. Some could find nothing better to do than jump up and down or climb the riggings, to the chagrin of the more contemplative. Others stared blankly out to sea. All, however, had to devote some part of the day to a task which, as Faber put it, "albeit loathesome, is very common, daily, and necessary – I mean the hunting down and catching of lice and vermin" on one's person.

The great diversion was eating, though it was hardly a gracious affair. A trumpet sounded, and there was a desperate scramble for a place at one of the three tables on the poop deck; latecomers had to take their plates to the rowing benches, with the galley slaves. Amidst smoke and angry shouts from the kitchen, the food was served: an aperitif of *malvoisie*, followed by lettuce salad, mutton (salt fish on Friday), and then either a grain pudding or biscuits and cheese. There was also watered wine, but sometimes wine and water ran short on the return trip. After the meal, the tablecloths were snatched up and the trumpet blew again, signalling the diners to clear off for the second seating of the captain and his honoured guests. Women did not join the company at mealtimes but ate in their berths.

Diversions were also provided by the various hazards of the galley. The pilgrim had to be on the lookout against falling ropes and beams; against cursing, hurrying sailors who would shove him roughly out of the way; against theft, by the galley slaves or equally by fellow passengers, "especially in the matter of trifles, such as kerchiefs, belts, shirts. . . . For example, while you are writing, if you lay down your pen and turn your face away, your pen will be lost, even though you be among men whom you know"; even against inadvertently sitting in a pool of pitch melted by the sun. The most serious danger came from pirates; in the second part of the fifteenth century the pilgrim was in frequent apprehension of attack by the Turks. He would be expected to aid in the ship's defence. Often pilgrim galleys were insufficiently armed – then sailors and travellers seized whatever came to hand. The German pilgrim Martin Baumgarten described such an event, with men throwing stones as "their knees struck against one another in fear".

Nor were the nights a tranquil respite. First, there were recurrent, often violent quarrels over berth space. Next, there were those who insisted on keeping everybody awake with talk or candlelight – until a neighbour extinguished the candle by emptying his chamberpot over it. After that, out came the creatures of the night: all the vermin, and sometimes the food animals who had broken out of their pen and ran over the sleeping passengers. The stench of the bilgewater grew more and more powerful. Oftener than not, one awoke ill-rested next day.

Happily for the pilgrim, this grimly monotonous succession was broken by visits to various ports. On Faber's 1483 voyage, the first stop was Rovigno, where the friar climbed a hill for a view of the sea – an avante-garde taste of his at a time when rugged scenery was not widely appreciated. The next stop was unplanned; the boat had to land on a desert island to avoid unfavourable winds. Faber went botanizing. He found purslane for salad and aromatic agnus cactus to sweeten his berth.

At Crete, the Faber party couldn't find an inn, so they stayed at a brothel – emptied of working women, Faber hastened to assure his readers – where they received an excellent supper, including the celebrated Cretan wine. Other travellers, presumably, availed themselves more fully of the brothel, where they could practise the handy Greek phrases given in von Harff's manuscript:

"Woman, shall I sleep with you?"

"Woman, I am already in your bed."

"Woman, shall I marry you?"

Despite, or perhaps because of, the pleasures Crete offered, the tourist had a low opinion of the Cretans. Baumgarten declared, "the excellence and fruitfulness of the soil emasculated the inhabitants. . . . The Cretans are always liars, evil beasts, and slow bellies." Furthermore, as the Latin guidebook *Innominatur* pointed out, they could not be trusted because "they even have an alphabet of their own".

After Crete, there was a stop at Rhodes, where von Harff saw his first ostrich. He noted, "When these birds have laid eggs in the hot sand, they hatch out the young with their piercing sight alone. . . . I was told they digest iron and steel, but this I have not seen."

Pietro Lando, the captain of Faber's galley, insisted on stopping at Larnaca to spend time with one of his wives. The passengers were disgruntled, but Faber and a few companions made good use of the delay with an excursion to the holy Mount St Croix, where reposed the cross of Dysmas, the penitent thief. They travelled by night, on mules, under the light of the moon when "the shrubs of that land breathed forth the sweetest fragrance, for almost all the herbs of that isle are spices of divers sorts, which smell by far sweetest in the night time, when they are moist with dew". After breakfast they saw the miraculous cross – supposedly suspended in mid-air; Faber noted that it appeared indeed to be so, but that he could not verify it – and thence to look at the sea. The next land they would behold would be the Holy Land itself.

It came into view, several days later, and rejoicing was great. *Te Deum* was sung, reported Faber, simultaneously in Latin, Italian, French, German, English, Hungarian, and Spanish, with numerous regional variations. The trumpeters sounded their horns, and the jongleur beat his drum. What greeted the pilgrim next was the perennial bane of tourism: crossing a difficult border. He landed at Jaffa, but with political relations between Venetian and Saracen shaky at best, it might be some time before he disembarked and still longer before he was out of "quarantine" and headed for Jerusalem. As the fifteenth century progressed, tolls grew heavier (about £350 per passenger, by 1980 values) and more numerous, and red tape increasingly complicated. It was the proliferation of tolls that ultimately put Contarini out of business.

As time went on, more and more officials were required to examine and vouch for the pilgrims: the Emir of Ramle, the Governor of Jerusalem, the Father Guardian of Mount Zion. These dignitaries, with their entourage of "revolting and corpulent men with long beards", as one pilgrim described them (no doubt the first natives of Jaffa he had ever seen), pitched their "customs and immigration" tents on the shore, soon to be joined by donkey boys and uninhibitedly curious onlookers. After some preliminary wrangling, which sometimes took days, the pilgrim was rowed ashore, but not before the ritual of tipping the galley slaves. It was an essential ritual, for the galley slaves made an aggressive appearance rattling their silver cups and assured the passengers that the ungenerous would have a hard time getting off the boat.

The captain paid the collective tolls. There was an additional charge for being non-Muslim, but groups paid discount rates. Then each pilgrim was examined by customs. It was illegal for non-Muslims to carry swords, and illegal to carry wine. Baumgarten, however, got some contraband past the officials by smuggling it inside a large piece of pork, "which they abominate above all things", so much so that they wouldn't touch it. Next came the issuing of visas, and then the mandatory waiting period in the stinking and dripping Caves of St Peter while arrangements were made for leaving Jaffa (guides, donkeys, settling on the Jaffa exit fee). Waiting in the caves offered possibilities for spiritual advancement – they had bona fide indulgence status. However, there was a thriving market in the caves, set up by the locals, to make the stay more bearable: rushes and muslin for a bed; Damascus rosewater, frankincense, and sweet soap to improve the air; fried eggs, bread, salads, hotcakes, and drinking water. There were mandatory expenditures, too: impromptu tolls collected by the guards. It was also hoped to lure the pilgrim into a fight, which would then necessitate his paying a heavy fine. To this purpose the Saracens applied all their ribald ingenuity; one young man of Faber's party was so upset by the rude jokes that he went back to the ship and never came ashore in the Holy Land again.

When at last the arrangements were made, all gathered for the trek to Ramle, next stop *en route* to Jerusalem. Every donkey owner in Jaffa turned up in hopes of work for himself as a guide and for his animal, and the pilgrim found himself violently tugged in opposite directions. Wey advised the pilgrim to be on the spot early, since the best donkeys were quickly claimed. But travellers like Canon Casola were not to be seen displaying such unsophisticated eagerness. Casola wrote, "I always let the Ultramontanes – who trod on each other's heels in their haste to leave – rush in front."

It was a morning's ride to Ramle. At the gate, the pilgrim had to dismount and walk, since Christians were forbidden to ride in the city. He stayed in the hospice built under the auspices of Philip the Good of Burgundy, an elegant establishment with vaulted rooms and date palms and fountains in the courtyard, where excellent food was on sale from the Arabs: roast chicken, almond and date confections, fine breads and a cornucopian variety of fruits. At Ramle, the Father Zion delivered a sermon on touristic deportment: no carving graffiti or chipping monuments; no skimping on ecclesiastical donations; keep out of mosques; never share wine with an Arab, look at his woman, or giggle at his antics – "the pilgrim ought to turn himself away and look grave so he will have peace". There was often occasion to put this advice to the test, because at Ramle Arab–European relations were notoriously strained, and the town was reputed to have the naughtiest street-urchins in the Holy Land.

More dangerous miscreants lurked ahead. It was written of the Jaffa–Jerusalem road that all along the way, Arabs

lay hidden in caves and crevices, waiting day and night for people travelling in small parties or straggling behind their groups. At one moment they are everywhere, the next they are gone. Their presence is felt by everyone who passes on that fatal road.

The governors of Ramle would not grant permission for pilgrims to leave if there were thought to be hostile tribesmen lurking. Even without them, it was a barren, ill-graced stretch of country. Casola commented in distaste, "These are not like the countries of Italy." Some members of Faber's party became so depressed that they fought. But the ultimate reward of the pilgrimage was not far away.

From the Jaffa road, wrote Faber, the city of Jerusalem came into view "like a flash of lightning": a holy revelation. Walled and crenellated, with domes and minarets rising above the fortifications, and behind them the sacred Mount Zion, Jerusalem appeared to the pilgrim literally as it was depicted in the medieval Books of Hours. On sight of the great city, Margery Kempe swooned and nearly fell off her donkey, whereupon Wey's recommended medicinal spices came in handy to revive her. For the most part, the circumspect pilgrim kept his devotions in check. He murmured his *Te Deum* in an undertone, so as not to provoke his infidel guides unnecessarily.

He entered Jerusalem via the Fish Gate, so named because it gave on to the road from the sea. There, he found hundreds of starving pilgrims begging for the entrance fee (one gold piece); some had been there for days. But the package tourist transcended such hardships. Removing his shoes to enhance piety with penance, he made his way to the forecourt of the Church of the Holy Sepulchre, built where the last events in the life of Christ had taken place.

The guide delivered a brief historical lecture, and a pandemonium of devotion was let loose: weeping, howling, shrieking, beating of breasts, outstretching of arms in the manner of one crucified, flinging of bodies on the ground to soak up holy vibrations. By the fifteenth century Faber was remarking that much emotional display arose "not because of the power which the place exercises . . . but because of the ease with which they weep". Like other aspects of the tour, the naïve rhapsodies were now being deliberately manufactured, too – by the pilgrim tourist himself. Once the first devotions were over, the pilgrim and his party advanced to the church itself and had a look through its narrow windows. To go inside, appointments had to be made in advance, for one or more night-long vigils. In the meantime there was plenty of sightseeing to be done in and around Jerusalem.

The fabric of no other city was so closely overlaid with religious significance. Every stone told a story. The rich accretion particularly appealed to the late-Gothic imagination, with its penchant for the elaborate, and the whole city had been quantified and versified so that the pilgrim missed nothing. John Poloner, an English pilgrim of the 1420s, left precise instructions: "From the place of weeping one goes 195 steps to the place where the angel Gabriel brought the palm branch to the glorious Virgin. . . . Two stone-throws higher up is the house of Caiaphas." For those of a non-arithmetical turn of memory, William Wey supplied rhymes. His style was heavily reminiscent of the *Stations of Rome*:

> Beside the school in a temple small,
> That some time was Saint Annys hall,
> A little forth in the way
> Is Herod's hall as I you say.

Secular sights were not ignored. The pilgrim couldn't help but be interested in the exotic bazaars, the haunting Arab music, the strange devotions of the Muslims. Though it was prohibited to visit mosques, a few Christians gained entry. Faber noticed an unlocked door and sneaked in; von Harff bribed a Mameluke and, no doubt making use of his heathenish dress and veil, walked in.

The women, too, were fascinating and disturbing. Santo Brasca, observing the black veils that covered their faces and the diaphanous fabrics that swathed them from head to foot, thought the women looked like "devils from Hell". Though veiled, they were bold: they took mischievous pleasure in waving and calling to the male pilgrims, and on one occasion drilled a hole in the wall of a hospice to peep at them. Von Harff reported that the Muslim women "often deceive their husbands, taking leave to go to the baths"; their veils provided the perfect disguise. More than one beauty, he added, had tried to tempt him from his Christian faith.

Other days, the pilgrim made short excursions outside Jerusalem. An obligatory one was to the Mount of Olives, taking in the Pool of Bethesda, the Garden of Gethsemane, and the Valley of Jehosophat. In the Valley of Jehosophat, the Day of Judgement would one day occur; to provide for that eventuality, the prudent pilgrim left piles of stones for himself and his loved ones, to be used as seats. Friar Faber was dubious – how would every soul that ever lived find room here when "all the Swabians who are now alive could barely find standing room"? Singing hymns to keep up their spirits in the heat, the touring parties tried to maintain a brisk pace. On such excursions, remarked Faber, many had cause to regret the "costly shoes" they wore for sightseeing.

After a few days, the party would receive notice that they were on that night's entry list for the Holy Sepulchre. Following supper, a crowd gathered in the church forecourt: up to 150 pilgrims; the turbaned and disdainful Saracen church keepers, with their official guest list; and assorted merchants – foodsellers with provisions for the night, candle vendors, and cloth and gem dealers who would pass the night inside the church selling their wares to the pilgrims. When everyone with permission had been admitted, the doors were locked until eight the next morning.

Inside, the pilgrim blinked, getting used to the dark; he scratched, perhaps, since the cathedral was infested with fleas, and kissed whatever stones were to hand, until the friars commenced their preliminary lecture and protocol instructions. No graffiti, beware of pickpockets, no shoving, don't waste alms on non-Roman worshippers.

Then came the three-hour guided tour of the cathedral, illuminated by the visitors' candles and accompanied by their hymns and exhortations. There was an underground chapel whose pillars were perpetually moist (a miraculous manifestation of weeping over Christ's judgement), and a giant seashell through which one heard the noises of Hell, said the guide. There was the rock of Calvary. Ultimately the pilgrims came to the Chapel of the Sepulchre, housing Christ's tomb. When the tour was over, there was an hour's rest. Then, at midnight, came the masses, when the pilgrim could consummate his visit with communion in the chapel on the rock of Calvary.

The pilgrim was left to his own devices after mass. Serious scholars like Wey could investigate theological questions: had the column to which Christ was bound been sprinkled with his blood? What was the true nature of the Holy Fire, and of the lamp above the Sepulchre? Aesthetes like Casola could get a more serene view of the displays: "As soon as I saw that the crowd of Ultramontanes had diminished, I went again with my lighted candle . . . and I touched the places and relics . . . without any impediment." Others bargained for fabric, chatted, picnicked, got drunk, or slept. Some went about leaving graffiti, despite the prohibition; knights especially liked to carve their coat-of-arms. Furtive sexual encounters in dark corners were not unknown. What the medieval Christian pilgrim from Europe found most offensive was the behaviour of the Oriental Christians: the Syrian priests who struck hammers on strips of iron, and members of other alien sects who jumped up and down, yelled, and clapped their hands. Most atypical was the sophisticated Martin Baumgarten, who remarked, "It is very well worth one's while to observe the great variety of sects that are in this temple, to hear so many different languages, voices, music, to see how they differ in their rites and ceremonies."

In whatever spirit they had passed the night, the pilgrims appeared loath to leave in the morning when the doors were unlocked. The visitors scattered, kissing all the holy places again, and the Saracens finally drove them out by force.

Outside, the pilgrim stocked up on souvenirs. Those he bought here would be the gems of his collection. The emblematic souvenir of Jerusalem was the palm frond: flourishing in the desert, it symbolized Christian regeneration and the triumph of faith over sin. In the eleventh century, pilgrims had to venture into the desert to pick their own palm fronds, but by the twelfth century these could be purchased in town; also popular as mementoes were lengths of string measuring the doorways, pillars, and other fixtures of the Church of the Holy Sepulchre. By the late Middle Ages, souvenir merchants had branched out considerably, selling paper crucifixes, paintings on paper and cloth, and small wooden models of the holy places. Wealthier tourists bought rings or silver bells and had them consecrated, touching them to the Sepulchre; some came home with dozens. The exotic fabrics purchased during the Sepulchre vigil had both sacred and worldly value as souvenirs.

There were two additional obligatory excursions, to Bethlehem and to the river Jordan. Bethlehem, five miles from Jerusalem, was a half-day's journey and entailed an overnight stay, including an all-night mass. The journey was leisurely, because it was "through woods full pleasant", as Mandeville said, and because there were so many Biblical sites along the way: the tower where Jacob wrestled with the angel, Rachel's tomb (rebuilt), the Virgin's halting places. Less pleasant delays might also befall the pilgrim: when Faber made the journey, his party was set upon by a gang of Arabs, one of whom found it uproariously funny to spear the friar's cap off his head.

At Bethlehem's Church of the Nativity, the pilgrim was shown an underground cave whose walls oozed a white substance, said to be essence of Virgin's milk; a sweet-smelling stone where the infant Jesus had lain; a well that still reflected, to the eye of the true believer, the star of Bethlehem; and the marble crib of the ox and ass which, when polished, produced an image of St Jerome and a lion. There was also said to be a great hoard of bodies of Holy Innocents; Friar Faber disbelieved the Arab guides who made that claim, but several of his companions scratched around in the dirt hoping to unearth fragments of bone. Not far from Bethlehem, wrote Mandeville, were the graves of the Patriarchs in the Vale of Hebron, although the locals discouraged Christian visitors, reviling them as hounds.

Also essential was the two-day trip to the Jordan, despite its perils. For one thing, the way entailed a precipitous, twenty-mile, 3000-foot descent in tremendous heat; for another, there might be bandits. In 1480, reports of marauders on the Jordan road necessitated an armed guard for the Contarini tour; Contarini insisted on an extra charge for the guard; the tourists refused to pay. The Muslims supplied the guard in the end, which Contarini had to finance. It was not much later that Contarini went out of business.

There were few sights of note on the way – fortunately so, since it was undesirable to linger in that dangerous, desolate place. The pilgrim was shown Lazarus's tomb, the Magdalene's house (subsequently occupied by goats) and the house of the traitor Judas, where the pilgrim was encouraged to express his contempt and anger, no doubt a welcome release after his desert trek.

At last the river Jordan came into view, long, meandering, narrow and muddy. To bathe in the Jordan had threefold spiritual significance: it was an imitation of Christ, it was a purification and healing act said to cure even leprosy, and it was a veneration of a holy relic. The pilgrim immersed himself as deeply and as far as he dared – though it could be unsafe, because there was a swift current in the river. Drownings were not uncommon, and swimming across was forbidden by the Saracens, although this was frequently disobeyed. Often the pilgrim went in fully clothed, not so much from modesty as to sanctify his garments. He also dipped whatever he could, especially the little silver bells bought for that purpose. Flasks of Jordan water were prized but illicit souvenirs; they were believed to cause disasters at sea, so the galleys forbade them on the return trip.

The Saracens watched the Christian ablutions with some impatience and disquiet. When the water ritual seemed to have gone on long enough, the pilgrims were summarily ordered out of the river and chastised if they tarried.

Next came another gruelling ride, to the Mount of Fastings. The way was through the notoriously xenophobic city of Jericho, where Faber's party was driven out of town. To their particular disappointment, they didn't even have a chance to stop in Jericho for dinner, though afterwards they picnicked most agreeably in a shady glen where there was a sweet stream from which they drank "like cows, without stint".

The Mount of Fastings was steep and rocky – the last part of the ascent, to the Chapel of Temptation, had often to be made on hands and knees. The hearty octogenarian ladies in Faber's party, despite excellent intentions, finally gave up. Margery Kempe got stranded on a ledge; when she howled for aid, her companions were ready to abandon her, but a Saracen guide went back and, for a tip of one groat, dragged her up to the chapel. It was, after all, what the Devil had done in leading Christ to that perilous spot.

All around were the anchorites' caves; the pilgrim noted their recessed bookshelves, sleeping platforms, cooking facilities. There was also a stupendous view, a vast Biblical panorama that stretched down to the sea. It was a spectacular culmination to the Holy Land tour.

The pilgrim now proceeded homewards as directly as possible. Any new sights would be anticlimactic. His tour did not describe a circle but a straight line ending at the major destination – after that, he was anxious to present the "new man" travel had made of him to his friends back home.

The moment of return itself was significant. Canon Casola detached himself from his companions so he could enter Milan alone, humbly attired in pilgrim's garb. He went for a solitary prayer at the Church of Our Lady, and only then did he visit the archbishop. Others received a ceremonial greeting. If a pilgrim belonged to a guild, for instance, his fellow members might contrive to meet him at the city gate and accompany him to the monastery for his return blessing. The pilgrim's trip was not complete until all who had blessed his departure had sanctified his return.

There were souvenirs to distribute and social calls to be made. But, like the modern tourist who returns home eager to share his travel snaps and exotic anecdotes, the pilgrim often met with a dour reception. Margery Kempe got back to King's Lynn full of elation and bubbling with travel stories. The vicar found her high spirits most unsuitable in a pilgrim. He frowned and said, "Margery, I wonder how you can be so merry."

Nor was the pilgrim's newly decorated costume properly appreciated. "I pray you," said a typical townsman, "what array is this? . . . Methinks your clothing is of cockleshells. On every side you are weighted down with brooches of lead and tin. How prettily garnished you are with coronets, and how full are your arms with snakes' eggs." This speech, from a play by Erasmus, expresses on one hand the perennial resentment of those who have missed out on a vacation. On the other it shows the pilgrim through the eyes of the Renaissance man, whose time had nearly come, and with it a new era in tourism.

CHAPTER THREE

The Elizabethan

It is an afternoon in May 1608, and there is rough sailing on the English Channel. The boat is a sixty-foot-long wooden cargo carrier, its deck stacked with boxes of freight amidst which the seventy-odd passengers try to find space. Seasoned travellers – merchants, soldiers, political envoys – have been wise enough to eat plenty of cooked quince and coriander before they set out, and above all never to look at the waves (the latest anti-seasickness tips). So they are weathering the journey pretty well, though not without uttering an angry oath or two – unless the boat is Dutch-owned, in which case swearing is punishable with a fine. Those of a pious bent buoy up their spirits with a round of the new Reformist hymns that are just coming into fashion. But one passenger, in plumed hat, white ruff at the throat, short velvet jacket and velvet knee breeches, leans over the deck and elaborately heaves out his dinner, to "varnish . . . the exterior parts of the ship with the excremental ebullitions of my tumultuous stomach . . . to satiate the gormandizing paunches of the hungry haddocks . . . with that wherewith I had superfluously stuffed myself at land".

He is an inexperienced traveller, or he would have known to eschew that last meal at Dover, but the hardships don't bother him much. They will all be matter for his travel diary; besides, he finds them interesting. As quintessential Renaissance man, he finds everything interesting. Nature's ways – the waves' roughness, the predisposition of the human digestive system to reverse itself when subjected to them – are particularly worth investigating; and if one's velvet jacket is soiled in the process, it's a small price. Come to that, it's even an advantage: this kind of thing makes a man of you. As

Thomas Coryate (the seasick tourist cited above) went on to quote, "Who is so tender, effeminate, and cowardly whom the heat of the sun, cold, snow, rain, hard seats, stony pillows and such infinite inconveniences . . . will not make more courageous and valiant?" The Elizabethan Renaissance tourist wanted to experience all of it – at least once.

With the sixteenth century, the Protestant Reformation dispelled the sanctified aura round the miraculous shrines that pilgrims had flocked to see. As the otherworldly attractions of pilgrimage waned, the enquiring spirit of the Renaissance generated great interest in this world, here and now. All kinds of study flourished, and scientific humanism emphasized immediate knowledge, seeing for oneself. For "to run over and traverse the world by *hearsay* . . . other men's eyes . . . is but a confused and imperfect kind of speculation, which leaveth but weak and distrustful notions"; whereas with "the eye . . . as through a clear and crystal casement we . . . in one instant comprehend half the whole universe". So began the *Instructions for Forraine Travel* by James Howell, a distillation of the Elizabethan tour. Francis Bacon called the Elizabethan traveller a "merchant of light" – original of the tourist who goes abroad to be broadened. His subject was modern life: natural resources, military strategy, medical science, machinery, weights and measures, law and the judiciary, ecclesiastical structure, punitive practices, childbirth and burial techniques, and everything in between. The pilgrim had set forth as part of something larger than himself, to touch a mystery; the Elizabethan set off in a spirit of independence, to make things clear.

All kinds of people became tourists in the age of pilgrimage. But the Elizabethan tourist was typically an unmarried English male in his early twenties, recently down from Oxford or Cambridge, travelling abroad to see how the world was run and thus prepare himself for membership of the ruling class. Married men ought not go, because their duty was to the family. Old men could not go, because they tired too easily and could not stomach foreign food. Women dared not go, because it jeopardized their chastity. In every sense, the Elizabethan tourist was privileged.

Money was rarely an obstacle if the tourist was a member of the wealthy class. However, in the belief that there was no better preparation for a government career, Queen Elizabeth herself sometimes paid part of the way. How would a young diplomat take part in foreign court life if he were ignorant of foreign affairs and lacked continental graces? Universities gave travel fellowships, too: in 1591, Fynes Moryson got £20 a year for two years from Peterhouse College, Cambridge, where he had studied law (Moryson also took a few courses at Oxford before he left, because an Oxford degree had more cachet abroad). In 1600, £50 or £60 a year (equal to about £2500–£3000 in 1980) covered expenses for a moderate young man like Moryson, provided he didn't over-eat like a German, fornicate like an Italian, or gamble like a Pole. Some extravagant young lords, however, easily spent four times that amount on themselves, and then some more on their servants. To be sure of having cash upon his return, the tourist could take out a travel wager, the prototypical travel insurance policy: a wealthy merchant laid odds that the tourist would *not* complete his journey, to be paid if he did. It was thought slightly disreputable, but Coryate staked £60 with one Joseph Starre, draper, and received £320 (equivalent to roughly £18,000) when he got back.

Since his aim was to penetrate, the Elizabethan tourist did not want to be lumbered with too many bags, but his documents were essential. First came the travel licence, which granted permission to leave England. It told how long he could stay away (usually two or three years), where he must not go (any place where the papist influence was too strong), how much money and how many horses and servants (usually three) could go with him. If the tourist also travelled with a gentleman companion-cum-tutor, the latter got a licence of his own. (The most intrepid Elizabethans went alone: Moryson, Coryate, and the dour Scotsman William Lithgow, "Cutlugs Willie", who left the British Isles summarily after his ears were lopped off in punishment for an amorous indiscretion.) The tourist had a passport, too, but that was surrendered, along with his exit fee, when he left England; new passports were picked up *en route* for each new kingdom.

The tourist also needed proof that he was a student; then as now there were student discounts throughout Europe on fares, entry fees, tolls. Letters to scholars, nobles, and especially to eminent English expatriates were equally crucial if he were to see art treasures (often private) and court life. There were also letters of credit, superior to cash because, like travellers' cheques in the present era, they couldn't be used if stolen. What coins he took were best sewn into his waistband or stuffed into the heel of his stocking – Moryson got blisters that way.

Besides his documents and money, the tourist required writing materials, a good holy book, a watch (not a striker, because that would alert robbers), a broad-brimmed hat, good boots, and a linen overall to wear in case of dirty bedclothes. Well prepared but streamlined, he was then ready for take-off, confident in the belief that he was simply obeying the law of nature. For, as Moryson summed it up, "Men were created to move, as birds to fly."

The ultimate goal of the tour was undisputed: apex of culture, flower of the Renaissance, Italy. But, one German scholar indignantly demanded, what kind of tourist "searched the ruinous theatres of the ancient Romans and the rubbish of their decayed buildings . . . also crept into the stews, brothel houses and bordellos of Italy", when he could instead be visiting Germany with its "most elegant towns" and "well-governed commonweals"? Besides, Germany was a good place to begin a tour because there the young tourist was forced to look after himself: the shops were mostly self-service (nobody to help one try on a new pair of boots) and the social arrangements were painfully egalitarian. Moryson reported that the tourist would have to "learn to admit the company of mean men, where many times . . . yea, very coachmen shall be thrust to be our bedfellows, and that when they are drunk". The tourist smiled to himself: he was ready.

Via the North Sea, his first stop was elegant, well-governed Hamburg, with handsome brick buildings and such ingenious innovations as wooden water-pipes (to avoid freezing). The tourist looked around him with approval. But Hamburg frequently meant trouble, too. The docks were rough, and after lunch, when they had tanked up on beer, the longshoremen were all too ready to pick a fight with an English traveller strolling by the harbour. When Moryson was there, it was suggested that a packing crate be smashed over his head. Hamburg was also renowned for its streetwalkers, whose practice was to entrap unwary clients; the client was arrested as soon as he reached the woman's room and forced to pay a fine, to be shared between streetwalker and magistrate. Even if the tourist had avoided that particular snare, he would be fingering his wallet nervously and wondering how his money would hold up, because Hamburg was expensive. "The dearest thing and most pinching that I find is drink, twopence sterling [about 50p today] the poor pint of English beer," fretted Henry Wotton, the future English ambassador to Venice, aged twenty-one when he started his tour from Hamburg. So the sensible tourist made his stay at Hamburg brief and headed instead for a university town – Wittenberg or Leipzig to the east, or Heidelberg to the south – where he could rent an inexpensive room, get his continental bearings, and take lessons to improve his German. Later on in Italy, to conceal their national identity from the Inquisition, many Elizabethan Protestants would pose as Germans; so mastering the fine points of German enunciation and grammar was of more than academic interest. That done, one was more ready to see Germany properly as well.

When he was ready to set off again, if he had no horses of his own, the English traveller asked around until he found five or six people going his way, and they shared the hire of a coach. At £3 per mile (1980's equivalent), the cost was very high, though the coach was no luxury conveyance: a covered wagon with wooden plank seats and convertible top of leather or heavy black cloth. It rolled across the flat, wooded countryside with ponderous slowness, and the journey was no pleasure. The passengers were crammed against each other on the hard, backless seats, and the aristocratic young man had to endure the beery breath and stodgy observations of his companions. He raised an eyebrow imperceptibly and turned his attention to the local agriculture instead.

At night, the coach party stopped at an inn. They were coldly greeted by the innkeeper, who rarely favoured his guests with even a hello. But the front room, with its built-in earthen oven, was very warm indeed. Unfortunately there was bad ventilation, so eventually the room reeked of sweat – especially when the less distinguished clientele was present.

Then, warmed, the party filed in for dinner, a strictly scheduled affair with no latecomers permitted. This cost about £3 at 1980's equivalent value. The dishes were stacked in sequence on a great iron tripod at the centre of the table: first course was a soup of sauerkraut, bread, and beer; next, typically, came beef with black cherry sauce; and last of all, bacon and sausage, the *pièce de résistance* (the German desideratum was "*Kurtz predigen, lange worsten*" – short sermons and long sausages). Other specialities included sour anise-flavoured bread, and cheese fermented in wine, so ripe that, as Fynes Moryson reported, "They eat the mouldy pieces and the very creeping maggots for dainty morsels." Wine was plentiful, but the surly German servants, to avoid making trips round the table to refill the cups, stood in one place and used a pitcher with a very long spout, rather like a twentieth-century oil can.

Table talk might be jocular, but it was not bawdy; under the table was a little bell, to be rung if anyone "speaks immodestly of love matters . . . to remind a wise man of his error". The inflammatory subject was politics. The tourist was forever pumped about England, though English law forbade his discussing affairs of state. There were inevitably thieves at table, too, so he was wise to avoid reference to personal wealth. He kept his eyes open, and tried to listen more than he spoke.

Soon the company would be too drunk to talk. The fellowship grew heartier and heavier, with much fervent hand-clasping wherein the tourist risked a crushed thumb. According to Moryson, there was "no shame . . . even to spew at the table and in their next fellow's bosom, or to piss under the table, and afterwards in bed". The best way to avoid these excesses was to go straight to bed when the dinnercloth was lifted from the table. If the tourist did not leave promptly at that moment, he would be charged for all-night drinking, a fixed percentage of the total consumption.

Besides, the tourist remembered, he needed time for his travel journal and correspondence. Since this was a study-trip, it was imperative to keep notes. Also, diary and epistle were stylistically important genres; the gentlemanly arts of wit and story-telling were vital skills, especially for a statesman, and letter writing was taught at the best Renaissance universities. However, the tourist was here wise to couch his more incisive comments in code, lest his notes be discovered and he be accused of treason. His writing completed, the tourist put his purse under his pillow, secured his sword at his side, and went to sleep – though he would surely wake with a chill in the night when his bedfellows joined him, because the duvet was never wide enough for two.

Happily, his stay at the inn was not protracted. In Germany – except for any period when he took classes at university – the Elizabethan tourist "made time" when he travelled. In the morning he was off to an early start.

Thomas Coryate visited fifteen German cities in under three weeks: a heavy itinerary. At the same time, the tourist was determined to fully "cover" each one. He started the visit to a new town by climbing the highest steeple for an overview. Then, following Francis Bacon's instructions, he systematically checked out each and every court, church, monument, fortification, harbour, antiquity, library, college, disputation, army, navy, arsenal, magazine, bourse, warehouse, fencing school, riding academy, theatre, treasury, cabinet, and museum, measuring all accessible structures, noting all available statistics, and copying all legible inscriptions into his travel notebook. If possible he also enquired of a local informant about the town's nightwatch system, water-usage rights, divorce laws, famines, floods, fires, leper colonies, local recipes, and anything else pertaining to social life that he could think of. He always tried to fit in lunch with an eminent scholar, provided his Latin was up to it – and that the scholar was willing. One German professor, Zacharias Ursinus, was so surfeited with English visitors that he had a plaque mounted over his door reading, "My friend, whoever you are, if you come here please either go away again or give me some help with my studies." The tourist's days were nothing if not full.

Besides these staple attractions, there were a few that particularly appealed to the Renaissance penchant for the elaborate and the unusual. Augsburg's great curiosity was *der Einlasse*, the automatic night gate: one deposited money in a box, stepped into an iron cage and, after an unseen guard gave the OK, an invisible mechanism released the lock. Some people deliberately stayed out after curfew just to see it work, but nobody could report back to Queen Elizabeth what the secret was. At Heidelberg the tourist inspected the world's largest wine tun – capacity over 24,000 gallons. When Coryate had climbed to the top, he was offered a sample of the contents, but he warned future visitors not to accept "as much as the sociable Germans would persuade thee unto" or it would be impossible to climb down. At Strasbourg everyone marvelled over the Gothic astronomical clock, a mechanical extravaganza with movable Roman gods telling the days of the week, Death announcing the hour, and at noon St Peter's cock crowing while Christ blessed the Apostles – a great occasion for the tourist to hold forth in his journal on science, religion and universal order. Coryate hoped that his account would prompt somebody to build one in London.

Pleasure was incidental in the Elizabethan's travels; he did not go looking for it. But continuing his socioeconomic survey of the region, he could not avoid a charming interlude when his itinerary dipped south to the spa town of Baden in Switzerland. Mineral spas in that era served much the same purpose as holiday resorts in the present one: the visitor simply took a little tonic exercise, relaxed, ate well, and made new friends. The days were spent "around the pool", dipping, or sipping if the waters were to be taken internally, and socializing; in the evening, a leisurely meal (Baden's speciality was crayfish with a light Swiss wine) and perhaps a session at the gaming tables.

Baden was a serious medical establishment. For the proletarian visitors, those with serious infirmities, there were two big public baths – sometimes their waters ran deep red from all the cuppings and bleedings, as the student of modern sciences observed with interest. Paying guests used the felicitous private baths attached to the inns. The walls were painted and the windows glazed, so the rooms were colourful and luminous; private compartments featured a window to the compartment adjoining, so one could chat or raise a glass with one's neighbour; floating tables for a snack or a book or a deck of cards were available. The greatest attraction, however, was the mixed bathing: men and women, young and old, married and single, climbed in together naked from the waist up, to flirt and dally. "Many having no disease but that of love, howsoever they feign sickness of body, come hither for remedy and many times find it," observed Fynes Moryson. There were always lots of courting couples, the young women delightful with breasts bare and heads garlanded with flowers and wreathed with long golden braids. Older married couples were no less demonstrative, and not only with each other. The cardinal *faux pas* at Baden was a display of jealousy. Such cool continental comportment was beyond Thomas Coryate. "Let these Germans and Helvetians . . . observe these kind of wanton customs as long as they will," he declared – no wife of his would be permitted to bathe nude with strange men. "For I might have just cause to fear lest if she went into the water with the effigies of a male lamb characterized upon her belly, the same might within a few hours grow to be a horned ram" (mark of the cuckold). Happily, the bachelor Elizabethan tourist could sample the pleasures of Baden without a pang; it was always instructive to compare sexual mores in different parts of the world and muse upon the consequences of social institutions.

On the subject of special events and pageants, Francis Bacon counselled, "men need not be put in mind of them; neither are they to be neglected". One special event on no account to be neglected, however, was the biannual book fair at Frankfurt. As sumptuous, solemn Easter at Rome was the peak touristic experience for the medieval pilgrim, so for the Elizabethan tourist was the Frankfurt book fair, an international gathering of publishers, scholars, and wits, a dazzling marketplace of contemporary ideas. Young Philip Sidney was at the fair in 1573; Henry Wotton attended in 1589; Fynes Moryson saw it in 1592; Thomas Coryate met the Earl of Essex there in 1608 – any "merchant of light" made it his business to be there if possible.

Since 1462, when Mainz came under siege, forcing the original printers under the auspices of Gutenberg to flee that city, Frankfurt had been the European capital of book publishing. As an early stronghold of the Reformation, Frankfurt was deeply imbued with the spirit of popular enquiry appropriate to that enterprise, along with a sizeable market for books, especially the Bible. The city was ideally placed to attract and disseminate wisdom and wealth: right at the crossroads of Europe, with Berlin to the north, Basel (the second city of printing) to the east, Paris to the south and Leipzig to the north. The fertile Rhine valley provided food and wine to sustain the multitudes, and a "fair and navigable" waterway led right into town. "Especially must we believe that it is by the same divine providence that the River Main so holds its course as to wash against this city," as the French visitor Henri Estienne pointed out in 1574. Clearly, the Frankfurt fair was a key feature in the universal plan.

The tourist began to inhale the fair's cosmopolitan atmosphere on the boat up from Heidelberg. On board with Thomas Coryate were "some few of every principal nation of Christendom", from Wittenberg to Padua, Cracow to Cambridge. Just outside the city, Coryate also espied from his place on deck the "most rueful spectacle of hanged men suspended from the gallows", but those going to the fair hoped that the light of reason and the healthy bustle of commerce would go far to rid the world of such antisocial characters before long.

Once inside the walls of the city, thoughts of humanity in the abstract gave way to the real thing: Frankfurt was packed. Besides the book fair there was a vast merchandise exposition, and the population normally tripled at fair time. The crowds were so dense that rubbish disposal regulations were suspended because it was often impossible to get a cart through the streets. Unless he had a letter of introduction to a bookseller with a guest room, the tourist's first order of business was to secure himself room at an inn. German visitors had their usual lodgings: Augsburgers stayed at the

Augsburgerhof, Heidelbergers put up at the Heidelbergerhof. Foreign tourists, though, had to push their way through and reconnoitre. The innkeepers didn't put out a sign, but it was obvious which were the best places by the number of heraldic escutcheons, left as a kind of "tip" by satisfied patrons of noble blood, displayed by the door outside.

His bag deposited, the visitor could sate his curiosity more fully. Fair-time Frankfurt went on all night: the sky was bright with fireworks, the midnight drinking curfew was lifted, and the prostitutes were out in full force. Alternatively there was the usual drunken bonhomie of the inn to entertain the tourist. In any case, he would want to be up early in the morning, with all there was to see in the light.

He started the day with a slice of gingerbread washed down with *aqua vitae*, a standard German breakfast for travellers, sold round town. Then he wandered about Frankfurt in amazement at "wealth inconceivable, so great that it was impossible for a man to conceive it in his mind that had not first seen it with his bodily eyes . . . the richest meeting of anywhere in Christendom", as Coryate exclaimed. In 1574, Henri Estienne found at Frankfurt "as much merchandise as there are stars in the sky": livestock, agricultural produce, silver and gold (resplendently on show at the Unten den Roemer), armaments, glassware, linens, veils, tapestries, fine paintings (displayed for sale in the cloisters of St Bartholomew's), wines, spices, sausages, and "a chariot and four of ivory which could be hidden by the wings of a bee". Or, put another way by the scowling Martin Luther, the Frankfurt fair was "that silver and gold hole through which flows from German lands everything that flows, grows, or is coined and beaten": a distinguished contemporary "trade show". The Elizabethan tourist was not normally a buyer of souvenirs, but he gathered a quantity of ideas about manufacture and commerce, key issues of the age.

At the same time, there was every sort of fairground attraction in the streets. Sideshows presented an elephant, a pelican (demonstrating the range of nature's cunning – more matter for the travel notebook), a tightrope walker who could push a boy in a wheelbarrow across a high wire attached to the Nikolai Thurm. Mountebanks, known as "treacle sellers" for their sweet-talk, purveyed potions and unguents, displaying gallstones they'd removed and teeth they'd pulled; but whereas Italian mountebanks charmed the crowds with wit, observed Moryson, German ones just wore them out with bragging. Fencing displays were a unique attraction of the Frankfurt fair; the fencing masters picked up and laid down their arms with great flourish, but they rarely did much fighting. More high-toned were the impromptu, perambulating music and poetry contests: after a drumroll, artists competed for the crowd's approval. Most popular of all were the English travelling theatrical players, despite their ragged props and costumes, their reduced company and the fact that the crowd could not understand a word they said. However, Fynes Moryson was not surprised, because it was well known that German wandering players were "more deserving pity than praise, for the serious parts are dully penned and worse acted, and the mirth they make is ridiculous and . . . less than witty".

The Elizabethan traveller recognized more than one kind of wit. As a contemporary social commentator pointed out: "By the Germans' wit the art of printing was first invented, of all arts that ever were as the most profitable, so the wittiest invention." To steep himself in that heady stuff, the tourist made his way round to the book fair, the "Fair of the Muses".

The main street of the book fair was Buchgasse, and it spread from there to Leonardskirche on one side and the river Main on the other. Booksellers' booths had a sign over the door giving the proprietor's name and fresh posters advertising current titles. The range of subjects was wide: the Reformation Bible remained most popular (and most controversial), but there were also many works on religious theory, grammar, philology, philosophy, and law. Additionally there were "trade books": chivalric romances, adventures, droll stories, and especially cookbooks. In the streets men, women and children hawked broadsheets (diatribes against drink were prevalent), newspapers, novelettes (evocatively called *Mordenwundergischichten*), calendars, and popular songs. Freelance translators offered their services for difficult transactions – the *linguae francae* at the fair were French and Latin – and so did assorted "book people" from all over Europe: typesetters, binders, engravers, proof-readers. Coryate declared the bibliographic spectacle better than St Paul's Churchyard in London, the rue St Jacques in Paris, or the Venice Merceria: "the very epitome of all the principal libraries in Europe".

Most illustrious of all that there was to behold at Frankfurt were the great and learned men. The tourist was awed. The foremost thinkers of the age appeared, along with hosts of lesser but no less ambitious philosophers, logicians, historians, mathematicians, orators, and poets. In the year Henry Wotton attended, Giordano Bruno was also at Frankfurt, unnerving his colleagues with ultramodern metaphysics. As Henri Estienne enthused, "Here very often right in the shops of the booksellers you can hear them discussing philosophy no less seriously than once the Socrateses and the Platos discussed it in the Lyceum." Every nuance of rhetoric held political overtones, in both the broad and narrow sense of politics – philosophical issues were "hot". And, as the shrewd Bacon counselled, it was most instructive to meet great men "to see how the life agreeth with the fame". The tourist drank it in: circumspect, speculative, but not without an eye on his main chance.

At the book fair he had at last been able to savour a draught of continental brilliance, that rare elixir that he hoped most of all to imbibe on his travels. He had been missing it till then, for while the Germans had a reputation as advanced free-thinkers and methodical scholars, they had never been known for sparkling wit. "All writers," reported Moryson, "commend the Germans for Modesty, Integrity, Constancy, Placability, Equity, and Gravity . . . but somewhat inclining to the vice of Dulness" – a rather stodgy specimen beside the quick, articulate Elizabethan gentleman. While the tourist had great respect for such matters as drainage systems, he found the German burgher's description of them long-winded and tiresome. For that "more complete polishing of . . . parts and studies" that the tourist was after, he turned his face first of all towards Paris, Europe's most civilized city north of Milan. Brushing the German mud from his boots and touching up the points of his moustache, the traveller approached the city gates.

What greeted his eye when he arrived at Paris was a curious mix of Renaissance elegance and medieval squalor. When Philip Sidney came in 1572 he found a quarter of a million people crammed into two square miles within the city walls alone. Though the Tuileries and the Louvre were already erected, there were only two stone bridges across the Seine, which was congested with ferrymen. Plumbing was nonexistent and there was a brisk street-trade in river water, bought by the bucketful from water carriers who went about with a pail in each hand. Mules trod the reeking, narrow streets, awash in mud and sewage. As to the populace, William Lithgow, arriving in 1609, saw a mass of poor people, a nest of rogues, a tumultuous place, a nocturnal den of thieves and a confused multitude; where contrariwise London is adorned with many grave, prudent, and provident senators, civil, well-taught and courteous people.

The city of Paris was in process of a vast transformation from wood into stone, so that it seemed perpetually under construction, with veritable armies of roofers, masons, and plasterers at work. The Gothic edifices were interspersed with palatial new buildings of luminous stone, fancifully adorned with cornices, pediments, mullions, medallions, statuary, all the playful conceits of the Italian Renaissance. And by 1577 there were no less than 250 tennis courts in Paris. Paris was something to behold, but the tourist withheld his highest praise: he was fascinated, but not overwhelmed.

Luxury accommodation was not to be had. The Elizabethan visitor would probably be staying with someone of consequence, but even the aristocracy lived in elegant discomfort, in large rooms hung with new Italian art and graced with imposing staircases but unheated and always faintly pervaded with the stench of the water closet. The inns were squalid, though they served good cheap food, much less expensively than their London counterparts. New wine – never aged – was plentiful.

The great tourist attractions, then as now, were the Louvre and the Tuileries. Coryate pronounced the gilded roofwork at the Louvre "so unspeakably fair . . . that a man can hardly comprehend it in his mind", and he found that the Long Gallery "excelleth . . . not only all those that are now in the world, but also all whatsoever that ever were since the creation thereof". By the end of the sixteenth century the Louvre was also a great museum: François I had acquired works by Fra Angelico, Raphael, and da Vinci. The Elizabethan visitor was much more interested in applied arts than fine arts; he passed over these treasures with rather cursory notice. At the Tuileries, he was fascinated by the artificial echo which caused one's voice to return from three places at once, and by the plumbing of the fishponds. As for Notre-Dame Cathedral, it was second rate compared to the one at Amiens.

The tourist's main reason for stopping at Paris was to observe French court life. News of France, England's nearest neighbour, was always of first importance to Queen Elizabeth. Such was the practice of statecraft then that a turn of phrase or the serving procedure at a royal table was scrutinized with the same attention that a news briefing or statistical report receives today; only a first-hand observer, a "merchant of light", was privy to the information. Every young tourist would, it was hoped, find a highly placed person from home to show him the ropes at Paris and make the necessary introductions; the English ambassadors were besieged with requests. Thus the Earl of Leicester wrote to Francis Walsingham on behalf of his nephew: "He is young and raw, and no doubt shall find these countries and the demeanour of the people somewhat strange unto him; and therefore your good advice and counsel shall greatly behove him for his better direction." The raw youth in question was eighteen-year-old Philip Sidney, whose wit and grace won instant favour with Charles IX. After a short acquaintance, Sidney was invited to the wedding of Marguerite of Navarre, and the King created a title for him, "Baron de Sidenay".

After Henri IV ascended the throne in 1589, the court was even more open to English visitors. They required no invitation to stroll about Fontainebleau freely and observe the royal entourage at leisure. Paris was already renowned as a capital of fashion, and silk was all the rage – particularly when the courtiers amused themselves by performing the ballet, which in those days was conceived as a form of social dancing. Stylish extravagance was everywhere at Fontainebleau: Thomas Coryate was especially dumbfounded by the royal guard, in red or green stockings, blue and yellow doublet with enormous counterpaned puffed sleeves, velvet cap with long, nodding plume, and prominent codpiece, "by that merry writer Rabelais styled the first principal piece of armour". Privately the stalwart Englishman found his French cousin too light and frothy for his tastes.

There were other noteworthy cities in France – yet why tarry in France when one could be in Italy visiting the most important cities in the world? Besides, France at the turn of the seventeenth century was dangerous; armed bands of unemployed soldiers roamed the countryside, hungry, broke, and ready for a fight. Fynes Moryson was assaulted in Burgundy and stripped of nearly all he had – but with characteristic prudence he had stashed sixteen crowns in a box daubed with "a stinking ointment for crabs", and another six were wrapped in a spool of thread stuck with needles "as if I had been so good a husband as to mend my own clothes"; his assailants never found them. Clearly, these were not places to linger. The typical itinerary led summarily down to Lyons and then via the Savoy Alps to Italy: conqueror of the world, nurse of the arts, earthly paradise, garden of Circe.

The Alpine scenery along the way pleased the Elizabethan no more than it had the pilgrim. James Howell described the mountains as "uncouth excrescences of nature", and the sound of a waterfall gave Coryate a headache. Nor were the dangers that the pilgrims had faced crossing the Alps in any way abated. In fact, they could be greater, because pilgrims tended to travel in larger groups. Fynes Moryson crossed the Alps with only a footman running at his side. In some places the way was so precipitous that Moryson found himself lying on the horse's neck and hanging on by its mane (he saved his presence of mind by *never* looking down). In another stretch of forest, the footman became paralysed with fear by the howling of wolves; he begged his English master to scare them off by firing his pistols (Moryson wouldn't). But when the traveller emerged on to the Lombard plains, he beheld a landscape of fecundity and measure; civilization triumphant.

Everything displayed that cardinal Renaissance virtue, symmetry. It was almost as if laid out by a mathematician. The vineyards and orchards were perfect rectangles. The vinestocks and trees were exactly equidistant. The roads were as straight as if they'd been drawn with a giant ruler. At precise intervals, the fields were framed with streams. Even the cows in the meadows had a fancifully decorous charm, attired in a long, white, fringed garment called a *housse* (rather like a twentieth-century upholstery cover) to keep off flies. Sweet human order prevailed, gracious nature yielded.

Usually the tourist travelled on horseback, but this was a most pleasant part of the journey to make on foot. He could always nip into a vineyard and refresh himself with a bunch of grapes – unlike the German boor who knocked Coryate's hat off when he filched a bunch, the civil Italian raised no objection. Coryate said of the north Italian countryside that it "did ever refocillate my spirits and tickle my senses with inward joy".

The way took the traveller past princely Milan, the Spaniards' stronghold (thus also a stronghold of the Inquisition and dangerous for Protestants); past beautiful Mantua where the Commedia del Arte flourished. It was in this setting of northern Italian high civility, around Cremona, that Thomas Coryate picked up one of the first forks to reach England. He explained,

The reason of this . . . curiosity is, because the Italian cannot by any means endure to have his dish touched with fingers, seeing all men's fingers are not alike clean. Hereupon I myself thought good to imitate the Italian fashion by the forked cutting of meat, not only while I was in Italy but also . . . in England since I came home.

Thereupon he acquired the nickname of *furciferus* – "only for using a fork at feeding but for no other cause", as he hastened to assure posterity. Coryate was well ahead of his times; for another century, even the most aristocratic Englishmen continued to grasp big slabs of beef, mutton and fowl in their fists. Not even the French had forks at the turn of the seventeenth century; the essayist Michel de Montaigne was always complaining that he'd bitten his fingers or run out of clean napery.

In the same region, Coryate found another couple of fetching novelty items, the fan and the umbrella, also virtually unknown in England. The latter, made of leather "hooped inside with diverse little hoops that extend the umbrella in a pretty large compass", was especially used on hot, sunny days by horsemen, who fastened the handle to one of their thighs so they could ride in the shade. Fynes Moryson advised caution: he knew one physician who suggested umbrellas were "dangerous because they gather the heat into a pyramidal point and then cast it down perpendicularly on the head". Not for centuries would rainy skies and businessmen with "brollies" come to be emblematically English.

Continuing south, the tourist came presently to Florence, "La Belle", golden city of the Medicis, and wanted to stay. Moryson, however, suggested taking in Florence on the way back instead. It was smart, he said, to get to Rome as soon as possible – because if the Englishman had been spotted by the Inquisition when he passed through Milan, the Roman Catholics might already be waiting to entrap him, so there was no time to lose.

Even if he were not imprisoned and tortured, the traveller could expect the worst. The *Essay of Travels into Foreign Countries* counselled darkly,

Beware of Rome, the forge of every policy that setteth princes at odds . . . the seller of all wickedness and heathenish impieties or Machiavelli of evil policies and practices that are unmeet subjects for these worthy travellers to spend their time about.

"You cannot sit in a coal cellar and keep your shirt white," insisted a friend of Philip Sidney, hearing of the latter's intention to visit Rome (the plea was heeded, and Sidney never made the trip). The moral stench carried all the way to Siena, declared William Lithgow, though he went anyway. The tourist had been warned.

Even to enter Rome was arduous, because the guards at the city gates were among the toughest to be encountered anywhere. Plague threatened Rome every summer, so the tourist had to present a duly stamped *bolletta* (bill of health) or else go into quarantine for forty days. Because the surrounding countryside was particularly infested with bandits, there was a strict search for weapons, which were illegal in many Italian cities. The customs men exhaustively examined every piece of printed matter for signs of heresy; one traveller, arriving in 1581, had his books retained for four months – and he was a bona fide Catholic.

The moment had come for the English Protestant to assume his carefully prepared German disguise. His enunciation had been perfected in Leipzig or Heidelberg, but he had to Teutonicize his comportment as well. Henry Wotton arrived wearing a broad black hat with "a mighty blue feather", and once in town he made sure frequently to be seen drunk in public. He explained,

I was reputed as light in my mind as in my apparel (they are not dangerous men that are so). And . . . no man could think that I desired to be unknown who, by wearing of that feather, took a course to make myself famous through Rome in a few days.

Fynes Moryson wore his German identity more discreetly, congratulating himself with the thought that he was thereby improving Germany's image abroad. To be doubly ensured against the Inquisition, he clandestinely introduced himself to the English Cardinal Allen, head of the English expatriate Jesuit community at Rome, who extended a few days' protection to Protestant tourists in the hope that they might convert. To conceal his identity from the world at large, Moryson then had to shake off the English Jesuit guides that the cardinal pressed upon him; quickly avert his glance if he saw a familiar face from Cambridge; and try to look especially nonchalant when passing the English college. He made sure to be seen leaving his inn every morning as if he were going to mass. Another Englishman had tried the same trick, but he got the time wrong, and gave himself away by announcing that he was on his way to mass in the afternoon.

His disguise in order, the Englishman then set off to see the sights as fast as possible. Perhaps paradoxically, he did not spend much time on the classical antiquities. For the Elizabethans, ancient Rome was the greatest civilization the world had ever known: potent, brilliant, supremely accomplished. However, unlike the medieval pilgrim, whose Gothic imagination had been darkly stirred by its devastation – and unlike the later Romantic, who would be moved to melancholic raptures by decay – the Elizabethan traveller derived no sentimental *frisson* from beholding the "mere carcass" that presented itself to his sight. The ruins had not yet been cleared and restored so, like the pilgrim, the tourist would merely pick his way over vast heaps of rubble pulverized beyond recognition. His literal, virile sensibility simply shuddered; *this* was not the grandeur that was Rome. What he really wanted to see was the currently reigning power: the Mother Church, the "whore of Babylon".

Like the pious pilgrim before him – though in a very different frame of mind – the Elizabethan made the circuit of the great religious shrines; it could be completed in two days. Above all, he tried to be inconspicuous, because the least *faux pas* might give him away as a non-Catholic. Moryson's first mistake was hiring a mule to carry him from one place to the next. An irate pedestrian demanded, "What, do you ride to heaven while we poor wretches go on foot?" From then on, he walked.

The great churches seemed to be perpetually crowded, not so much with foreigners as with affluent Romans. Apparently they had no jobs, and were free to make leisurely peregrinations from one indulgence station to the next, every day of the week. The Protestant Elizabethan mingled with the throng, admiring the statuary and gilding. He never asked to see any relics, because he'd be expected to worship them. Such confrontations of belief were best avoided. Certain passionate Reformists like Lithgow had been known to rip the clothes off plaster saints rather than "with indifferent forbearance wink at the wickedness of idolators". But the circumspect Moryson advised, "Let them stay at home who are so zealous that they will pull the host or Sacrament out of the priest's hand . . . inordinate desire for martyrdom is not approvable." Still, when nobody was looking, Moryson was not above stealing a coin from the collection box as a covert gesture of anti-Popery; and Tom Coryate, visiting a church in another city, even pocketed a votive offering as a souvenir.

A few tourists got a more intimate view of the Church. The crafty Henry Wotton penetrated to the Pope's chamber. He wrote, "The whore of Babylon I have seen mounted on her chair, going on the ground, reading, speaking, attired and disrobed by the cardinals . . . in both her mitre, in her triple crown, in her litter, on her mule", and in other "private parts" he dared not mention.

The gorgeousness of the Church and the mood of high ceremony – white horses, red velvet, gold lace, and Latin litany – seemed to colour the whole life of the city. Walking about Rome, the tourist never seemed to see anybody at work; when they weren't strolling from church to church, the natives idled about their villas, all pale green marble with miniature vineyards set like gardens with fountains and fishponds, where they dined *al fresco* on capon under glass (the tourist just glimpsed them over the garden wall). Wotton sighed, "Rome's delights on earth are sweet and her judgements in heaven heavy."

In other moods, the "whore of Babylon" was confounding, paradoxical. What was the traveller to make of the flagellants, mercilessly scourging themselves and covered with raw wounds, yet chatting amongst themselves with nonchalant cheerfulness as they did so? And there were strangely affecting sights such as a boy of fifteen in a blue taffeta gown, crowned with olive branches and holding a lit taper, standing by the altar on Palm Sunday – a murderer, just pardoned by the Pope.

No matter how deeply the tourist despised the "bribing hands of the simoniacal minions", in Lithgow's scathing description, he could not fail to be impressed with the charitable works of the Church. There were hospitals staffed by high-born ladies in gowns of beaten gold who spent all day making bandages or washing the wounds of beggars. Lithgow himself wrote approvingly of the free meal, with four kinds of meat, bread, and wine, offered to pilgrims at St Peter's; they even provided clean paper to wrap the leftovers. As another Elizabethan ruefully concluded, "This I must say to the shame of our Protestants: if good works may merit heaven, they do them – we talk of them."

As predicted, the tourist's investigation of Rome had been fraught with danger. Pursued by the Inquisition, Lithgow was obliged to hide out in a tower for three days and finally to climb over the city wall at midnight. But the Church remained a fascinating phenomenon. So, unless he was willing to brave the bandit-infested way to Naples, the tourist might make his way next to the pilgrimage shrine of Loreto, on the Adriatic coast.

The journey took four days, and the way was lively with sinners, to Lithgow's grim satisfaction. A couple of Italian gentlemen *en route* to Loreto with their concubines insisted on sharing the journey with him. They all put up at the same inn where "each youth led captive his dearest darling to an unsanctified bed". For the last part of the way, when penitents were meant to go on foot, Lithgow observed that "the vermilion nymphs were slipping like wanton lambs on grassy mountains and quenching their follies in a sea of unquenchable fantasies" – penitents indeed!

Loreto itself was tiny: just a single street leading to the shrine of Santa Casa. The street was packed solid with dirty inns and expensive souvenir shops. Inside the shrine, the Elizabethan visitor confirmed his worst opinions of the Church. It was there that Fynes Moryson saw his first exorcism. The ritual took place in a chapel kept deliberately dark "to increase religious horror" – a familiar papistical device. As the priest worked up to a pitch of fervour, the silently outraged Moryson reflected,

How much more skilful was he in the devil's names than any ambitious Roman ever was in the names of his citizens. . . . If he had eaten a bushel of salt in Hell . . . this art could never have been more familiar to him. He often spake to the ignorant woman in the Latin tongue . . . and at last the poor wretch, either hired to deceive the people or drawn by familiar practice with the priest or at least affrighted with his strange language and cries, confessed herself dispossessed.

Lithgow, too, saw some "notable illusions" at Loreto. When he was there, he noticed a woman, clearly drunk, in the midst of a noisy prayer fall suddenly into a swoon. Immediately the crowd acclaimed her as a saint, overcome with holiness – whereupon she woke up, vomited her lunch, and was instantly acclaimed as a devil instead. She would have been stoned to death had Lithgow not intervened. "And here," he drily concluded, "was one of their miracles."

So much for the dead past and the forces of darkness. It was, after all, for the present – and hence, the future – that the "merchant of light" had come to Italy. Having scuttled in and out from under the "whore of Babylon's" skirts he was now free – in his own guise – to see Florence, elegant paragon of urbanity, and Venice, cosmopolitan hub of power. The Elizabethan's imagination spun like a top – he was only getting started!

Florence was set in the countryside like a jewel in a medallion. The tourist approached through fertile meadows, into a ring of prosperous suburban farms and vegetable gardens, through the gates into a stately city of warm russet and ochre brick. It was paved in flagstone and all made to human measure, with small open squares, fountains, and graceful stone bridges across the Arno decked with marble statuary. Where London teemed and bustled, Florence hummed like a gold watch, a model metropolis.

In the enlightened mode of the Renaissance, the spirit of commerce attained its rightful place, the tourist noted. "Not only the gentlemen but even the princes of Italy openly profess to be merchants (which our men, with leave may I say foolishly, disdain)," commented Fynes Moryson. There were barbershops, dressmakers, fancy butchers with meat laid out on marble slabs. Most keenly interesting to the tourist were the banks. While he was redeeming his letter of credit, he eagerly took note of all the procedures, and especially of the new financial vocabulary. "Cash", "bankrupt", "traffic" – all came into English from the Italian in the Elizabethan period, brought back by the travellers.

The look and tone of Florence dated from the Medicis, so for the Florentines it was nothing new by the late sixteenth century. But the English tourist was discovering it for the first time – he took it all to be ultra-modern. *Toscanismo* (the Tuscan manner) had represented the apex of style at Oxford and Cambridge. The tourist felt he had truly arrived.

The arts of living were practised with an enchanting lightness – none of the heavy sumptuousness that prevailed in the north. In Florence the tourist might taste for the first time such delicacies as caviare or frogs' legs. He admired the way everything was made ingeniously appealing, even the dainty portions of fried guts for sale in the street markets. Dining ambience could be delightful, as Fynes Moryson noted:

In their inns from morning to night the tables are spread with white cloths, strewed with flowers and fig leaves with . . . glasses of diverse coloured wines . . . and delicate fruits . . . being all open to the sight . . . through their great enlarged windows. At the table they touch no meat with the hand but with a fork of silver or other metal. . . . In summertime they set a broad earthen vessel full of

water upon the table wherein little glasses filled with wine do swim
for coolness. . . . The meat is served to the table in white glistening
and painted dishes of earth.

However, it could be expensive, especially if the tourist paid *al pesto*
(at a set rate, like the modern table d'hôte) rather than *al conto* (à la
carte). Unfortunately the sleeping accommodation was less delightful – expensive and dirty. It was imperative to ask for clean sheets,
Moryson warned, because Italians "are troubled with an itch"; you
could tell by the way they were always scratching inside their
trousers, even the nobles.

The essence of *Toscanismo* was the art of being a gentleman, in
itself a revolutionary Renaissance concept. The French variety was
something of a silly fop, adjudged the tourist; he reckoned that the
perfection of the type was the Italian. The aspiring Elizabethan
courtier wanted all the fine points; these matters had not begun to be
articulated in England. He read eagerly from Castiglione's *Book of
the Courtier* and Giovanni della Casa's treatise on "The Perfect
Gentleman":

The perfect gentleman will not wash his hands in public (lest others
ask themselves the cause), nor give people smelly things saying "Foh
I see pray you how this does stink." And when you have blown your
nose, use not to open your handkerchief to glare upon your snot as if
you had pearls and rubies fallen from your brains.

Nor, della Casa went on, should the gentleman sneeze too loudly,
pare his nails in public, breathe on others when he spoke, or bore
them reciting his dreams. "Without which proportion and
measure," he concluded, "that which is good is not fair." Restraint
was the requisite mode; Italians were appalled, reported Moryson,
by certain young Englishmen who might "presently call men by
nicknames . . . as Tom, Jack, Will, Dick and the like, yea will leap
upon their friends' shoulders and if they will be merry presently fling
cushions, stools, yea custards". The young Englishman had much to
learn.

Of all the graces a gentleman might possess, grace of speech was
the highest. Florence was renowned for purity of language, and for
innovative spoken wit as well. Around the turn of the seventeenth
century there developed in Florence several academies devoted to
versification and highly sophisticated *jeux de mots*. The members

played word games like the present-day "Call My Bluff", and tourists with an exceptional mastery of Italian might be invited to join in. The Svogliati Society extended that honour to the poet Milton in 1638.

Yet, ultimately, the Englishman was wary of all that fancy talk.

They are reputed the authors of all flattery spread through all our transalpine nations . . . forced with hyperbolical protestations and more than due titles to all degrees. . . . Thus Tacitus sayeth truly, the more things are feigned which men do, the more they do them.

Thus Moryson averred. Come to that, the Florentine was "close, secret, crafty, and the greatest dissembler in the world". No wonder, either, given such a national character, that the covert art of poisoning reached its high point here, even "reputed worthy of Princes' practice". Taken to its extreme, the process of civilization must turn sinister, *sinistro*. The visitor was of two minds about it, a not uncommon condition among those attracted to foreign cultures.

Gentler arts also flourished in Florence, however. The tourist duly admired the Pitti Palace – "the most magnificent and regular pile in the Christian world", declared Wotton. Everyone knew of the Florentine Michelangelo, hailed all over the Continent as the greatest artist of the Renaissance. But the Elizabethan traveller, who did not hold fine art in awe, was apt to view the man with a sanguine matter-of-factness. Fynes Moryson saw Michelangelo as an opportunistic, audacious *enfant terrible*. When commissioned to paint the Pope's chapel, recounted Moryson, in a fit of petulance against the clergy Michelangelo peopled his scene of Hell with likenesses of prominent ecclesiasts, including the Pope himself (after much persuasion he agreed to paint them out); and when the Duchess of Urbino ordered some portraits of saints, Michelangelo sent her instead a picture of "the Father of all Saints, which . . . was the privy part of a man".

Straightforward curiosities could be much more salutary. Florence's great attraction was the duke's palace. With a proper introduction to the duke, the tourist could see the treasury, which featured bejewelled furniture and vestments, a nail turned half to gold by an alchemist, a lizard in amber, an egg-sized emerald worth 100,000 crowns (nearly £1.5 million today), and – as the tourist was especially gratified to note – a painting of Queen Elizabeth. Then at the duke's zoo he saw lions, tigers, wolves, eagles, a fierce Indian mouse, and a leopard with black, white and red spots. For the

visitor's amusement the animals might be let loose in the zoo
courtyard, where men in wheeled cages provoked them with
firecrackers.

For aesthetic gratification, more than any Michelangelo painting
the Elizabethan tourist favoured the art of moving water: fountains.
Besides mere beauty, they displayed mechanical ingenuity; they
could animate statues, make music, and be employed in practical
jokes which the Elizabethan found hilarious. The best example, just
outside Florence, was on the estate of Pratolino. The tourist's visit to
Pratolino was a high point of his trip. Impelled by the force of water,
Pan stood up to play a sweet tune on his pipe and then sat down
again, his expression shifting from hope to melancholy; a tiger
drank, swallowed, and looked around; a laundress, sculpted out of
white marble (the sculptor happened to be Michelangelo), wrung
water from linen over a bubbling cauldron; predators hunted, ducks
dived, a hundred figures came to life. Then, sitting down on a garden
bench, the tourist found he had triggered off a mechanism that
drenched his backside, and if in confusion he then ran up the stairs he
was squirted afresh with every step. It all made a splendid splash,
and the aristocratic Elizabethan was as naïvely delighted as any
twentieth-century provincial seeing Disneyland for the first time;
he never let a little shower put him off sightseeing.

Getting serious again, the tourist continued up across the heart-
land of Italy and came to the two university cities of Bologna and
Padua. Padua was reputedly the greatest university on the Continent, particularly in the sciences; there, the late-Elizabethan traveller could attend a lecture by Galileo. A heady atmosphere prevailed
that was something of a revelation to a Cambridge or Oxford man.
The student population was cosmopolitan and aristocratic:

not such students . . . as most commonly are brought up in our
universities (mean men's children set to school in hopes to live upon
hired learning), but for the more part of noblemen's sons, and of the
best gentlemen, that study more for knowledge and pleasure than
for curiosity or lucre.

With non-mandatory class attendance, and a highly innovative
student government, Padua was a haven of liberalism, even to the
point of lawlessness: swords and firearms were legal and murder was
punishable by mere banishment. Most visitors stopped at least long
enough to brush up their Italian; some stayed to take a degree, which

would be highly respected back in England – though the cynical Italians said of the foreign student, "We take the fees and send back an ass in a doctor's gown."

A student card from Padua would exempt the bearer from all tolls in Venice, the next major stop on the itinerary and the apex of the tour. Since Parson Torkington proclaimed it the last word in beauty, pleasure, and sophistication, Venice's touristic reputation was in no way diminished. More important for the Elizabethan, Venice was a hub of internationalism. There, the "merchant of light" could pick up intelligence about the Turks (the sixteenth-century equivalent of the Communist bloc to Western Europeans in the present era: sworn enemies and inscrutably alien thinkers), and about the Vatican. Venice was also the oldest republic in Europe, with a venerable constitution and a formidable Doge – a political education in itself. This was by far the most popular city on the Elizabethan tour: in 1612, the English ambassador reported that there were nearly eight times as many Englishmen in Venice as in all the rest of Italy put together.

Yet, since there was so little contemporary travel literature before 1600, the visitor's image of Venice, though dazzling, was imprecise. It often came as a shock, for instance, that Venice was a city of canals, because "a certain English gentleman, a man that much vaunted of his observations of Italy", as Coryate tartly described him, had written about riding post through Venice on horseback. But the shock was an agreeable one, and the tourist was enchanted with his discovery of the gondola. Since 1560, all gondolas were required by law to be painted black, but they had nonetheless a quality of gaiety and lightness, with upholstery edged in bonelace, and prow and stern gracefully lifted in the shape of a dolphin's tail. Thus ensconced, the tourist glided past the great edifices of the Renaissance, freshly embellished by the masters of painting: the Doge's Palace by Tintoretto, the Fondaco dei Tedeschi by Titian. While the apogee of art was well past by then in Rome and Florence, Venice was enjoying a second golden age in the late sixteenth century: Titian, Tintoretto, Veronese, Palladio, all were contemporary with the Elizabethans; never had the city been more visually resplendent. Because there were no horses, the streets were quiet, and so impeccably clean that, as James Howell averred, one might walk about with nothing on one's feet but silk stockings and satin slippers.

The tourist in no way viewed Venice as a museum. He disembarked from his gondola to walk down the Merceria, still the most expensively sumptuous high street in Europe, purveying the latest in fine fabrics, tapestries, and jewellery, scented by the perfumeries and sweet with the music of nightingales, kept by all the shopkeepers in little cages. Then, he was endlessly intrigued by St Mark's Square, the international gathering spot for talking politics and making business deals. Every day between six and eleven in the morning and again from five until eight in the evening there assembled Poles, Slavs, long-haired Greeks, turbaned Turks, Jews in red hats (symbolizing the blood of Christ, prescribed apparel by law), and Europeans from every nation. A little distance away, the tourist chuckled at the mountebanks on their makeshift stages, playing music on home-made instruments and making up words as they went along, "seasoned with a singular variety of elegant jests and witty conceits"; as well as more sensational tricks, such as gashing an arm and healing the wound on the spot with one of the ointments offered for sale. Also the food market, half on land and half floating, was as popular with tourists as ever. There were rafts of grapes; shop windows hung with pheasant, peacock, and partridge; mountains of vegetables that the tourist had never dreamt of in England: asparagus, spinach, artichokes, cauliflower, pimentoes, tomatoes. Clustered together in the canal, two dozen sailboats loaded with melons made a small island. "Then" (in the words of Aretino, whose works were known to every Englishman who admired Italy) "comes the business of counting, sniffing and weighing them to judge their perfection" by "beautiful housewives, shining in silk and superbly resplendent in gold and jewels". Whatever might transpire at Elizabeth's court, market day was never like this in London.

The crowd itself was a great attraction. Where the pious pilgrim stole furtively scandalized glances at the Venetian beau monde, the Elizabethan studied them with frank interest. Fashion was a serious matter to him. On the one hand, it spoke volumes about contemporary life; on the other, a man of the world was known in great part by his manner of dress, and it behoved him to keep up to date. The late-sixteenth-century Venetian was Europe's best-dressed man; with black felt cap, short hair, short black cape and discreet small collar, close-fitting black doublet and breeches, he looked trimly business-like, even soldierly, a Renaissance man of action. The fashionable Venetian, Thomas Coryate pointed out, was quite

without those new fangled curiosities and ridiculous superfluities of
panes, plaits, and other light toys used with us Englishmen. . . .
Whereas they have but one colour we use many more than are in the
rainbow, all the most light, garish, and unseemly colours in the
world.

If the Englishman laughed at himself for his attire, the Venetian was
all too ready to join in. Three travellers arriving there in 1581 with
long hair, colourful clothes and, most conspicuous of all, large lace
collars had a crowd around them in no time hooting at their
"enormous lettuces". But the Venetian women, to the Elizabethan
eye, represented the opposite extreme: utter sartorial vulgarity.
Their platform heels, of red or yellow leather, were up to eighteen
inches high, and they were frequently seen to topple over in the
street unless they had a ladies' maid to lean on. They veiled their faces
but bared their bosoms. It was reputed that their hair, elaborately
arranged in peaks and pompadours, achieved its blonde shade
through dyeing in urine.

Venice's foremost attraction – perhaps the foremost single attraction of the entire Elizabethan tour – was the Arsenal, the biggest and
most modern military outfit in the world. So efficient was the
Arsenal's technology that it was said they could build from scratch
a galley and three cannons while a man ate his dinner; and so
prodigious, that a tourist visiting in 1589 saw over a hundred new
warships that had not even once been used. At the same time, the
Arsenal employed nearly three thousand workers, all of whom
could retire on a pension – a model of enlightened labour policy.

The visitor needed connections to see the Arsenal, and a special
permit was required. Many lesser government enterprises were
open to the public at large. Coryate was most impressed with an
alabaster gallows reserved exclusively for the hanging of dukes
convicted of treason. St Mark's was an especially popular spot for
executions. Moryson saw two young noblemen progressively dismem-
bered at various places round town where they had committed
mayhem, finally losing their heads to a kind of guillotine in St
Mark's Square. William Lithgow, who smelled smoke, arrived just
in time to see "a grey friar burning quick at St Mark's pillar . . . for
begetting fifteen noble nuns with child, and all within one year; he
being also their father confessor. Whereat," he added enthusiastically, "I sprung forward through the throng and my friend followed

me, and came just to the pillar as the top half of his body and right arm fell flatlings in the fire."

In a cooler mode, St Mark's Church was one of the art treasures of the city. Practical man that he was, the Elizabethan was most impressed by workmanship and verisimilitude: Moryson praised the realism of the classical bronzes, and Coryate marvelled over the intricate mosaics, an art form he had never heard of before. The contemporary Renaissance masters were more admired as artisans than revered as artists. They were craftsmen whose skills were to be employed. Philip Sidney commissioned a portrait by Veronese which was executed in a mere four days (though the artist's assistants took a little extra time to fill in the background). The truly exalted art, for the Elizabethan, was music. For the first time at Venice, he heard madrigals exquisitely performed by the *castrati*; and also "concerts of grave, solemn music, sometimes running so sweetly with soft touching of the strings as may seem to ravish the hearer's spirit from his body", as Fynes Moryson said in a moment of rare feeling. In sum, Venice so abounded in beauty that even Lithgow was constrained to pronounce that "the glory of Gallants, Galleries, Gallies, Galleasses and Gallouns make this incomparable mansion the paragon of all cities in the world". However, the earnest Sidney kept his sightseeing to a minimum and would not be seduced by the "*magnificorum magnificis magnificentiis*", as he put it dismissively.

More than high art seduced the Elizabethan tourist from his serious business. Venice was renowned throughout Europe as the great city of courtesans: twenty thousand registered professionals by the turn of the seventeenth century, more beautiful, more cultivated and wealthier than anywhere else in Christendom. This was a large number when the entire city had a population of well under half a million, but then, in Moryson's somewhat shocked tones, the Italians were so beset by "fleshly lusts that a man of these northerly parts can hardly believe . . . how chastity is laughed at among them". The courtesans were tolerated because they paid enormous taxes – enough to support twelve galleys – and because they were seen to protect the sacred institution of marriage. If men were free to go to the brothel, they wouldn't be tempted to seduce other men's wives. Thus the wife could remain on her pedestal; for Italians, commented Moryson, preferred to "adore them as images rather than love them as women". He added that the adored wives themselves were, consequently, "much sooner inflamed with love" than most.

The traveller had no trouble locating a courtesan because, like certain taxi drivers of the present epoch, most gondoliers doubled as panders, and they usually knew a few crucial words of French, German and English to overcome the language barrier. The tourist would be taken – sometimes even against his wishes – to a fine house and shown into a room tastefully and expensively furnished, with plenty of books and some crucifixes in evidence. Then the lady herself appeared, equally a combination of opulence and refinement: perfumed and bejewelled, in a damask gown with gold fringe and carnation silk stockings (nothing like the tottering, overdressed Veneziana seen about town). "Moreover," enthused Coryate, "she will endeavour to enchant thee partly with her melodious notes that she warbles out on her lute . . . and partly with that heart-tempting harmony of her voice. . . . Also thou will find her a most elegant discourser." Italian was the ideal language for love-making, with its "sweet pronunciations" and "insinuating and piercing accents"; but the courtesan could hold forth on intellectual topics too. She was made to please the whole man. Many Renaissance men visited courtesans for an evening of conversation – especially travellers, who were without feminine companions. Even so, all customers had to pay the full price: for the most exclusive, four crowns per visit (about £50 today), down to about a quarter of that for someone more common, the type "esteemed so loose that they are said to open their quivers to every arrow". If courtesans were not to the tourist's tastes, there was

beastly Sodomy . . . rife . . . in Rome, Naples, Florence, Bologna, Venice, Ferrara, Genoa, Parma not being exempted nor yet the smallest village in Italy: A monstrous filthiness, and yet to them a pleasant pastime, making songs and singing sonnets of the beauty and pleasure of their Bardassi, or buggered boys.

So runs the seething account of William Lithgow. Either way, having thus sampled the pleasures of the night, the tourist could be said to have roundly "done" Italy.

He had now seen a little of everything and more of some. To the northeast lay Prague and Vienna, remote outposts of Empire, and, well beyond the pale, Moscow; to the southwest, Spain, politically brilliant abroad and stagnantly impoverished at home, and, in any case, too hot. On the way back the tourist might take in the Netherlands and meet the shrewd, industrious Dutchmen, but the principal points had been covered. His ship thus laden with fresh information, the traveller finally pulled into his native harbour.

It is a commonplace in the annals of tourism that one comes home feeling changed, but that nobody else notices the difference; they've heard all the travel stories before, and they're not impressed. For the Elizabethan, the opposite was true: everyone was interested, though not always without apprehension, to see what the "merchant of light" had brought back.

Many expected the worst. If the Englishman had prejudices against lightminded Frenchmen and sinister Italians, those prejudices were fully extended to anyone who had been in contact with them. The unadulterated, home-grown Englishman was not impressed with fancy table manners, connoisseurship of wine, "desperate hats", trailing French cloaks or form-fitting Venetian doublets. The popular satirist Thomas Nashe wrote of the Frenchified traveller, "You shall see a dapper Jack that hath been but over at Dieppe, wring his face round about, as a man would stir up a mustard pot, and talk English through his teeth like . . . Monsieur Mongo de Mousetrap." Far worse would be those returning from Italy: mincing, hypocritical, debauched, godless. In Nashe's words, "It is now a privy note amongst the better sort of men when they would set a singular mark or brand upon a notorious villain, to say he hath been in Italy."

The stereotype was not without its counterpart in reality. Sir Edward de Vere, seventeenth Earl of Oxford, spent something like twenty times more than the recommended sum of money on his continental pleasures; when he returned from the tour in 1576 he divorced his wife; and sometime afterwards he followed the Italian practice of hiring assassins to murder Sir Philip Sidney. Yet (apart from the very darkest of his deeds) he remained one of Queen Elizabeth's favourite courtiers, unequalled in her eyes for gallantry, good looks, and grace on the dance floor. The Queen was especially delighted with the gifts he brought her from Italy: sachet, a perfumed leather jerkin, and scented gloves trimmed with silk roses.

For each visitor who returned an over-refined sybarite, there was one like Fynes Moryson, so bedraggled by the rigours of the journey that a servant who had known him for years nearly threw him out of the house when he got back. Clearly, such a traveller had achieved a genuinely thorough exposure – and was quick enough to live to tell the tale.

Telling the tale was an important business. It was thus that the Elizabethan rewarded those who had sponsored his journey; more than that, he owed it to society, a debt he did not take lightly. The foremost stylistic requirement was objectivity; one avoided, above all, the fabulous excesses of Thomas Mandeville. In fact, most accounts were so dry as to be unreadable. But Fynes Moryson's comprehensive *Itinerary*, Thomas Coryate's exuberant *Crudities*, and William Lithgow's *Painful Peregrinations* (the adjective was his) were well received in their own time and have survived. All three men continued to be travel writers and went well past the usual boundaries of the Elizabethan tour.

Other Elizabethan tourists found their travels crucially formative for their subsequent careers. Philip Sidney became a foreign envoy to the Queen. Henry Wotton was for many years the ambassador to Venice; during one low point in his career, he worked as a spy at the Scottish court, calling himself Ottavio Baldi and posing as an Italian – a feat he could never have carried off without his previous experience as a flamboyant German in Rome. More broadly, the Elizabethan tourists brought back all kinds of innovative continental techniques, from the abstract forms of commerce, statesmanship, and gallantry to concretely practical methods of gardening, plumbing, and cooking. They also brought news of the great artistic Renaissance.

The trip was a success, and it inspired others. The "tickling humour" to go abroad that Philip Sidney had described soon grew into an epidemic itch. The Elizabethan experiment shortly became an accepted system: the Grand Tour, mandatory for every gentleman.

CHAPTER FOUR

The Grand Tourist

The year is 1731 and the place is Rheims, in northeastern France. Rheims's Cathedral of Notre-Dame has often been called the greatest cathedral in all France, its architectural harmony comparable to that of the Parthenon, its elaborate encrustation of sculpture depicting nearly every form of life known to medieval man. The English tourists are apparently in no hurry to see it. For one thing, they have just "done" Paris, so they are somewhat *ennuyé* with sightseeing, though even at Paris they visited only a few places. For another, the cathedral is Gothic, therefore quite out of fashion – so cluttered and *heavy*. And for another, they don't seem to be up and about much before the end of the day. Typically, at "four o'clock in the afternoon, and about an hour after dinner – from which you may conclude that we dine at two o'clock" – the tourists are to be found "picking our teeth around a littered table and in a crumby room, Gray in an undress, Mr Conway in a morning grey coat, and I in a trim white night-gown and slippers", as Horace Walpole wrote.

Entertainments, tea parties, and balls make up the more active sector of their daily (or nightly) round: games of quadrille, provincial theatricals, Mme Lelu's revealing new gauze gown. Yet, says Walpole, "I don't know how to make 'em look significant, unless you will be a Rhemois for a little moment." Finally, he concludes, "I won't plague you any longer with people you don't know, I mean French ones, for you must absolutely hear of an Englishman that lately appeared at Rheims" – much more likely, in his view, to be interesting. A hundred and fifty years after the heyday of the Elizabethan tour, the itinerary has been pared down to some selected works of a particular aesthetic style, and the fascinating foreigner reduced to a predictable national type who is rarely interesting. Instead of the total immersion that his predecessor favoured, the Grand Tourist preferred to skim off the cream of Europe. Ultimately, if not sooner, his cup of tea was English tea. He sipped the delights of the Continent, but kept his cool distance.

The progress (or reduction) from an eager enthusiast like Coryate to a languid aesthete like Walpole occurred in stages. In the Elizabethan era, nothing had better recommended a man for worldly success than a wide knowledge of the modern world, and an earnestly eager demeanour to go with it. As the seventeenth century advanced, the idea grew that this character, "somewhat solemn, coy, big and dangerous of look" (as the typical courtier was described), could use some lightening touches. The serious man of ideas was succeeded as an ideal type by the dashing man of action. And instead of the grave and insinuating Italian, the new masculine model was that stalwart but lightminded cavalier, the Frenchman.

Exterior graces shone brightest: riding, fencing, dancing, wooing fashionable ladies. All but the last – which came easily once the others were mastered – were best acquired at the new academies for manly arts at Paris that began to flourish in the early seventeenth century. The daily round alternated physical exercise with lessons in French language and conversation, equally necessary to the courtier and equally arduous: "The French tongue by reason of the huge difference 'twixt their writing and speaking will put one often into fits of despairs and passion", but one must "set upon her again and again, and woo her as one would do a coy mistress, with a kind of importunity", declared James Howell in the *Instructions for Forraine Travel*.

"He must," Howell continued, "apply himself also to know the fashion and garb of the court, observe the person and genius of the Prince, and enquire of the greatest noblemen and their pedigree." Imbibing the atmosphere of the aristocracy – not, as the Elizabethan tourist had done, to analyse its elements strategically, but rather to absorb them – was the most important reason to frequent continental high society. Richard Lassells's guidebook, published in 1678, dwelt on the matter at length. Something must be done with that great bear

my country gentleman that never travelled, can scarce go to London without making his will or at least without wetting his handkerchief

. . . that never saw anybody but his father's tenants and Mr Parson; and never read anything but *John Stow* and *Speed*, thinks the Land's End to be Worlds-end; and that all solid greatness, next unto a great pasty, consists in a great fire and a grand estate.

Later, Lord Chesterfield, singular mentor of manners and mores, expanded the theme in his letters to his son, who was travelling on the Continent:

It must be owned that the Graces do not seem to be natives of Great Britain; and I doubt the best of us here have more of the rough than the polished diamond. Since barbarism drove them out of Greece and Rome, they seem to have taken refuge in France. . . . Among men, how often have I seen the most solid merit and knowledge neglected, unwelcome, or even rejected for want of them! While flimsy parts, little knowledge, and less merit, introduced by the Graces, have been received, cherished, and admired. . . . The scholar, without good breeding, is a pedant; the philosopher a cynic; the soldier a brute; and every man disagreeable.

"The Graces, the Graces! remember the Graces! Adieu!" signed off Lord Chesterfield. In all the world, the place where a young man learned best how to *be* was Paris.

Italy, however, now cast in a new light, was the place to *see*. Along with graces, the young tourist was developing an eye for beauty. For the first time, he began really to notice the art of the Italian Renaissance. The tour of Inigo Jones and his patron the second Earl of Arundel set an early precedent. In 1613 they travelled the length of Italy and back. Jones made an exhaustive exploration of the ancient classical ruins, with a copy to hand of *I Quattro Libri dell' Architecture* by the Renaissance master Palladio. The Earl of Arundel bought art: medallions, engravings, statuary, paintings, books, and coins, by the crateload. Jones returned to England to build the Banquet House in Whitehall, the Queen's House in Greenwich, St Paul's Church in Covent Garden: spare, stately edifices with cupolas and columns in the Palladian mode, never before seen in England. Meanwhile the Earl of Arundel's collection gave the English their first look at the original artistic masterpieces of classicism and the Renaissance: luminous, shapely, made to the measure of human perfection. It awakened the desire to see more art – and also to buy art, which became a most important aspect of the Grand Tour.

Italy as the academy of statecraft was finished. With the new enthusiasm for democracy, the despotic governments of Italy were regarded with downright distaste:

> We envy not the warmer clime that lies
> In ten degrees of more indulgent skies.
> 'Tis Liberty that crowns Britannia's Isle,
> And makes her barren rocks and her bleak mountains smile.

Besides, one no longer needed to go to the source to study government or current events. News circulated briskly with the proliferation of journals and gazettes, and from the early eighteenth century one could read modern history at Cambridge or Oxford. Italy had moved from the present into the past, where the tourist stood back and beheld it, a dazzling still-life.

The new approach was elegantly articulated by Joseph Addison (later to establish the *Tatler* and the *Spectator* in London). In 1699, a Latin scholar just down from Oxford, Addison set off on the Grand Tour with the idea for a new kind of guidebook. It would be based on the works of Horace, Virgil, and the other great poets of Latin antiquity, describing the landscapes and temples of their verses, seeing Italy as they had. It was an excellent course of study, and – more immediately – an aesthetic delight. Addison wrote home in a rhyming letter:

> For whereso'er I turn my ravished eyes,
> Gay gilded scenes and shining prospects rise,
> Poetic fields encompass me around,
> And still I seem to tread on classic ground.
> For here the muse so oft her harp has strung,
> That not a mountain rears its head unsung,
> Renowned in verse each shady thicket grows,
> And every stream in heavenly number flows.

To tread the classic ground in Italy, to pick up flourish in France: the appeal of the Grand Tour widened steadily as the eighteenth century continued. As England was growing steadily more prosperous, so more and more country squires had the wherewithal to turn their sons into gentlemen.

There was a brief hiatus between 1756 and 1763, with the Seven Years' War. When peace resumed, the Grand Tour was more popular than ever. Great colonist abroad and great industrialist at home, Britain had never felt more powerful. There was more money than ever for travel, and social aspirations soared. More and more young men made the tour, until by 1785 – just before the French Revolution and the Napoleonic Wars put an end to it – there were an estimated 40,000 Englishmen travelling on the Continent.

Lest the country squire hesitate to send his boy abroad, an increasing number of books appeared arguing in favour of the Grand Tour, and telling how to go about it. It was best, opined the *Treatise Concerning the Education of Youth*, for the master to travel when he was young and impressionable. Then, he could be more easily dissuaded from rude ways and bad habits, more easily remoulded. If mothers were worried about exposing their sons so early to foreign dangers, the *Treatise* pointed out that the English countryside was equally hazardous, what with the marshes and bogs. The optimum age was about sixteen, just after graduation from university. At that age a chaperon was required: the tourist's father knew all about the preening sots of France and the atheist lechers of Italy. Choosing the right tutor, or governor, was most important. He was the one who would guide the youth towards the refinements of the Continent, and steer him away from its debaucheries; it was a crucially intimate relationship. As Richard Lassells (himself a tutor) explained, the tourist's

lackeys and footmen are like his galoshes, which he leaves at the door of those he visits. His valets de chambre are like his nightgown, which he never useth but in his chamber . . . his groom is like his riding cloak, and never appears near him but on the road. But his governor is like his shirt, which is always next unto his skin.

In the slang of the day, the tutor was called a "bear-leader" – he required the *savoir-faire* to take a rough rustic and make a man of fashion. He should also be a man of letters. Originally he was supposed to be Protestant as well; a Scots edict of the early seventeenth century even made it mandatory. Later it mattered less: Lassells himself was Catholic. At the very least the tutor had to be an Englishman; otherwise he would probably have formed all sorts of disagreeable foreign liaisons. That could only spell trouble for the ingenuous tourist, who might get stuck for months in some provincial town where the tutor had friends; installed as a boarder at the house of the tutor's mistress; enrolled in an inferior academy where the tutor got a kickback; locked in a country hotel room with a local bawd; or even married off to a country girl whom (thanks to the tutor's connivance) the tourist had compromised. Beware, concluded Lassells, of "needy, bold men" who might apply for the job, especially if they were foreigners.

Several distinguished men served as tutors early in their careers. A handful became world-renowned later on: Adam Smith, Thomas Hobbes, Joseph Addison, Ben Jonson (though Jonson distinguished himself on tour by getting dead drunk, to the triumphant glee of his charge, the young Sir Walter Raleigh). The typical tutor was neither the cultivated paragon nor the duplicitous rogue that the essayists characterized. Most often he turned out to be a down-at-heel pedant in his middle years, who had probably taken religious orders but never found much of a post, a modest type who might himself be going abroad for the first time. *The Bear Leaders*, a pamphlet published in 1758, described the meeting of the governor and his charge:

The Oddities, when introduced to each other, start back with mutual Astonishment, but after some time from a frequency of seeing, grow into a Coarse Fondness one for the other, expressed by Horse Laughs, or intimated by alternate Thumps on the Back, with all such other gentle insinuations of our uncivilized Male Hoydens.

Besides the tutor, the tourist's entourage could include several more members. There were the aforementioned valets, lackeys, coachmen and footmen, though some books recommended hiring new domestic servants at each new place: local servants would be more efficient shopping in foreign markets and finding the way on foreign roads, and it also gave the young master practice issuing orders in foreign languages. Additionally there could be "specialists": the third Earl of Burlington travelled with an accountant, a portrait painter to copy monuments and statues, and a landscape painter to do the scenery.

There was plenty of luggage. The Grand Tourist tended to travel heavy. As the period of the Grand Tour progressed, guidebooks concentrated more and more on practical hints, as opposed to educational theory, reflecting – or stimulating – the tourist's increasing preoccupation with comfort. Besides the "basics", he was variously instructed to take a portable tea caddy, an inflatable bath with bellows, a pocket inkstand, a complete medicine chest, and at least a dozen changes of linen (since you couldn't trust a foreign laundress). Most important, he needed good clothes. A minimal travelling wardrobe included a summer suit of camlet with gold thread buttons, a winter suit of worked flowered velvet with velvet buttons, red-and-white pumps with diamond buckles, white silk stockings, at least four pairs of fine Swiss ruffles, several Spanish lace handkerchiefs, and a fancy snuffbox and toothpick case. With all of that, the tourist was usually obliged to travel with at least one coach. Burlington set off with two, followed by an immense outrider of liveried servants on horseback. However, he sent all but one coach and four horses back when he got to Dover; owing to the vagaries of continental roads, it was the tourist's practice to buy or hire new vehicles at several stages of the journey.

Thus handsomely provided with cultural insulation, with as much of "the best from Britain" as he could possibly carry along, the traveller and his party arrived at Dover full of confidence and high spirits. If the winds were ill, he might have to wait for a while before the next boat set sail – a damned nuisance, since the town was not charming. Still, it gave him a chance to get acquainted with the other young voyagers who were headed for the Continent. By the time the boat departed, to the timid tutor's silent chagrin, the boys were enthusiastically gossiping about mutual friends from Cambridge or Oxford or Edinburgh, singing their favourite songs at top volume, and trading off-colour jokes – in much the same mood as a crowd of young backpackers setting off on the Channel boat nowadays, with the important difference that, since there was no bar service on the Channel boat as yet, they couldn't get drunk.

A few hours later, the atmosphere shifted, from one of rosy camaraderie to the greenish yellow of seasickness, the first great trial of the voyage. It gave the travel journal an opening note of high drama. Nineteen-year-old John Lauder declaimed,

What a distressed brother I was upon the sea needs not here be told, since it's not to be feared that I'll forget it, yet I cannot but tell how Mr John Kinkead and I had a bucket betwixt us, strove . . . who should have the bucket first, both being equally ready; and how at every vomit and gasp he gave he cried God's mercy as if he had been to expire immediately.

Unlike the jaunty Tom Coryate, and despite Lord Chesterfield's admonition always to be cool, the Grand Tourist tended to complain, especially if there were fellow Britons about who agreed with him: a frequent effect, throughout history, of travelling with a party from home.

Many crossed to Calais, and thence made straight for the Loire valley, to start off with a course in the manly arts and in languages. The region was particularly recommended for the study of French, because the accent there was said to be the purest in all of France. The tourist could also study Latin. James Howell recommended taking "an ancient nun for a divota, with whom he may chat at the gates [of the convent] when he hath little else to do – they have all the news, and they are very talkative, especially if you give them English gloves, knives, or ribbons".

There were schools at Angers, Blois, Saumur, Tours, heavily patronized by young German and English "bloods" in attendance upon the graces. Student *pensions* were numerous, and a young gentleman was sure to run into somebody he knew. The high times continued well past bedtime: John Lauder's journal enumerates,

when two lay in a chamber together, there are many ways to fly on one another. We might take a little cord or a strong thread when the other is sleeping, bind it to his covering or bedclothes, then going to our own bed with an end of the string in our hand, making ourselves to be sleeping, draw the string to us and the clothes will follow, and he will be very ready to think that it is a spirit.

One could also drag a chair along the floor; squeeze one's roommate till he broke wind; and so on into the night. The chief entertainment, however, was drinking each other under the table and on to the floor. After a time, the tourist's journal tended to repeat the phrases "I found my head sore with the wine I had drunk", and soon afterwards, "I was very light of money, whence I borrowed from Mr Kinloch." There – for the moment – the tourist paused.

Other Grand Tourists crossed instead to Ostend and began with an informative survey of the Netherlands. That was followed by a gallop through the German Empire, a dress rehearsal at the minor courts of Europe before appearing on stage in Italy and then in the ultimate performance at Paris.

In the Low Countries the British traveller purchased antiquarian books, modern maps, binoculars, and tulip bulbs. He also took some notes on social welfare, canal construction, and agriculture. His father, the country squire, was most interested to know how the Dutch got their cows' coats so clean, and their dung so sweet-smelling; and he expected regular letters from his boy giving evidence that the tour was useful.

Then the tourist headed northeast. He crossed the Rhineland – lovely, of course, although its brooding Gothic castles were out of fashion. Soon he was at charming Berlin and then at Potsdam, for a look at Frederick the Great. "It was," declared James Boswell, who was there in 1764,

a glorious sight. He was dressed in a suit of plain blue, with a star and a plain hat with a white feather. . . . The sun shone bright. He stood before the palace with an air of iron confidence that could not be opposed. As a loadstone moves needles, or a storm bows lofty oaks, did Frederick the Great make the Prussian officers submissive bend as he walked majestic in the midst of them. I was in noble spirits, and had a full relish of this grand scene which I shall never forget.

Some visitors were so much excited by the image of the Prussian soldier that they even contrived to join an army: young Thomas Coke signed up with the Prince of Vienna as a gentleman volunteer for the liberation of Belgrade and spent a considerable sum on camping equipment and horses before his distraught tutor managed to dis-enlist him. In the Elizabethan age it would have been looked upon as valuable experience for a statesman, but for the eighteenth-century youth it was no more than an escapade.

Mostly the miniature armies of the German Empire looked to the British Grand Tourists like little sets of toy soldiers: quaint. Boswell chanced upon the tiny court of Coswig, with a fighting force of 180 whose sentry boxes were "painted in lozenges of different colours like the stockings of harlequin". Most amused, Boswell engaged the troops in conversation, questioning them about their operations. They were sure he must be a spy, and carried him forcibly to the magistrate. Coswig hadn't seen such excitement in years, but Boswell giggled throughout the proceedings, until at last the burgo-master threw his case out of court.

The tourist's important conquests in the Empire, however, were to be social ones. His chances of success were excellent: "Provided you are six feet tall, have a proud look, wear a little gold lace on your coat, and have little or no religion, you will be abundantly equipped to please," wrote one commentator, adding: "But if you go to France, it is quite otherwise. There, the women rule."

The protocol was simple: arrived in a new domain, the tourist sent his servant round to the local castle with his card, and shortly afterwards he could expect an invitation to dinner, supper, or a ball. The only remaining requirement was that he be dressed properly. Boswell was denied admittance to the court of Dresden because they were in mourning and he had no black coat. A few days later he tried to get in again, wearing his scarlet coat with a black armband and some crêpe in his hat, in hopes of passing himself off as a British officer; but the Dresden Elector's master of horse stopped him with, "Sir, that is not a uniform." In Gotha, Boswell wore a five-coloured suit of flowered velvet, and the Princess herself complimented him.

Having double-checked his costume, the tourist set off for the castle, where he was warmly received. First, the master of the house would want to show off his treasures: the Baron of Kleve was proud of his English clock, which played ten tunes; the Duke of Wolfenbuttel had a lead ink-horn that Martin Luther had hurled at the devil (badly crushed and dimpled from the impact). Then, after a sumptuous meal, there were the court entertainments. The Duke of Brunswick put on a sacred music concert performed by eunuchs and opera singers accompanied by organ, French horn, flute, fiddles, and trumpets. Commented the tourist, "Quite heaven. I adored my God, and I hoped for immortal joy." Also diverting were the diamond-bedaubed dwarfs kept by many of the high-ranking German nobility.

The chief entertainment was provided by the guests. As the tourist saw them, the ladies were large, florid, and friendly, the men gallant, comely, cordial, and stupid. The German aristocrats were agreeably surprised by the tourist: one lady told Boswell she had "imagined the British to be rude like Russians or Turks . . . What would I have given," he said, "that Mr Samuel Johnson had heard a German talk thus!" While sipping tea and eating little sugar cakes with fortunes inside them, the tourist was invited to play party games such as "seek-the-pin", hardly his fantasy of the sophisticated continental soirée. Apart from that, the local society spent most of their time gossiping nastily about each other, the chief point of contention being who had the right to the title of Excellency. The visitor was encouraged to take sides, and pressure mounted with each successive dinner party. Lady Mary Wortley Montagu wrote from Ratisbon in the eighteenth century,

I know that my peaceable disposition already gives me a very ill figure, and that it is publicly whispered as a piece of impertinent pride in me, that I have hitherto been saucily civil to everybody, as if I thought nobody good enough to quarrel with. I should be obliged to change my behaviour if I did not intend to pursue my journey in a few days.

To visit the chief court of the Empire, the tourist travelled to Vienna; it was declared the most sumptuous city in the world in the definitive guidebook, Thomas Nugent's *Grand Tour*. Vienna's streets were closely lined with tall apartment buildings, richly decorated inside with damask upholstery and curtains, hangings of velvet and lace, japan tables, crystal and porcelain *objets d'art*, and enormous mirrors in silver frames. The mirrors in turn reflected the extravagant finery of the Viennese ladies: enormous, powdered hairdos studded with diamonds, pearls, and gemstones ("it being a particular beauty to have their heads too large to go into a moderate tub"), and fancy dresses over whalebone petticoats which "cover some acres of ground", as Lady Montagu observed. The dinner parties where they presided were equally lavish, featuring as many as twenty different wines, with a wine menu for each guest, and oysters imported from Venice ("which they greedily devour, stink or no stink", added Lady Montagu).

Most bizarre of Vienna's opulent entertainments was the royal shooting gallery. The Empress's ladies-in-waiting, armed with hand pistols, shot at paintings to win bejewelled trinkets as prizes; the gentlemen watched but were forbidden to play. Lady Montagu was diverted, but in the end she wrote, "I cannot endure long even pleasure, when it is fettered with formality and assumes the air of system." Thomas Coke found the spectacle unaesthetic because the participants' bosoms were twice too big for his tastes. "Magnificence carried to excess" was the final judgement on Vienna (as phrased by Lady Montagu), whereas it was elegance that the tourist admired. He was ready for Italy. As Lord Chesterfield put it, "You will now have been rubbed at three of the considerable courts of Europe – Berlin, Dresden, and Vienna; so that I hope you will arrive at Turin tolerably smooth and fit for the last polish." Before arriving at this state of greater refinement, the tourist was obliged to pass through that rude, raw zone, the Alps of Switzerland.

Just outside Geneva, however, there was one more eminently civilized attraction: the château of the philosopher Voltaire. Some got only as far as the gate, where they peered in like visitors to a zoo, until the infuriated Voltaire himself drove them away; at times, the crowd numbered more than fifty. But if the traveller wrote politely in advance, he was usually invited to look around inside and then to stay for dinner and theatricals afterwards. Boswell even went back for a second, overnight visit, which he further prolonged by secretly ordering his coachman to be late in fetching him away. Voltaire, who usually appeared in his dressing gown and nightcap, enjoyed a lively encounter, but he didn't make things easy for his young visitor. The tourist was by no means on safe ground by sticking to small-talk, either: even so innocuous a question as "Do you speak English?" brought the disconcerting answer, "No. To speak English one must place the tongue between the teeth, and I have lost my teeth." The visitor looked down at his shoes and thought of the sophisticate he would be when his tour was completed.

With that behind him, the Grand Tourist went back to Geneva, to prepare for his great trek across the mountains, a test of another order. Preparations were major, since he was a tender traveller with many items to protect, and the *voiturins* (mountain guides) drove a hard bargain, knowing that the customer had little choice. The standard rate from Geneva to Turin was £31 (equal to almost £1700 in 1980), which included six mules, three voiturins, six bearers, one sedan chair, and all meals except breakfast. Four of the mules would carry the tourist's own coach, which had to be taken to pieces to get through the mountain passes, and if any part weighed more than 350 lb there was an extra charge. Two mules would carry the sedan chair until it was time for the young man to be mounted in it, whereupon the six bearers would take over (eight if he were "lusty", ten if he were "extremely corpulent" – and if the tourist thought the voiturins were overestimating his weight, he'd have to take the matter up with the Syndicate of Judges). Then the tourist assembled his own outfit: hare-lined boots, bearskin wrapper and hood, beaver-skin mask and mittens, taffeta eyeshades.

The tourist was tolerably amused at first, until the party came to the steep bit. Thereupon he mounted his sedan chair, or "Alps machine": two slender tree trunks attached by strong cords for the youth to sit on, with a back, arms, and a footboard. Since the direction was uphill, he found himself "thrown back like a bishop in his studying chair" – ridiculous; but on the way down, he might have to go by sled – terrifying.

It was hard, in such awkward circumstances, to be cool like Lord Chesterfield. The tourist didn't relish the undignifying experience of "clambering up and sliding down these horrid mountains", as Walpole sputtered; to complete Walpole's indignation, his pet spaniel Tory was seized by a wolf and dragged off to be devoured in the Alpine woods before Walpole's eyes. "Such uncouth rocks and such uncomely inhabitants!" The people still suffered from goitre, which made great swellings like turkeys' wens on their necks; they had crude mountain manners – even their lusts, said one guidebook, were "quenched by snow". "I hope I shall never see them again," declared Walpole categorically.

Other reactions were more equivocal. "Barren mountains . . . cannot delight a traveller. Yet they may amuse him," said Samuel Sharp. Joseph Addison, passing through the Alps, confessed to "a sort of agreeable shuddering at this most misshapen scenery". Boswell pronounced them "horridly grand". Though the eighteenth-century tourist was not ready to find the Alps beautiful, he was beginning to get a certain thrill out of them. Where his predecessors would have liked simply to shut their eyes to the Alps, the Grand Tourist was at least curious. By the 1760s, day-trips out of Geneva for the express purpose of looking at glaciers and waterfalls had begun to be organized; and in 1765 the first tourist inn was opened at Chamonix.

Nonetheless, in the age of the Grand Tour such amusements were incidental. It wasn't till he emerged from the Alps that the tourist came at last to something important: "A man who has not been in Italy is always conscious of an inferiority, from his not having seen what it is expected a man should see," pronounced Dr Johnson. At Turin, the tour *really* began.

At last, a modern city: Turin had been largely rebuilt at the turn of the eighteenth century, after a siege by the French. The high street featured well-stocked shops; the central square, Piazza San Carlo, was lined with columns in the style of London's present-day Covent Garden piazza. Shiniest of all was the palace of the King of Sardinia, stuffed with expensive pictures, gilt furniture, and many mirrors. Yet the Grand Tourist generally looked down on glitter: Walpole commented, "very costly, but very tawdry: in short, a very popular palace". The tourist could install himself in high comfort, too – a vast relief after the Alps, where some inns had offered, in place of mattresses, sacks stuffed with leaves that prickled all night. There was luxury accommodation at the Duke of Florence and the Spit. Or, if he wanted to economize, the Auberge d'Angleterre cost just seven shillings per day (£9.50 in 1980), and the name was sure to attract other Britons, whom the tourist was always glad to see.

At Turin the traveller would also see his first Italian *contessa*. His chances would be excellent with the Contessa di San Gillio, a woman of fifty with "a great predilection for young Englishmen", who often invited one Grand Tourist, or several, to join her for tea or at the theatre. There were so many fine ladies at Turin that some visitors were quite distracted and, new at the game, went for several at once. Boswell simultaneously courted three: he pressed the knees of one *contessa* between his at the theatre; two nights later, at the same theatre with another *contessa*, he loudly declared his love, whereupon a man sitting near "said without the least delicacy, 'A traveller expects to accomplish in ten days as much as another will do in a year.'" A week after that, he wrote to a third, begging her to show mercy and meet him in a dark corner somewhere – inadvertently quoting his letter to countess number two in the process. At the end of two weeks, Boswell lost out with all of them, though he believed it was because he was too modest. Next time, the tourist might promise himself, he'd do better; anyway, Turin was only the beginning. The next stop, Milan, would be the first major city on his Italian itinerary.

The journey passed through Piedmont and Lombardy, a land that "flows with milk and honey", as John Evelyn exclaimed with pleasure; "a vast garden surrounded by a noble moundwork of rocks and mountains", observed Joseph Addison, with the classicist's eye for form. Richly planted with wheat, rice, orchards, vineyards, and green pasturage, the landscape delighted the eighteenth-century gentleman as it had delighted the Elizabethan before him. Then he passed into Milan through one of its ten gates and beheld a metropolis: ten miles square, its population over 300,000 by the turn of the eighteenth century, an ecclesiastical stronghold, a treasury of art and merchandise.

First, with a vast collection of books (72,000 volumes), manuscripts (1400) and drawings (including several by Brueghel, Dürer, and da Vinci), there was the Ambrosian Library. Behind that stood the picture gallery, with works by Carraci, Fratini, Bramantino,

Visconti, Raphael, Titian, and more Renaissance masters. In the cabinet of Signor Settala one could find a mandragore, a petrified mushroom, a piece of a thunderbolt, a sample of asbestos, and "many other exotic rarities which are better seen than described". Next, the Palazzo Simonetta, where Addison had fired his pistol to obtain an echo that returned fifty-six times (Boswell got the echo fifty-eight times); plus the archbishop's palace, the seminary, the 4000-bed hospital, the citadel, eighty monasteries, fifty convents, and two hundred churches. Milan provoked countless exclamations for the recent arrival.

The single most impressive sight was the Church of the Duomo, begun in the fourteenth century and still being built in the age of the Grand Tour; Addison found the effect largely spoiled by all the scaffolding. The soaring, multi-pinnacled edifice had 160 marble pillars, each, averred Lassells, worth 10,000 crowns (£70,000 in 1980), and 600 marble statues, each worth 1000 crowns. The whole had a grandiose solidity that rang of the genuine article: "massive white marble, not candied and frozen over with a thin crust of marble", Lassells said.

Rich stuff – but then, the tourist read in Addison, Italy was full of marble, so that was no great reason for admiring the Duomo. Besides, in general one did not admire the Gothic style. Elsewhere Addison characterized the Gothic cathedral as one whose

very spouts are loaden with ornaments . . . columns finely engraven with fruits and foliage that run twisting about them from top to bottom, the whole body of the church . . . chequered with different layers of black and white marble, the front covered with such a variety of figures and overrun with so many little images and labyrinths of sculpture that nothing in the world can make a prettier show to those who prefer false beauties and affected ornaments to a noble and majestic simplicity.

The tourist sniffed. But with the night, surely, would come something appropriate to his notion of elegance: he was going to the opera, at the immense and opulent La Scala opera house. There, too, he might hope to press between his the knees of another *contessa*.

The ambience, however, did not live up to its setting. For one, the Italians used the theatre as a place to socialize: the doors of the boxes were forever slamming shut, and noisy conversation and the loud smack of kissing often drowned out the music. Then, they ate in the theatre, not just snacks but roast meats and macaroni pies, so the place smelled like a restaurant. Boswell complained:

Rough dogs often roared out *brava*. The singers seemed slovenly. Blackguard boys held the sweeping female trains and often let them go to scratch their head or blow their nose with their finger. I wished to have gingerbread or liquorice to give them.

As for the opera itself, the music was exquisite, but the tourist found it incongruous that squeaking eunuchs were cast in heroic roles (in his heart of hearts he had always suspected Latins to be of dubious masculinity). Anyway, Milan was good for souvenirs: for the ladies at home, some gold jewellery, scented soap, and crystalware; for the visitor himself, another set of pistols and swords. Thoroughly satisfied with those, he continued on through the lyrical plains to the east towards Venice, the next major stop.

En route, he passed through Cremona, where Thomas Coryate had picked up a fork, a fan, and an umbrella. The eighteenth-century visitor might buy a violin – for Cremona offered Amadi, Guarneri, and Stradivari. Strictly speaking, such a purchase constituted a *faux pas*. Lord Chesterfield had written,

If you love music, hear it . . . but I insist upon your neither piping nor fiddling yourself. It puts a gentleman in a very frivolous, contemptible light; brings him into a great deal of bad company; and takes up a great deal of time which might be better employed.

Next came Vicenza, home of the architect Palladio. Vicenza presented the tourist's first sight ever of the master's work: elegantly simple, disciplined but light, tranquilly perfect in its plane surfaces opened with windows and its classical pillars and domes – a new design for living for the man of state and the man of taste. Now, *this* was the sort of thing one came to see in Italy. The tourist's imagination came to life. He could see *himself* in a house like that.

As he approached Venice, the procession of Palladian mansions grew more and more impressive, especially if he came by barge along the Brenta. It was one of the great touristic approaches in Europe. Drawn along in an elegantly appointed barge called a *burchio* (one shilling per person – just under £1.50 in 1980 – or £1 17s 6d to hire the barge for a private party of up to twenty), the tourist passed one exquisite villa after another, surrounded with fanciful topiary and sculpture, with frescoes by Veronese and Tiepolo, the perfection of the Renaissance. (It would seem silly to come in on the night boat, but even that trip was picturesque in summer because the way was often brightly illuminated by glow-worms.) He arrived at Venice enchanted, and the mood of delight stayed with him.

Venice for the Elizabethan had been the city of the future. For the Grand Tourist it was a city of the past, charming but not exigent. Where it was once the hub of European politics, by the eighteenth century it was languidly sinking into the mud. The formidable Arsenal was now virtually a military museum: the suits of armour outnumbered the guns, and such guns as there were had inconveniently placed triggers; the swords were unwieldy; and there were far more boats than sailors to man them. So where the Elizabethan had hurried past the *palazzi* to try to get into the Arsenal, the Grand Tourist took a cursory look at the Arsenal, smiled to himself, and glided about admiring Renaissance art and architecture. He bought himself some pretty things: an original by Canaletto, who specialized in landscapes for the English market (landscapes were never an important part of Italian Renaissance art), and some of the little stamps showing the great buildings of the city; then, perhaps, a new snuffbox: they were made in the London style (where before they were done *à la parisienne*), and the fancy shops boasted most particularly of items "made in England" – which greatly pleased the tourist. At the glassworks of Murano there was a great variety of souvenirs: different drinking vessels for each nationality (metre-high ones for the Dutch, crystal tankards for the English, wide goblets for the Italians), fully rigged glass warships, glass organs which made music if you blew into their pipes, and huge mirrors for ladies; the only problem was that they might break in one's luggage.

The tourist was beginning to know Italy. Now, surely, for a *contessa*! Yet, she eluded him. It seemed she was always taken up with one or several *cisisbei*: her official lovers, who attended upon her on all social occasions and were also permitted to share her more intimate favours, while her husband enjoyed those of another man's wife. The institution of the *cisisbei* fascinated (and "shocked") the Grand Tourist endlessly. Yet a personable young Englishman might himself attain the role of *cisisbeo* for the duration of his stay. He would, however, first have to put in many hours at the *conversazione*, intimate gatherings for chat and card games.

The visitor went along, and wondered whether it was worth the effort. The exchange of banal civilities droned on endlessly and the men far outnumbered the women – so he usually found himself talking to other disconsolate tourists. Not only that, but the Italians were notoriously stingy about food: after hours in the parlour he might be offered no more than a *demitasse* of coffee and a slice of watermelon. To top it off, the houses were usually unheated. Walpole wrote,

There are scarcely any chimneys, and most of the apartments are painted in fresco, so that one has the additional horror of freezing with imaginary marble. The men have little earthen pans of coals upon their wrists and the women have portable stoves under their petticoats to warm their nakedness and carry silver shovels in their pockets with which their cisisbei stir them – Hush! by them I mean their stoves!

If the tourist got too impatient, there were always the courtesans. By the golden age of the Grand Tour, the courtesan had come down in the world. No longer the proud and cultivated woman of parts that Thomas Coryate had shaken his head over, she had become something closer to the standard streetwalker. But the brusque young squire was not dissatisfied, judging from his patronage.

In addition, there was the great release of Carnival. The pageantry was fantastic: extravagant costumes, floats, street theatre, contortionists, wrestlers, performing animals, dentists in spangled garments pulling teeth to the accompaniment of drumbeats, fortune tellers encircled by crystal balls talking through long tin tubes. At Carnival time the tourist's day was an uninterrupted round of pleasure: mornings in the coffeehouse, afternoons marvelling at the sights and dancing in the streets, evenings at the opera or at a private ball, of which there were several every night. Masked and cloaked from top to toe, he could let off more animal spirits by running through the streets with the mob and throwing eggs filled with sweetwater (it was nothing compared to what the locals got up to during Carnival; some had been known to fire at each other with carbines from passing gondolas). He might even get next to a *contessa*. After that, the tourist smiled, adjusted his ruff and betook himself and his tutor to Florence, where the art of the Renaissance burst fully upon him.

He was charmed. His eye was particularly taken with the fountains. Where the Elizabethan had delighted in their mechanical ingenuity, the Grand Tourist loved the coolness of the stone and the play of light on the water, which "breaks upon a round of emboss of marble into millions of pearls", in John Evelyn's words. The art treasures, too, had a bejewelled luminosity: Florence was an Aladdin's trove. At the St Lawrence Chapel, one saw "lapis lazuli full of veins of gold . . . and stellified with mother-of-pearl". At the Duke's Palace he came upon a cabinet of ebony, then one painted sanguine red, inset with mother-of-pearl, lined in green silk, and hung with Titians, Raphaels, Holbeins, interspersed with enormous gems: total value £125,000 in the late seventeenth century (£3.5 million in 1980). He went to the Uffizi and looked at more Raphaels, Holbeins, Rubenses, Rembrandts, Michelangelos, Cellinis, del Sartos, Donatellos. His tutor explained that Raphael was the great colourist; Michelangelo the best draughtsman; del Sarto the consummate realist. The colours were all deep scarlets, celestial blues, shining golds, gleaming whites, tender skin tones; the bodies supple, muscular, reverentially true to life; the faces expressive of all manner of emotion "as God made them, pulpy and rising up like living flesh". The tourist remembered what he had read about humanism, at Oxford or Cambridge, and the subject was illuminated in a new way.

There was so much to see – Lassells reckoned the tourist should devote a full month to Florence – and so much to remember. The travelling painter would be put to work in earnest now, and the young man might get out his own sketchbook, too. A favoured few were themselves immortalized in Zoffany's *Tribuna*, a painting commissioned in 1772 by Queen Charlotte of England, to be set in the Octagon Room of the Uffizi depicting the cream of the English visitors then in Florence. It took Zoffany six years to finish the painting, and in that time he was courted by many who hoped to have their portraits included in the scene. Zoffany usually obliged, and then when the tourist left town his face was painted out and another put in its place. When the work was done, Horace Walpole (who was not included) commented that it was "crowded by a flock of travelling boys, and one does not know or care whom". Sir Horace Mann (who was included) also ventured that "the naked Venus which is the principal figure will not please her majesty so much as it did the young men to whom it was shewed".

The other major cultural attraction of the city of Dante and

Boccaccio was its academies of poetry and wit. In 1678 Lassells particularly noted the Academy of the Crusca, famous for its dictionary, and instructed the traveller that it was "much better to spend the week in making of orations and verses than in drinking of ale and smoking of tobacco". The Italians themselves, however, often smiled at the tourist's adulatory view of the academies; to them the academicians were rather silly, addressing each other in the antique Latin mode and quibbling over trifles of diction. One hundred years after Lassells's writing, there were 500 academies in Italy, but their main function by then was the manufacture and sale of diplomas to Grand Tourists. Still, opined the tutor, a visit to an academy was better than a visit to an ale-house.

Finally, the young Englishman loved Florence for its southern charm. Walpole found it relaxing, and it suited his genteel nocturnal schedule perfectly:

Up at twelve o'clock, breakfast till three, dine till five, sleep till six, drink cooling liquors till eight, go to the bridge till ten. . . . delicious nights on the Ponte de Trinita . . . in a linen nightgown and a straw hat, with improvisatori and music, the coffee houses open with ices. . . . sup till two and so to sleep till twelve again.

A perfect vacation from Grand Touring.

Still, the tourist had his father to think of; a letter came presently from home wondering what was taking the youth so long, with the dubious paternal conclusion, "I perceive your mind is still wandering, and when your eye will be satisfied with seeing I know not, nor can I be informed by those wiser than myself that this voyage now undertaken by you can turn to the advantage you pretend unto." So the tourist and the tutor had their coach readied once more, engaged a *vetturino*, and set off for Rome.

Possibly the party had increased – at his Florence *pensione* the tourist might well have struck up a friendship with another young traveller bound for Rome and persuaded the tutor to make room in the coach for him. If the newcomer were good company, the three might pass the hours reading aloud from Montesquieu and discussing moral points; if bad, the tutor's ears burned while the two boys exchanged bawdy stories. After all, put together they were bigger than he was, so he often kept his counsel. Other boys, like young Lord Burlington, had no friend along but the dog. Instead of looking out of the carriage window, Burlington travelled the length of Italy with much of his attention fixed on the doings within. Was his spaniel Dye comfortable in her new basket? Were she and her pups warm enough under their new quilt? Did they have enough milk?

From Florence, the tourist and his party headed for cinnamon-coloured Siena, through "millions of little hills planted with trees and tipped with villas and convents". Arrived there, he visited the Gothic cathedral and pronounced it, with Addison, "too much". It was time he got to Rome.

The Apennines had to be negotiated first. Barren and difficult to cross, with accommodation to match – the ceilings were festooned with spiders' webs; the windows were without curtains or glass, just shutters; the walls were hung with gory representations of saints in agony, and the bed had damp and dirty sheets, a mattress stuffed with "wet leaves, potatoes and peachstones", and no headboard. There was no privy, so one had to stare at the chamberpot all night. To eat there might be giblets in eggwhite, fried frogs, roast bluejay or magpie, and several scrawny chickens cooked to oblivion – often ten times more than he could eat (he was paying table d'hôte), but none of it edible. The traveller sighed for his powdered beef and potted venison, and did not make the best of things.

He tried consoling himself with the chambermaid; she was definitely on the itinerary, to judge from the guidebook. *The Gentleman's Pocket Companion for Travelling into Foreign Parts* offered the following piece of sample conversation, translated into five languages:

– Sweetheart, is my bed made? Pull off my stockings and warm my bed, for I am much out of order. I shake like a leaf on a tree. Warm a napkin for my head and bind it well. Gently, you bind it too hard, bring my pillow and cover me well. Draw the curtains and pin them together. Where is the chamberpot? Where is the privy?
– Follow me, I will show you the way. . . . If you see it not you will soon smell it.
– Put out the candle and come nearer to me.
– I will put it out when I am out of the room. What is your will? Are you not well enough yet?
– My head lies too low. Raise up the bolster a little. My dear, give me one kiss, I shall sleep the better.
– Sleep, sleep, you are not sick since you talk of kissing. I had rather die than kiss a man in his bed or any other place. Take your rest, in God's name.

Perhaps, in deference to the tourist's father, the author had tacked on an unsuccessful ending.

Enough of all that. The tourist squared his shoulders, adjusted his breeches, and prepared to meet the queen of cities, the capital of antiquity: at last he was coming to Rome.

He passed through the portals of the "academy of the past", and looked round in dismay. How dingy it seemed! The streets were narrow, dirty and curiously empty. Many people seemed underfed, and many were beggars. Much more offensive than that, however, was the city's contemporary vulgarity. What had the grandeur that was Rome to do with greengrocers, English warehouses, garlic-reeking sidewalk cafés, or the sign of the shaving plate (signifying a barber's shop)? From the minute his coach pulled up to the customs house the tourist had been surrounded by clamorous *servitore di piazza* (would-be valets) who jumped on board and insisted on taking him to the Spanish Steps. "I entered Rome with full Classical enthusiasm," said Boswell, "but when I arrived at my inn and found myself surrounded by the landlord, by valets de place, by scoundrels, my fantastic sensibility was wounded": the perennial plight of the tourist with high hopes.

Settling in was simple, anyway. Rome catered widely to the English trade, with English coffeehouses where the London newspapers could be read, English restaurants, and inns with names like the Albergo Londra. After a day or two, the tourist would want to rent a flat; he'd be staying for several weeks at least, and a flat was much less expensive: including full service, just over £4 per week in the mid-eighteenth century (about £100 in 1980). Once he'd made himself at home, the youth took a second look at the city, and its power began to work on him.

A guidebook was essential in Rome. There was a great variety for sale, most of them large and expensive. Piranese's was still definitive, a handsome tome full of copperplate engravings. Also of excellent value was the three-volume set of *Roma Antica e Moderna*, price ten shillings (£13.50 in 1980). The best background reading on the antiquities was the classical authors themselves. The writing was so graceful, said Addison, not like the muddled and lugubrious Christian stories that explained the religious art.

To see the city properly, the tourist also hired an antiquarian guide. Rome's most distinguished guide was the German Johann Joachim Winckelmann, the Superintendent of Antiquities from 1773, "a gentleman of exquisite taste and sound learning", available to tourists with the most cachet; but Winkelmann was highly intolerant of know-it-all philistines, and said so. Otherwise there were many British expatriates who offered their services as guides; in general they were Catholics who'd moved to Rome for the sake of their religion.

By the mid-eighteenth century, Rome had been systematized into a standard six-day tour of arts and antiquities. On the first day, the guide and his charge viewed the city from the Capitoline Hill, and the tourist received a lecture on historical geography. The second day, they visited the Forum, now crowded with artisans' huts and animal pens, and the Coliseum, where there were heaps of animal dung, beggars, and a few old women praying at the Stations of the Cross which had been erected there. The squalid modern touches were regrettable, but Boswell described his feelings as "sublime and melancholy" all the same. On the third day, they saw the Palatine Baths and the house of Cicero, where Boswell was "seized with enthusiasm", and broke into Latin; his guide, the Scots Jacobite Colin Morison, followed suit, and they conversed in Latin from then on. On the fourth day, they re-climbed the Palatine Hill and then the Capitoline, saw a fragment of Jupiter's temple, and a church on the site where Vercingetorix was once imprisoned. The fifth day took them to the Diocletian Baths. What the tourist found most exciting, he reflected, was the exaltedly *human* quality of the Roman gods and goddesses – just as, in the classical writings, the deities were so much of this world. Again he thought of humanism and had a moment of enlightenment. On the sixth day there was a visit to the Pope's chapel – where, inevitably, Protestant tourist and Catholic guide had their first argument about religion.

The young visitor could hardly neglect the churches. For one, they held the Renaissance masterpieces of painting and sculpture, hundreds more that he had to see. Tobias Smollett was irked by the preponderance of Madonnae over Christs – too much feminine influence, he thought; and he found the Pietà "indecent" because it showed a nearly naked man in a woman's arms; but in these sentiments he was rather ahead of his time, anticipating the Victorians. Archetypically, the Grand Tourist simply pursed his lips at the content and smiled on the form and the execution. Then, too, many churches were themselves architectural masterpieces. Addison enthused at length over the exquisite proportions of St

Peter's, and especially over the lovely light that poured down from the cupola, making the people below look like angels. What did it matter if the original architects had been papists more than aesthetes?

In the same way, the church ceremonies were enjoyed with cool aesthetic detachment. Horace Walpole wrote, "We are not very fond of sights; don't go a-staring after crooked towers or conundrum staircases. . . . Now and then we drop in on a procession or a high mass, hear the music, enjoy a strange attire." He was most amused, at a candlelit rite set out with crimson damask throne, purple armchairs and gold trim, to see "a mighty pretty cardinal-kind of habit; 'twould make a delightful masquerade dress". Popery was no longer sinister – just rather quaint and backward.

Along with this new tolerance, a high point of the eighteenth-century Roman visit was being presented to the Pope. He was quite willing to receive Protestants now; and the tourist had also relaxed his scruples. Lord Chesterfield wrote to his son, "Go through the necessary ceremonies for it, whether of kissing his slipper or his b–h——, for I would never deprive myself of anything that I wanted to do or see by refusing to comply with an established custom." The Pope, reported Samuel Sharp, was a "goodnatured old man", especially tickled when Englishmen bowed before him. After the formal prostration, he would chat for a few minutes on neutral topics such as travel or the Italian language, and the visitor came away pleased with himself and culturally "broadened" regarding the religious question.

Rome offered other broadening experiences. His classical enthusiasm restored, Boswell decided to "remember . . . the rakish deeds of Horace and other amorous poets and . . . allow oneself a little amorous indulgence in a city where there are prostitutes licensed by the Cardinal Vicar". At seven shillings (less than £10 in 1980) for a *fille charmante*, it was an eminently accessible pleasure. Besides that, wine was cheap and plentiful, there were many miles between the tourist and his father, and numerous compatriots were eager to join forces with him.

According to prescription, the English youth was to have spent his mornings in academic study with the tutor and his afternoons in instructive sightseeing, but that programme might have long since been abandoned. Tourists rarely have a good reputation, but the Grand Tourist in Rome made an especially bad name for himself: an insular, drunken, profligate ruffian, it was said, who

> Down Italian vistas startles
> Whore-hungry amidst groves of myrtles

according to one emblematic couplet.

Lady Mary Wortley Montagu did her best to improve the situation. She established herself in Rome in 1740 and had a regular entourage of Grand Tourists who, she was pleased to report,

> really paid a little court to me, as if I had been their queen, and their governors told me that the desire of my approbation had a very great influence on their conduct. While I stayed there was neither gaming nor any sort of extravagance. I used to preach to them very freely, and they thanked me for it.

But by 1758 she had amended her judgement, admitting with shame:

> The folly of British boys and stupidity and knavery of governors have gained us the glorious title of Golden Asses all over Italy . . . by hoarding together and throwing away their money on worthless objects. . . . Since the birth of the Italian drama, Goldoni has adorned his scenes with *gli milordi Inglese* [a species of buffoon].

However, the Grand Tourist also came away with better things. He had seen much that was new and beautiful, and so he must have acquired some measure of *vertu* – taste, in the fullest sense of the word. He would bring it back to England, in spirit and in substance. During the Renaissance, the art collector had been particularly respected as one who combined both worldly power and cultivated sensibility. It was a most prestigious occupation, and the Grand Tourist's emulation of it was an important aspect of his trip. He was now ready to make major purchases.

Like wealthy tourists in every epoch, these young Englishmen naturally attracted predators. Rome swarmed with confidence men, many of whom were themselves English, ready to take in the unwary purchaser. Smollett cautioned,

> The English are more than any other foreigners exposed to this imposition. They are supposed to have more money to throw away. . . . This opinion of their superior wealth they take a pride in confirming, by launching out into all manner of unnecessary expense: but, what is still more dangerous, the moment they set foot in Italy they are seized with the ambition of becoming connoisseurs

in painting, music, statuary, and architecture; and the adventurers of this country do not fail to flatter this weakness to their own advantage. . . . One engages in play with an infamous gamester and is stripped perhaps in the very first *partie*; another is pillaged by an antiquated cancatrice; a third is bubbled by a knavish antiquarian; and a fourth is laid under contribution by a dealer in pictures.

On the other hand, it was easy to make a genuine "find" at Rome. The Italians were negligent of their artistic heritage; the tourist not infrequently came upon an exquisite marble bust lying face down in the dirt, or a fragment of antique frieze overgrown in the corner of somebody's garden. What he might pick up casually in Rome became a treasured rarity back in London.

Discerning young scions opened their purses to the maximum. In Rome alone, young Lord Burlington spent approximately £350 on a diamond ring (nearly £10,000 in 1980), 300 crowns on a painting of the Temptation of St Anthony, and another 1800 crowns on assorted paintings of the madonna, a marble table, a set of porphyry vases, and a set of marble columns which he presented to a convent. Thomas Coke (known to the appreciative Italians as *Cavaliere* Coke) bought paintings by Procacini, Garzi, Conca, and Luti, as well as several anonymous views and architectural drawings, a gigantic marble bust of the Emperor Lucius Verus, and a statue of Jupiter so big that it broke the wagon.

There was also a roaring trade in medallions, icons, prints, and small craftwares. The souvenir market was vast, but Lord Chesterfield reminded the tourist that he had not been sent to Italy to "run through it knick-knackically . . . [with] days lost in poring upon almost imperceptible cameos and intaglios; [to] become a virtuoso in small wares". The one memento his father unequivocally approved for the tourist, however, was a portrait done by one of the Italian specialists. Against a background of marble columns and antique busts, seated in a carved chair, his hand resting on the head of a mastiff and his tutor standing beside him, his likeness was taken by Pompeo Battoni or Angelo Trevisani. He sent the picture home as a kind of "progress report", so his father could see what kind of man-of-the-world the world was making of his son.

His course at the "academy of the past" completed, the tourist now made his way to "wanton Naples" "in the bosom of the Bay", the warmest, the ripest, the most voluptuous place he might visit without becoming positively uncivilized. The route led through countryside fragrant and fertile with olive, myrtle, bay, pomegranate, and citrus groves, perfectly *harmonious*: John Evelyn declared himself "delighted with the sweetness of this passage, the sepulchres mixed amongst the verdures of all sorts". With his eye for Italian *light*, the Grand Tourist remarked that the road itself was "so smooth and shining that when the sun shines upon it you may see its glitter two miles off, like a silver highway". For a guide, the tourist emulated Addison and read the poetry of Horace, who'd made the same journey in antiquity.

Arrived at Naples, the traveller found streets that teemed with life. Amongst the throngs were noisily serenading lovers, naked children dancing to castanets, insouciant half-clad beggars, and laughing prostitutes. The inn tables groaned; wrote Evelyn, "We seldom sat down to fewer than eighteen or twenty dishes of the most exquisite meats or fruits", including melons, cherries, and apricots in mid-winter. The tourist had to admit the food was good – but the people went too far. Just what he'd expected of Italians, he sniffed: pleasure-mad and lazy.

There wasn't much sightseeing to do in the city, but the Bay of Naples – where the Romans had taken their holidays – was rich in antiquities. The tourist rode out to Puteoli and Baiae in a fetching little two-seater and then clambered over the crumbled baths, collapsed bridges, broken Roman highways, and capsized statuary. It was a landscape of "magnificence in confusion", many times disordered by the eruptions of Vesuvius and the bubblings of the sulphur springs, and in no way restored by the negligent Italians – though the locals did a thriving souvenir business in antique medals, which they picked up in the fields. The most thorough classicists would go as far as the Isle of Capri where, in seclusion, the Emperor Tiberius had once pursued the most debauched pleasures. The Grand Tourist beheld the reflection of the ruins glimmering in the turquoise-blue waters, picked up a medal as a souvenir – something like Venus and Mars naked in each other's arms – and smiled to recall an aptly salacious verse by Martial. Most exciting of all the ruins was Herculaneum, buried by Vesuvius centuries before and just un-earthed at the end of the 1730s. Freshly opened to sightseers, it was astonishingly intact: a mile-square underground city, with its columns still standing, the marble seats of the amphitheatre still in place, even the frescoes still bright. Already, though, the King of

Naples had removed many works of art; despite repeated petitions by Grand Tourists who were keen antiquarians he would not allow them to be seen. Considering the Italians' characteristically casual approach to the treasures of the past, the tourist had no doubt that Herculaneum would probably be allowed to collapse again before long.

Though the English youth had a distinct preference for civilization, still there were a couple of natural wonders near the bay that he went to see. One was the Grotto del Cane, a cave that emitted poisonous vapours, which would kill a dog in a matter of seconds, though if the animal were plunged in the waters of the neighbouring Lago d'Agnano it revived. The local dogs ran whenever they saw a carriage of tourists approaching the cave, but the sanguinely curious visitors tried the experiment on several animals to be sure it was no trick, and Addison had it performed twice on a viper as well. Then the tourist climbed Vesuvius. He did it in the interest of science, not pleasure: it was a "troublesome march" and ruffled his dignity. The sides were steep and crumbly, so he was forever sliding backwards on to his bottom and covering his breeches in powder; at the top he got a hot-foot from walking on the stones, and his nostrils filled with sulphurous fumes. He lay down on his belly to peer into the crater, with its brightly multicoloured walls, till his eyes filled with smoke and he could see no more.

Back in Naples, he made himself presentable again and paid the requisite social calls. The English scene there was led by Sir William Hamilton, the British envoy, and his wife Emma, a former Cheshire barmaid and a great beauty several years his junior. Sir William was proud of his beautiful young wife and loved to show her off to the tourists, who were invited to improve their sketching by taking her nude likeness in classic poses. Then, in the true spirit of the ancient Romans, there were lavish dinners at the *palazzo* of the Prince of Francavilla: after the meal, the prince took his young English guests to the seaside where they could watch the prince's love-boy pages disport themselves in the waves. (The tourists asked if they could please have it done with girls next time, and were obliged.) With that, having "trod the classic ground", the Italian circuit was essentially complete. The tourist was now ready to show himself in Paris, and he made his way back north.

This time he might travel by water, with readings aloud from Virgil, who had made the same trip. He hired a felucca, an open boat fitted with lateen sails or with several oars, and a shelter for the passengers, with room enough to carry the *post-chaise* as well. If he went all the way from Naples to Nice, the hire of the boat came to about twenty louis d'or (just over £1000 in 1980); it cost more if the felucca were hired by the day, but then the tourist could stop as often as he liked.

At Leghorn he relieved himself of some of his baggage. There was a large colony of English businessmen there, including many shipping agents who would send back crates of precious souvenirs to England. *Cavaliere* Coke packed off several, but was arrested and nearly imprisoned when it was discovered that he was trying to export a headless statue of Diana without an extradition licence (in the end he was allowed to keep the statue, which is still on display at Holkham Hall). A short distance up the coast was Pisa, with its leaning tower. It was a standard attraction, but Richard Lassells disapproved. He wrote in his guidebook that a straight tower would have been better, for "there's no mystery to make things ill". While he was on the subject, Lassells went on to counsel his readers to be sparing with their exclamations, "for admiration is but the daughter of ignorance". The tourist stopped again at Genoa, all built on hills with the houses frescoed on the outside, "with its holiday clothes always on . . . like a proud young lady in a strait-bodied flowered gown", as Lassells described it. The next stop was in France.

The Riviera coast was rife with Barbary pirates, but with luck the tourist would make it to Marseilles unharmed. He docked there; and before proceeding north he had to have a look at that singular social phenomenon, the galley slave. Naked except for high red bonnets and canvas breeches, the slaves were chained at leg and waist to their rowing benches and beaten with a bullwhip on their backs or soles if their rowing pace slackened, "a miserable spectacle . . . strange and fearful . . . to one unaccustomed". Yet the slaves remained "cheerful and full of vile knavery". When they were not at their rowing benches, they passed the time fashioning small items to be sold for pocket money, and the visitor could chat with them. Boswell, always up for a philosophical dispute, put it to them that they probably enjoyed their servitude; the slaves wouldn't yield his point, but Boswell so enjoyed the chat that he bought them a round of drinks.

After fortifying himself with a girl for the night – ideally one recommended by another Briton – the tourist made his way up the valley of the Rhône, towards Paris. Inhaling the perfumes of Provence – thyme, bay, myrtle, rosemary, lavender – he passed through Avignon, Orange, Vienne. He looked at the Roman ruins with a practised eye now. At Vienne he tasted his first truffle, and appreciated it. Then he came to Lyons and turned northwest for the post route across central France.

Travelling nonstop by diligence, he covered about sixty-five miles per day at a daily cost of twenty livres (about £50 in 1980), including food. The seats were hard, the hours were long (one had often to rise at three a.m.), and the company was objectionable: the French talked ceaselessly, and the women offended the tourist's sense of propriety by adjusting their garters in full view of all. The provincial inns were no better than those in Italy, and the tourist didn't care for French food either. "One third of the dishes is patched up with salads, butter, puff-paste, or some such miscarriage of a dish," complained Walpole; at one inn, the indignant John Lauder was served a roast chicken with the legs of a different bird substituted for its own – "Such damned cheats be all the French!"

The tourist came to the Loire valley, and laughed to remember his academy days. Decorous and verdant, the Loire pleased his freshly cultivated regard as it had pleased that of the kings who chose to build their châteaux there; though the châteaux themselves were nothing special to the tourist who had now seen the Renaissance architecture of Italy. John Evelyn wanted particularly to visit Blois, whose *trompe l'œil* staircase was mentioned by Palladio, but when he did he found it to be "of greater expense than use or beauty". Then the tourist came to the great goal of his journey: Paris.

Immediately on arrival, the tourist's senses were besieged by a rush of "glittering clatter" (so it was put in *A Sentimental Journey*, Laurence Sterne's novel which constituted the ultimate distillation of the Grand Tour). His coach entered the city gates and promptly found itself in the middle of a traffic jam, with hackney cabs driven by snarling cabbies and drawn by seedy horses splashing mud on the pedestrians: the streets were so narrow that they couldn't step out of the way. Noise reverberated all around, and accidents were endemic. The tourist's own coach was assailed by bewigged, be-powdered, earringed young men in silks – looking much as the tourist would himself like to look – who wanted to be engaged as servants.

The best inns were all in the Faubourg St Germain; it was also the recommended quarter for leasing a flat (the cost was about two guineas per room per month – just under £60 in 1980). Beyond that elegant neighbourhood, inns abounded but, with names like the Ygrec, Venus' Toilette, and the Sucking Cat, they hardly made a suitable address for the young Englishman. In 1642, James Howell had counselled that the tourist's "chamber be streetward to take in the common cry and language and to see how the town is served and the world wags about him". But by the heyday of the Grand Tour, the visitor was more concerned with genteel interior ambience. Parisian plumbing was still execrable, but rooms now featured wallpaper (the most fashionable kind, called "domino", was patterned after playing cards), more furniture, and many knick-knacks.

His lodgings sorted out, the youth took his bearings: what had Paris to hold for him? Like Sterne's protagonist Yorick, he "walked up gravely to the window in my dusty black coat and looking through the glass saw all the world in yellow, blue, and green, running at the ring of pleasure". He must make himself equal to that occasion.

First, the barber came to give him a shave. The barber's technique was impeccable – he never nicked his client – but his fingers smelled funny, John Lauder warned, from wiping his bottom without paper. Then there was the wig: the tourist couldn't possibly get by with restyling the one he had; he must go to the perruquier for a new one, dashingly crimped and copiously powdered.

Next, from diamond-buckled pumps and white silk stockings (much less practical than English black, because he was sure to be splashed with mud) to gold-trimmed tricornered hat, he needed a whole new outfit, or several. Though the notion of being fashionably dressed was hardly a new one, fashion crazes as such – changing from year to year, from nuance to nuance – began with the eighteenth century, with the new social mobility in Europe. Nothing turned the rough-edged country squire into a "gentleman" so rapidly or so obviously as how he looked: the tourist was a sure customer. He was steered from shop to shop by his new Parisian servant, who knew just where to take him, and was well rewarded by the shopkeepers for doing so. In the end, the traveller surveyed himself in the glass and pronounced, with Yorick, "They order these matters better in France."

Thus made splendid, he went out to see the city. As ever, Paris presented a mixture of the sumptuous and the squalid which struck the tourist's classical sensibility as incongruous. There were high-fashion wigmakers and jewellers in one street, butchers' shops oozing offal in the next. A window richly curtained in damask and brocade was patched with paper in a dozen places. A shabbily dressed aristocrat rode past in a carriage covered in gilt cupids. The shopgirls, or *grisettes*, could be charming; in emulation of Yorick, the tourist must find some pretext to take the hand of one for a moment and practise his gallantries. But on the whole, the "common people" were hardly the kind of wholesome peasant that the Grand Tourist liked to see. Smollett observed

three lusty hussies, nieces or daughters of a blacksmith, who do nothing from morning till night. They eat grapes and bread from seven till nine, from nine till twelve they dress their hair, and are all the afternoon gaping at the window to view passengers. I don't perceive that they give themselves the trouble either to make their beds or to clean their apartment.

Everybody spoke a gallant, ceremonious French that, to the English ear, showed an unbecoming disregard for their station. "Nothing is more common," remarked Addison, "than to hear a shopkeeper descrying his neighbour to have the goodness to tell him what's o'clock, or a couple of cobblers that are extremely glad of the honour of seeing one another."

Having sampled the everyday ambience, the tourist then made the rounds of the usual attractions: the Tuileries, the Palais Royal, the Invalides, the Bastille, the tombs of Richelieu and Mazarin. At the Place Vendôme he examined one of many statues of Louis XIV, and was not transported. Lady Mary Wortley Montagu said of the royal statues that proliferated throughout France,

If the king had intended to express, in one image, ignorance, ill taste, and vanity, his sculptors could have made no other figure to represent the odd mixture of an old beau who had a mind to be a hero, with a bushel of curled hair on his head and a gilt truncheon in his hand.

The Louvre was not to be missed, for its collection of Renaissance masters. More recent French works pleased the Grand Tourist less. Smollett found the statues "quite contrary to the simplicity of the ancients" with their wild postures and extravagant clothing. And the faces in the paintings, Addison observed, always seemed to wear a smirk: "all men were *petit maîtres*, and all women *coquettes*. . . . What particularly recommends 'em to me," Addison said in conclusion, "is that they don't speak French and are not too talkative."

The pre-eminent attraction was outside of town: the palace of Versailles. Extra-fast cabs, evocatively called *enragés*, made the trip regularly; there was also the drastically overcrowded *coche d'oisiers* (some passengers travelled on the roof); or the boat down the Seine to Sèvres. Especially after Italy, Versailles came as a disappointment: as usual, the French went over the top. "The great front is a lumber of littleness, composed of black brick, stuck full of bad old busts and fringed with gold rails," pronounced Walpole. Entering, the tourist found treasures from past eras that he couldn't help admiring, though they seemed out of place at Versailles. The ornate gilding from the epoch of Louis XIV, however, and especially "the nauseous flattery and tawdry pencil of le Brun", a favourite artist of the period, were more French foppery. The interior ambience was hardly regal either. Walpole reported:

In the colonnades, upon the staircases, yea in the very antechambers of the royal family, there are people selling all sorts of wares. While we were waiting in the Dauphin's sumptuous bedchamber . . . two fellows were sweeping it and dancing about in sabots to rub the floor.

The tourist wandered outside, to get a breath of air and see the grounds. If he were a personage of importance, whose visit had been arranged in advance, the fountains would be turned on (many ordinary visitors, if they knew about it, came on those days also). Still the tourist was not impressed. Walpole described

avenues of water-pots, who disport themselves much in squirting up *cascadelins*. . . . 'tis a garden for a great child. Such was Louis Quatorze, who is here seen in his proper colours, where he commanded in person, unassisted by his armies and generals, and left to the pursuit of his own puerile ideas of glory.

Nonetheless, any tourist who had the chance was presented to the King and Royal Family at Versailles. The procedure took about an hour. First, explained Walpole, "you are led into the royal bedchamber just as [the King] has put on his shirt; he dresses and talks good-humouredly to a few, glares at strangers". Then you met the

Queen, much more talkative; then the Dauphin, who remained only for a second; the Dauphiness, who stood there looking cross; the Dauphin's sons, "who only bow and stare"; finally "The whole concludes with seeing the Dauphin's little girl dine, who is as round and fat as a pudding."

Back in Paris, there were souvenirs to buy, all sorts of last-minute trifles as gifts to take home. As early as 1644, Evelyn noted a gift shop in the Ile de la Cité which would be very much in place in Covent Garden in the 1980s: "Noah's Ark, where are to be had for money all the curiosities imaginable for luxury or use, as cabinets, shells, ivories, purselane, dried fishes, rare insects, birds, pictures, and a thousand exotic extravagances" (even the name, Noah's Ark, would be right nowadays). Horace Walpole bought fine china and pastilles for friends in England; Lord Burlington's Paris mementoes included two harpsichords, a bass viol, a set of silver dessert spoons, a sponge to clean his pictures, and several pairs of gloves. John Lauder spent £8 (just over £200 in 1980) on the unexpurgated works of Rabelais. And with the eighteenth-century English vogue in Paris, it was an excellent place to pick up a complete set of Shakespeare. However, Lord Chesterfield cautioned firmly against "fooling away your money in baubles at toyshops. Have one handsome snuff-box (if you take snuff) and one handsome sword; but then no more very pretty and very useless things."

Should one have wished to stop in the midst of these exertions for a drink or a bite, cafés had been ubiquitous since the opening of the Procope in 1686; and from 1770 there were restaurants in the modern sense of the term. *Haute cuisine* began in the mid-eighteenth century, so the tourist might order truffled turkey, pâté de foie gras, *terrine* of partridge, or *choucroute de Strasbourg*; the connoisseurship of wine was also in practice, with Burgundies and champagnes most highly recommended. One establishment was off limits; Lord Chesterfield wrote, "I must insist upon your never going to what is called the English coffeehouse at Paris, which is the resort of all the scrub English, and also of the fugitive and attainted Scotch and Irish."

The great cultural attractions of the evening were the theatre and the opera – Paris had over twenty performance halls. The well-travelled tourist was not so readily impressed with the opera. Boswell wrote that "French squeaking and grimacing were insufferable to a man who has just come from the operas of Italy." Addison described the usual French dish, all puff and no beef:

Every man that comes upon the stage is a beau; the shepherds are all embroidered, Pluto has his valet de chambre. . . . Alpheus . . . makes love in a fair periwig and a plume feather but with such a horrid voice that one would think the murmurs of a country brook much better music.

And Walpole said he'd rather go without dinner than have to take in an opera: "the music resembles a gooseberry tart as much as it does harmony". The theatre, with Corneille, Racine, and Molière, was easier to admire. Addison's only real objection was to the stock comic character of *un gros milord anglais*, the pompous, big-bellied Englishman – "as if corpulence were a proper subject for satire".

The night proffered other pleasures as well. First of all there were the gambling houses. Adventurers disguised as gentlemen and calling themselves *Monsieur le Comte* were quick to spot an English tourist at a loose end in a café or at the theatre and invite him for supper or a friendly game of cards – where his new snuffbox would not be all that the tourist lost. Lord Chesterfield announced categorically to his son,

No consideration in the world shall ever make me pay your play-debts; should you ever urge me that your honour is pawned, I should most immovably answer you that it was your honour, not mine, that was pawned, and that your creditor might even take the pawn for the debt.

Gaming, he stipulated, was acceptable only for low stakes and at the salon of a woman of fashion.

The brothels of Paris stocked a range of women, from shopgirls and unhappy wives to actresses and opera singers to thrill-seeking ladies of the aristocracy. A tourist could even write ahead to reserve one in advance, specifying the height, weight, and colouring he favoured. On that account, too, Lord Chesterfield was adamant; he would pay neither brothel bills nor medical bills:

A young fellow must have as little sense as address to venture, or more properly to sacrifice his health and ruin his fortune with such sort of creatures; in such a place as Paris especially, where gallantry is both the profession and the practice of every woman of fashion.

In fact, it was possible to spend all one's time going from dissipation to dissipation in Paris; it was as bad as Rome. Lord Chesterfield could not issue warning enough:

The life of Milords Anglais is regularly, or irregularly, this: As soon as they rise, which is very late, they breakfast together, to the utter loss of two good morning hours. Then they go by coachfuls to the Palais, the Invalides, and Notre-Dame; from thence to the English coffeehouse, where they make up their tavern party for dinner. From dinner, where they drink quick, they adjourn in clusters to the play, where they crowd up the stage, drest up in very fine clothes, very ill made by a Scotch or Irish tailor. From the play to the tavern again where they get very drunk and where they either quarrel among themselves or sally forth, commit some riot in the streets, and are taken up by the watch. . . . Their tender vows are addressed to their Irish laundress, unless by chance some itinerant English-woman, eloped from her husband or her creditors, defrauds her of them.

By then, the tutor might be tearing his hair in earnest. Mr Forbes was "a gentleman of parts, virtue and prudence, but of too mild a nature to manage his pupil", the young Earl of Derby. In Paris the earl first got mixed up with a "lewd, debauched" Englishman, the son of a physician; when Forbes timidly objected, Derby stood by while the physician's son pummelled the tutor. Then the earl fell in with a crowd of French rakes and, when Forbes took exception to them, "consented to his governor's being tossed in a blanket. The earl was wild, full of spirits, and impatient of restraint: Forbes was a grave, sober, mild man, and his sage remonstrances had no effect on his pupil." Finally Derby's father had Forbes replaced with a colonel, "roughy honest . . . [who] told him sharply that he was sent to govern him, and would givern him".

On the other hand, enjoyment was the proper object in Paris, pursued in the proper manner. "Pleasure is the remaining part of your education," Lord Chesterfield informed his son, on that last leg of the journey. He was even sanctioned to fall in love, so long as it wasn't with a strumpet. Most important, he was about to make his appearance in that crucial theatre, the Parisian salon. There he would make his reputation as a man of fashion, for everyone would be talking about how he behaved – and his father would be the first to hear about it.

The young man ought not to lack invitations, for Anglomania was rife in Parisian high society in the eighteenth century; very much in vogue were clubs, cold baths, horse racing, and tea parties. The French wouldn't admit it, though; as Walpole observed, "If something foreign arrives at Paris, they either think they invented it or that it has always been there."

Before setting out, the English visitor checked that everything was in order. His clothes and wig were right, his toilette was impeccable down to the finest detail. Lord Chesterfield admonished,

I would much rather know that a man's fingers were actually in his breech than see them in his nose. Wash your ears well every morning, and blow your nose in your handkerchief whenever you have occasion; but, by the way, without looking in it afterwards.

(Castiglione was not forgotten.) Then, preceded by page, lackey, and valet, the tourist made his entrance.

Privately, he might be less than enraptured with what met his gaze. Lady Mary Wortley Montagu described women of fashion:

so fantastically absurd in their dress! so monstrously unnatural in their paints! their hair cut short, and curled round their faces, loaded with powder, that makes it look like white wool! and on their cheeks, to their chins, unmercifully laid on, a shining red japan, that glistens in a most flaming manner, that they seem to have no resemblance to human faces, and I am apt to believe, took the first hint of their dress from a fair sheep newly ruddled.

But that was beside the point: the young man was there to show himself (unobtrusively, of course), and to gain intimacy with the graces. He took his place beside a sophisticated lady, and placed himself on the *qui vive*. If she was witty, he smiled; laughter, pronounced Lord Chesterfield, was vulgar. If there was dancing, he knew what to do: "Custom has made dancing sometimes necessary for a young man; therefore learn to do it well and not be ridiculous though in a ridiculous act" – Lord Chesterfield again. No matter how small the small-talk, he never looked at his watch. And then, if he chanced to be alone with a lady "with whom you are tolerably free, say frankly and naturally, *'Je n'ai point d'usage du monde . . . avez la bonté, madame, de me faire part de votre secret de plaire à tout le monde.'*" ("I don't know the ways of the world . . . be good enough, madame, to share with me your secret of pleasing everyone.") Tender looks and ardent sighs apart, the man who knew how to please women would also please men – the elements were the same, and that was the object of the exercise. In sum, declared Lord Chesterfield, "I should be glad to hear half a dozen women of fashion say, '*Où est donc le petit Stanhope?* . . . *Il faut avouer qu'il est aimable.*'" ("Where's little Stanhope, then? . . . One must admit, he's sweet.") It was the epithet to crown the tour.

By now the English traveller had been away for a long time: at least one year, maybe five. He had acquired as much *vertu* and *chic* as his constitution allowed; his tutor could do no more. His creditors, however, were keeping very busy on his behalf, and at last his father gave him final notice; it was

quite necessary now to put an end to peregrination. You have had full opportunity to be satisfied that pageantry, civil and ecclesiastic, gives no entertainment to thinking men, and that there is no end or use in strolling through the world to see sights before unseen, whether of men, beasts, birds or things, and will return with a proper taste and relish for your own country. For if that were not to be your disposition, I should most heartily repent that I ever agreed to your going abroad.

So, smiling at his fashionable reflection in the glass, the tourist dismissed his French servants, terminated the lease on his flat in the Faubourg, and prepared for the trip home. The task of packing might be considerable: Thomas Coke had to buy an extra two berlins to carry all his souvenirs, and Lord Burlington returned with a record 878 pieces of luggage.

The tourist journeyed up to Calais or Boulogne and remarked what "plump and snug" towns they were, more modern with every passing year. It must be due to the tourist trade, opined Walpole: "The crumbs that fall from the swarms of chaises that visit Paris must have contributed to fatten this province."

At Calais, the tourist put up at the fashionable Hôtel d'Angleterre (or just "Dessein's" to those who'd read *A Sentimental Journey* and were in the know). At table he deftly and elegantly cracked his crab, with a scornfully lifted lip for the new arrivals, rowdy young bloods and their "wet nurses", as the tutors were called among those who had dispensed with theirs, carrying on and calling for more wine. If their bearish high jinks went on all night, he would have no sleep – but then, this was the last foreign inn he would have to endure for a long time, for the next day he ought to be in Dover.

There were the usual annoyances returning through English customs: Walpole had to pay seven and a half guineas' duty (more than £250 in 1980) on a coffee set that had cost him only five. Burlington, however, got his 878 pieces past the officials with a mere ten shillings (£14 in 1980) bribe.

Now the tourist was home. What had the finishing school of the Continent made of him? Ideally, the outer man was an epitome of grace and ease in the world; while the inner man, refined by art and equally by the discipline of travel itself, of continual encounters with newness, had raised sensibility to its highest form. Sterne's Yorick is a gentleman and a hero precisely because he does very little more than register coolly exquisite sentiments: to feel the pulse in a shopgirl's wrist takes him to amorous heights; an old piece of wrapping paper sets him musing for hours on the process of history; a fleeting scene glimpsed in a doorway evokes "all the sentiments of a dozen French plays". Finally the sentimental traveller reaches nearly religious peaks (but coolly, never through excess): Yorick apostrophizes, "All comes from thee, great sensorium of the world! which vibrates if a hair of our head but falls upon the ground in the remotest desert of thy creation." Published in 1768, Sterne's book enjoyed an immediate vogue, especially in Germany, where the horn snuffbox, Yorick's souvenir from Amiens, became an emblem of friendship.

In England, not everyone took such a generous view of the fine fellow the tourist had become. He was no longer regarded as the sinister debauchee that his exotic Elizabethan predecessor was thought to be. But many found the "macaroni", as the eighteenth-century dandy was called, just very silly. From the capital, Alexander Pope waved him away (in the *Dunciad*) with:

> The Stew and Palace equally explored;
> Intrigued with glory and with Spirit whor'd;
> Try'd all hors d'oeuvres, all liqueurs defined;
> Judicious drank, and greatly daring din'd;
> Dropt the dull lumber of the Latin score,
> Spoil'd his own language and acquired no more.
> All classic learning lost on Classic ground,
> At last turned Air, the echo of a sound.
> See now, half-cured and perfectly well-bred,
> With nothing but a Solo in his head.

Back with the squire on the country estate, he was even more useless: worried about his wig whenever it rained, hanging about inside playing the guitar instead of out hunting, nagging the cook to prepare French sauces. "They talk about how much better a country France is and how much they eat or drink better there, which our neighbours will not believe and laugh at them for saying so," said the Earl of Clarendon firmly.

Elsewhere, the Grand Tourist produced a genuine revolution in taste. What began with Inigo Jones was taken up by such architects as Christopher Wren and John Vanbrugh. Noble houses like Blenheim Palace and Burlington House became showplaces of the Renaissance style; while in America, Thomas Jefferson's Grand Tour gave rise to the classical style of the White House. Inside the great houses, there were original treasures from Italy and France; and Robert Adam created a new style of furniture modelled on what he saw in the Louvre on his tour in the 1750s. Inspired by the paintings of Poussin and Salvatore Rosa there emerged a new style of landscape gardening, incorporating natural features with more formal designs. Especially in Kent, where the continental macaronis later became prosperous paterfamilias, they transformed the countryside with their new houses and gardens.

The most remarkable transformation was visible at the estate of West Wycombe in Buckinghamshire. Outside, the house was styled in the ancient Grecian mode; inside, it was Italianate, with walls covered in erotic frescoes – somewhat "shocking", but such matters were viewed more coolly in the eighteenth century. The garden was most extraordinary: strolling amidst its pillars, thickets, statues and knolls, the visitor saw that these features were laid out in such a way as to describe the form of a naked woman (though unfortunately the aeroplane hadn't been invented, so the garden was never seen at its greatest advantage).

West Wycombe belonged to Sir Francis Dashwood, a very singular Grand Tourist. The tone he brought back from Italy went outside the elegantly decorous measures of neo-classicism. It struck a wild chord, which wouldn't vibrate fully until several decades later, when the Romantics trod the classic ground in search of pagan deities and other outlaw spirits.

CHAPTER FIVE

The Romantic

The year is 1780, and the setting is St Mark's Cathedral, in Venice. This day, as usual, a dandified young English aristocrat and his tutor have arrived for the church tour. Such parties are familiar to the local guide: the young man can be expected to do plenty of writing in his notebook, and perhaps to murmur something coolly appreciative of the artwork, or drily disapproving of its subject matter – above all, nothing immoderate. So the guide is quite astounded when his usual disquisition on history and aesthetics is suddenly interrupted with a dramatic recitation. His young patron has broken into a passionate soliloquy from *Oedipus Rex*, "stalking proudly about like an actor in an ancient Grecian tragedy, lifting up his hands to the consecrated fanes and images around, expecting the reply of his attendant chorus".

When his soul, if not his tutor, has been satisfied, the young Englishman sails forth into the light again. The time would be right for a cup of chocolate or a water-ice at one of the coffeehouses or ice-cream parlours in the *piazza*, so popular with the other "macaronis". But this young man eschews such dainty pleasures. Instead he wanders into the maze of tiny alleys behind St Mark's, penetrating the most "murky quarters . . . in search of Turks and infidels". He likes to pretend that he is really in Constantinople. That's where his Grand Tour would have taken him, if his mother had not been the one paying for it. The young man is William Beckford, original of the Romantic tourist – that rare hybrid of rakish flamboyance and pastoral innocence who made a brief but significant appearance around the turn of the nineteenth century.

In the early eighteenth century, "Romanticism" was a term not yet in usage. But the Romantic sensibility – intensity of emotion and sensation, poetic mystery above intellectual clarity, individual expression above social cohesion – was in many ways prefigured in certain young rakes among the English aristocracy. They were already so highly steeped in culture that they looked for something beyond high culture, and they had the money and the freedom to seek out exotic pleasures and to indulge in imaginative experimentation. They were sent on the Grand Tour for the usual purposes of education and refinement. Once away from home, however, they might educate and refine themselves after their own fashion.

The perfection of the type was Sir Francis Dashwood, twenty-one when he made the Grand Tour in 1729. Dashwood extended his tour well beyond its conventional boundaries: he got as far as Russia, where he masqueraded as Charles XII and paid court to the Czarina. But Italy was the place he found most inspiring. One afternoon, he quite distinguished himself at a penitential church service: the ritual of wailing self-flagellation was underway when suddenly Dashwood emerged from the shadows of the church, cloaked in black, snarling, swearing, and cracking his horsewhip to right and left (the penitents were sure it was the Devil). He also discovered, on the one hand, exuberant art and architecture, whose pagan beginnings still showed through the classical formality; and, on the other hand, the darkly dramatic paintings of Salvatore Rosa, the popular Gothic horror theatricals, and the satanic arts of black magic at Venice and Verona.

Back in England, young men like Dashwood became arbiters of taste in more ways than one. Their gardens displayed mock-medieval remains, broken bits of Greek temples, dead trees, and enormous uncut boulders, suggestive of Gothic melancholia and voluptuous decay, though none outdid West Wycombe; and in fashionable London, amidst the already splendid powdered wigs, flowered waistcoats, and gold-braided breeches, there appeared Italian velvet jackets and Oriental silk turbans.

The "Italian craze" (direct descendant of that *Toscanismo* that had inspired Elizabethan tourists almost two centuries earlier) was formally honoured in 1734, when forty-seven young aristocrats recently back from the Grand Tour founded the Society of Dilettanti, with Dashwood as its first president. Their stated purpose was "encouraging at home a taste for those objects which had contributed so much for their entertainment abroad". As Horace

Walpole put it, the Dilettanti were in fact "a club, for which the nominal qualification is having been in Italy and the real one, being drunk". They went on to become serious about high art. They sponsored painters' and archaeologists' expeditions to Italy, Greece and Asia Minor. The founding members played it out in full regalia: the president's uniform was a Roman toga and the "arch master" wore a long crimson taffeta robe with a Hungarian cap, while the official presiding over the initiation rites was known as the "Imp".

In honour of Italy's satanic pleasures, the Hellfire Club was founded. Members gathered by night at the deserted Medmenham Abbey to say a blasphemous black mass, followed by an enthusiastic sexual orgy with sisters from a London "nunnery". The high priest was Dashwood, and most of the monks had been on the Grand Tour. Exotically voluptuary and recklessly individualistic, these young men foreshadowed the Romantic tourist in high dudgeon: a traveller in search of exquisite intensity and pagan abandonment.

Simultaneously, another kind of Romantic quest – for the innocently "natural" – was beginning, with the literary arrival of Jean-Jacques Rousseau. Rousseau came from the provinces to the intellectual salons of mid-eighteenth-century Paris to preach the doctrine of the natural man. He told the affronted encyclopédistes that intuition made a better path to knowledge than scholarship, and instinctive response a better guide to behaviour than prescribed moral codes. "Subjective" feelings meant more than "objective" reality. Civilization was corruption. Man had to return to nature.

Rousseau's philosophy was nurtured, appropriately, in the Franco-Swiss Alps. He was born in Geneva and came into manhood in the Savoie with Madame de Warens, the high-minded but overindulgent lady who initiated him into spiritual faith and free love. It was in the Alps, too, that Rousseau cultivated a taste for long country hikes, wandering for days in the mountains; the rhythm of walking, and above all the range of the view, would "throw me, so to speak, into the vastness of things". But sweet, level prospects couldn't carry Rousseau to the necessary heights. His favourite scenery was dramatic, even frightening:

I need torrents, rocks, firs, dark woods, mountains, steep roads to climb or descend, abysses beside me to make me afraid. . . . At a place called Chailles . . . there runs boiling through hideous gulfs below the high road . . . a little river. . . . I was able to gaze into the depths and make myself as giddy as I pleased . . . glancing every now and then at the foam and the blue water, whose roaring came to me amidst the screams of the ravens and birds of prey.

All these particulars were recounted in Rousseau's *Confessions*, published in 1781, a key influence in the philosophic shift to Romanticism. With that, too, the Alps were cast in a light of majestic beauty for the first time; and to hike among them, to "live" their vastnesses and abrupt declivities, was transformed into a transcendent pleasure. Rousseau stimulated a taste for "naturalness", and sharpened a yearning for unspoiled places with unspoiled people, that has remained with urban man ever since.

The decorously high culture that inspired the Grand Tour was being undermined, from one side by rakish impertinence, from the other by earnest Rousseauvian primitivism. Then in 1789 the French Revolution, followed by the Napoleonic Wars, rendered the Grand Tour a pragmatic impossibility. Travel to the starred attractions was effectively disrupted until 1814. But among the travellers in the interim period and just after were an extraordinary few whose sensibility – experience for its own sake, love of local colour, getting away from it all – has inspired masses of people ever since, even though their latter-day emulators may have only three weeks in which to do it.

Travel for culture or pleasure, with many quick changes, was bound to appeal to a devoted seeker after sensation like the Romantic. But he was often driven to travel for more pressing reasons. As one who favoured exquisite sensation and free expression, the Romantic was prone to the kind of unconventional behaviour that could lead to scandal. Thereupon, an absence from the scene of the débâcle became advisable. William Beckford – besides spending his days writing Orientalist fantasies whose heroes lived on coconut milk, or redecorating the ancestral home as an Aladdin's cave – greatly distressed his mother with an amorous interest in his twelve-year-old male cousin "Kitty" Courtenay. So in 1780 the nineteen-year-old was sent abroad in hopes that the world would take some of the romance out of him. Things did not go as planned. By the end of that decade, Beckford having returned to resume the passionate obsession, the scandal over Kitty Courtenay assumed such proportions that it made the London newspapers. The family hustled William off again. Thereafter he spent years at a time travelling around the more tolerant countries of Europe when the cold disapproval of England (the scandal was never forgotten) became too hard for him.

Beckford's great friend, the "*infinitamente* indiscreet" (as Horace Walpole described her) Lady Caroline Craven, also found London uncomfortable in the 1780s after she had been caught at a soirée in a bedchamber with the Duc de Guines. On the Continent her unconventional mores occasioned fewer comments – or at least she didn't hear them, being on the move. Lady Craven's views were not always Romantic, but her comportment was decidedly so: her companion was frequently the Margrave of Anspach, a divorcé with whom she maintained a chaste love affair for many years; carrying along a great cageful of songbirds, she visited places no English lady had ever been to before.

Another lady who found England too confining was Hester Stanhope, niece of Sir William Pitt. Her scathing wit was the terror of the local gentry, she was a formidable horsewoman, and she was six feet tall. She made her first continental tour in 1802, in the midst of the Napoleonic Wars; at Mont Cenis Pass, impatient with her companions, she galloped off on her mule and "left the rest of the party to their frights and fears", as she contemptuously wrote in her travel diary. In 1804, when Britain feared invasion, the twenty-eight-year-old Lady Stanhope was put at the head of a regiment of horsemen, the Fifteenth Light Dragoons and Berkshire Militia. After the danger subsided, and especially after Pitt's death, she couldn't find enough to occupy her in England. At thirty-four, to avoid the stifling destiny of a genteel spinster, she set off again for foreign parts. A perfect Romantic beginning: on the boat to Gibraltar she met twenty-year-old Michael Crawford Bruce, who became her lover for many years, though despite censorious letters from home she wouldn't marry him. Lady Stanhope too appeared where no English woman had gone before. Since she despised her sex – she once declared that she'd rather live with pack-horses than with women – she wore the opulent costume of a Turkish man: cashmere turban and girdle, gold-embroidered pantaloons, purple velvet waistcoat and pelisse, satin vest, red jacket trimmed with gold lace, and silky tasseled white burnous; she rode on a gold-embroidered crimson velvet saddle with a silver sabre at her side.

The Shelleys, Percy Bysshe and Mary, with their cousin Claire Clairmont, represent the Romantic traveller in the most pristine form. They made their first European tour in 1814, Shelley aged twenty-one, Mary and Claire both seventeen. Shelley and Mary were eloping, and the restless Claire, who spoke better French, went along to translate and for the adventure (to Mary's ultimate annoyance, as Shelley and Claire became more and more friendly). By the time of their second tour in 1818, the three were confirmed exiles: Shelley had a wide reputation as a dangerous proselytizer of atheism and free love; Claire was pregnant with Lord Byron's daughter Allegra.

The Compleat Romantic Tourist, however, was Byron: swash-buckler, decadent sensualist and dreamy melancholic by turns. He too was a social exile. His first trip in 1809 to Portugal, Greece, and the Near East with his friend John Cam Hobhouse was made partly to evade his creditors, partly to dampen an interest in young boys (though arguably his destinations were ill chosen for the second purpose). The second trip, commenced in 1816, to Switzerland and then to Italy, where he subsequently settled, was a consequence of the break-up of his marriage, rumours about his relationship with his half-sister, and the arrival of bailiffs at his London home for the collection of his enormous debts. Nonetheless, Byron travelled in high style. His 1816 entourage included a valet, a sparring partner, a guide and a personal physician. They travelled in an enlarged copy of the coach used by the Emperor Napoleon, including sleeping quarters, dining quarters, library, and a little perambulating zoo with birds, peacocks, a dog and a monkey. In the poet's own time, the "Byronic route" was followed by many who aspired to a Romantic sensibility. Still more tourists went that way in hopes of catching up with the famous man himself, to satisfy their curiosity.

Ideally the Romantic would have travelled as far from his familiar world as possible. Byron dreamed first of going to India or Iceland. Beckford fantasized endlessly about enchanted jungles and labyrin-thine medinas. Still, the Romantic tourist from England inevitably started off with a mundane Channel crossing. Regular packets made the trip almost daily, and passage was often fully booked.

More Romantic than most was the Shelleys' Channel crossing. To evade Mary's mother, the three set off before dawn and were in their *post-chaise* by five a.m. They got to Dover by late afternoon, but rather than wait for the morrow's packet boat they decided to leave that night in a small fishing vessel. A gale came up; the morosely seasick Mary dozed fitfully between her lover's knees on the floor of the boat; at one point lightning struck the sail and waves rushed in. Shelley, keeping vigil, asked himself whether "in death we might not know and feel our union as now". Later, they were glad they had left when they had, for while they recuperated at Calais "Captain Davidson came and told us that a fat lady had arrived who said Shelley had run away with her daughter."

Other tourists, more prosaically occupied in Calais with the retrieval of their baggage from customs, stayed, like Yorick, at Dessein's hotel. But, once cleared, it was a quick trip to Paris – two days in the diligence. To his disappointment, the tourist saw that he was not the only foreigner around, because road signs all along the way were bilingual, although the English versions were translated literally from the French, so not all "quaintness" was lost.

In 1790, when Paris was fully under the sway of the Revolution, few Englishmen ventured there. But the true Romantic devotee of intensified sensations and life in the raw found Paris fascinating and exhilarating. High contrast was everywhere, and the social structure was excitingly disordered; bewigged, silk-breeched gentry talked politics with butchers and ditch-diggers. Most of the nobles had already left Paris, but those remaining aristocrats still made a dazzling appearance on their promenades through the Bois de Boulogne. Now, however, when the Anglophile dandies on horseback and elegant dowagers in coaches passed by, the onlookers boldly jeered, "There goes the fishwife with her neighbour the shoemaker's wife", or "How about that seventy-year-old coquette!" Though many people had no bread, the tourist could still find a cheap, comfortable inn with excellent morning coffee; and on Sundays there was lunch at the taverns called *ginguettes* at the outskirts of the city for ten centimes.

William Beckford was in Paris in 1790, too. He found there had never been a better time to pick up valuable souvenirs; the fleeing nobility had flooded the market with art and antiques, and wartime inflation made Beckford even richer than before. The ultimate apolitical tourist, he wrote to Lady Craven,

I never amused myself better at Paris in all my days. The whole town is at my devotion. . . . What care I for Aristocrates or Democrates? I am an Autocrate, determined to make the most of every situation.

On the whole, the Romantics did not love France, still steeped in the essence of Louis XIV. Because it was usually on the way to voluptuous Italy or spectacular Switzerland, however, the Romantic tourist found himself travelling through, not without pleasure. France was the first foreign country that Shelley and his ladies had ever visited, and while they disapproved of the politics they could hardly refrain from rhapsodizing over the landscape. At every single stop, reported Mary sardonically, Claire Clairmont would declare, "O, this is beautiful enough! Let us live here!" In the perennial mode of young travellers in France, they picnicked in the meadows on bread and cheese. Mary remarked, "In England we could not have put our plan into execution without sustaining continual insult and impertinence; the French are far more tolerant." Picturesquely, the three young tourists bought an ass to carry their provisions, but the animal was soon so tired it had to be traded in for a mule. Shelley had sprained his ankle, and he rode the mule while the girls walked. Shortly, the mule too was exhausted and had to be changed for an unromantic hired carriage.

As they continued east to Switzerland, Shelley's party grew increasingly disenchanted. By the time they reached Langres in Burgundy, Claire declared, "Were it not for the grand ruins at its entrance I would have it pulled down and destroyed, for I observe that old towns are always dirty." The dingy inns were getting them down. There were places where they had to sleep on a sheet thrown over a heap of straw, and to dine on sour milk, sour bread, and stinking bacon. After the latest war with Prussia, depression was general; some people didn't even know the war was over. Everywhere were ravagement, scarcity, and the sullen demoralization of a conquered people. The group were glad to leave France behind.

Other English tourists approached the Continent via the North Sea, landing at Ostend. But the Low Countries, temperate, tidy and flat, represented all that failed to interest the Romantic. Danger and tragedy were nowhere in evidence – except on the plain of Waterloo, scene of the great battle. Napoleon, larger than life and so cast out from ordinary life, was a Romantic hero; Byron in particular identified strongly with him. Already by 1815, the tourist in Brussels saw posted a "Notice to English and American travellers: two four-horse mail coaches start from Brussels for Waterloo at Mont St Jean every morning. Price five francs, there and back." While the battle-field itself was already ploughed up for farmland and crossed with hedgerows, it was still crowded with souvenir sellers offering medals, buttons, breastplates, signet rings, helmets and weapons: a sword and guns cost eight francs (under £10 in 1980). Human remains were also sold, on a sliding scale of prices. A jawbone with a sound and regular set of teeth fetched more than one that would have needed dental work, and the old men and young boys who held them up for sale didn't fail to point out their orthodontic assets. "How sleep the brave!" murmured one visitor.

Otherwise, there was little to inspire the Romantic tourist here. He dutifully presented his letters of introduction and went to see the private collections of art, but he was not transported. Beckford wrote from Antwerp,

I went to Monsieur van Lencren's who possesses a suite of apartments lined from the base to the cornice with the rarest productions of the Flemish school. Heaven forbid I should enter into a detail of their niceties! I might as well count the dew-drops upon the most spangled of van Huysum's flower-pieces, or the pimples on their possessor's countenance; a very good sort of man, indeed, but from whom I was not at all sorry to be delivered.

The traveller on this route then went on to Germany, where the placidly ordinary atmosphere persisted. Beckford waxed scathing on the insipidities of German spas where visitors ignored the natural wonders in favour of a chat or a game of billiards. He characterized the busy social round and the townscape of "fountains in full squirt" as rather like an elaborate mechanical clock. Nor was he impressed with the expensive ecclesiastical art, with its "scraps of martyrdom studded with jewels". In the end, the prevailing essence seemed to be sauerkraut.

One great Romantic attraction was a cruise down the Rhine, bordered with steep crags and ruined medieval castles and abbeys. Shelley's party made the river trip and loved the scenery – Claire noted judiciously that "Ruins have a fine effect and henceforth I shall hardly think any scenery complete without them" – and they supplemented their appreciation with readings aloud from Byron and Shakespeare. The one drawback was their fellow travellers: "a most horrid set . . . drinking, smoking, singing and cracking jokes of a most disagreeable nature" (the Germans' humour, no doubt, was provoked to new heights of ribaldry by the Shelleys' unconventional *ménage à trois*). The German *canaille* "take advantage of [the] custom for men to kiss each other at parting . . . and kiss each other all day which with their horrid leers and slime has a most loathesome effect". So offended were the three English travellers that at one juncture the gentle Shelley was moved to knock a man down.

(Beckford had proposed another solution to the problem of cruise ambience: "to build a movable village, people it with my friends, and so go floating about from island to island, and from one woody coast of the Rhine to another". Immersing oneself in the life of the natives may work in Romantic theory, but the practical seeker after exquisite sensation has frequently surrounded himself, when possible, with a large, carefully chosen entourage of his own friends to keep the natives in the background.)

At last the Rhine brought the tourist to Switzerland: pristine, majestic, land of Rousseau. *This* was a moment he'd been waiting for, for nothing is so Romantic as anticipation; and Romantic anticipation has everything to do with tourism as well. He made his way to Geneva, where he put up at the Hôtel Angleterre, just outside the town gates and so convenient for late arrivals, because the gates shut at ten p.m. The Romantic signed the hotel register with a flourish: Byron wrote his age as one hundred; the more earnest Shelley filled in, under the space marked "profession", "Democrat, great lover of mankind, atheist", written in Greek.

Sweet, clean, and sedate, the Angleterre was a great relief to the tourist who had just come from eastern France with its sour suppers and bed-lice, or from the leering beer-guzzlers of Germany. It was also gratifying to the idealist to discover that there was no scolding of servants in Swiss hotels. Scolding was "an exercise of the tongue perfectly unknown here", Mary Shelley noted with approval, enjoying the consequent consternation of the "haughty English ladies" used to ordering their lackeys about. At the turn of the nineteenth century, Switzerland was admired as a stronghold of democracy and the closest approximation in Europe to a classless society.

Soon, though, to enhance his solitude and privacy, the Romantic traveller rented private lakeside accommodation; a cottage if he were of modest means like Shelley, a villa if he were rich like Byron. Byron especially wanted to get away from the Angleterre, where he was continually pestered by other tourists who had followed there to get a look at him. The "staring boobies" even went so far as to bribe his servants for bits off Byron's travelling coach – even more than the scenery, Byron was Switzerland's chief tourist attraction in 1816, and long afterwards people came just to remember him. Nor did the poet escape their prying eyes when he moved out of the hotel, because the Angleterre's proprietor Jacques Dejean obligingly installed a telescope in the back garden so guests could spy on the scandalous amours of the Romantics. Claire Clairmont was seen to arrive at Byron's villa almost daily with an excuse to see the reluctant poet; it was she who had timed the Shelleys' arrival to coincide with Byron's – she had "scrambled eight hundred miles to unphilosophize me", Byron complained. But the tourists at the Angleterre were largely disappointed by their spying; for although Claire eventually succeeded in making Byron her lover again, he was never an ardent one. He may have written his age as one hundred, but he acted more like two hundred, remarked Claire tartly.

Lake Geneva, however, was beautiful, an inspiration. Sometimes the tourist went rowing with friends, spending hours in earnest discussion of marriage, free love, art, and politics. Sometimes he went alone. Byron could be seen now immobile, staring at the sky, now writing furiously. He was particularly fond of rowing on the lake when the weather was stormy, and at night; he'd been known to stay out for eighteen hours at a time when it was most turbulent. At such times he was never without his pocket pistols.

A starred attraction on every early-nineteenth-century itinerary was the Rousseau tour around Lake Geneva, to the scenes from his novels and places where he stayed. By rowing boat, it took about a week, and while one manned the oars his companion read aloud from *La Nouvelle Héloïse*. The tourist was sure to stop at Meillerie, where in emulation of Rousseau's fictional lovers he dined on wild honey; and at Clarens, where he could meditate on love lost. From Clarens, Lausanne was within walking distance; the tourist visited the ruined house and garden of the historian Edward Gibbon, and plucked a sprig of acacia as a souvenir. (Strictly speaking, the sober Gibbon's house did not belong on the Romantic itinerary. Shelley wrote, "My companion gathered some acacia leaves. I refrained . . . fearing to outrage the greater and more sacred spirit of Rousseau.") It was perfectly lovely, the visitor reflected, casting his gaze back through time. But ultimately tourism in the sacred name of Rousseau had to do with confronting the Alps. The tourist now shifted his gaze up and away and made ready to dispense with civilization and plunge into pure nature.

He started over the lower slopes, and found nature at its sweetest, verdant, soft, decked with flowers. Byron was charmed by the landscape round Lake Jaman: "In the very nipple of the bosom of the mountain. . . . The music of the cowbells in the pastures . . . and the shepherds shouting from crag to crag and playing on their reeds". One might even be lucky enough to arrive on St Anna's Day, when all the young women by that name celebrated together. They all seemed to be tall, fresh-faced blondes with bright ribbons tied into their braids and a sweet smile for the gentleman from England. Sometimes, however, the pastoral imagery got out of hand: the Shelleys were driven to Neuchâtel by a kind but loquacious coachman, who provided a running commentary to their first view of the Alps in which "his associations with the mountains were those of butter and cheese – how good the pasturage was for the cows – and then the cows yielded good milk and then the good milk made good cheese – and so on from step to step". It tended to distract from the poetry.

The tourist climbed further, and there the elements were more vigorous – just what Rousseau liked – playful and a little threatening. He started his day at dawn with a breakfast of fried mountain trout and wine. Then he set off on the Alpine trail, switching from carriage to horseback to foot-scrambling, and also ducking small avalanches and waterfalls, hurling snowballs, losing luggage down ravines, sinking in fresh mud, tumbling off icy pinnacles. A German guidebook published in 1804 advised the tourist to equip himself with stout boots, a telescope, and a pot of paint and paintbrush so he could leave his name on the rocks.

There were all kinds of souvenirs for sale: gems and crystals, plant specimens, chamois horns. Mary Shelley bought herself a squirrel, which promptly bit her. But though the Romantic patronized the tourist boutiques, he denounced them. Shelley called the proprietor of the Natural History Cabinet at Chamonix

the very vilest specimen of that vile species of quack that together with the whole army of aubergistes and guides and indeed the entire mass of the population subsist on the weakness and credulity of travellers as leeches subsist on the blood of the sick.

The Romantic tourist was further disturbed when he ran into the unromantic tourist, who transformed Switzerland into a place just like home in the worst way. On the slopes of Mont Blanc, Byron overheard an English lady remark to her companion that the setting was particularly "rural". The poet raged, "As if it was Highgate or Hampstead or Brompton or Hayes! . . . 'Rural!' quotha, with rocks, pines, torrents, glaciers, clouds, and summits of eternal snows far above them – and Rural!"

But when the intrepid Romantic climbed high enough, he finally lost the others and reached that solitude and inhuman purity he was after. Felicitous nature gave way to nature implacable: stark, fierce, frightening. Byron crossed a river that was "rapid as anger". Two days later, he came to "a rock; inscription – two brothers – one murdered the other; just the place for it". Up above the timber-line, he saw "*whole woods of withered pines, all withered*: trunks stripped and barkless, branches lifeless; done by a single winter – their appearance reminded me of me and my family". And on the Mer de Glace (Sea of Ice) glacier, Mary Shelley took inspiration for *Frankenstein*.

Rousseau had prescribed mountain solitude for self-discovery; the nineteenth-century Romantics in the Alps took the self to its limits and beyond. Byron recalled, "Between metaphysics, mountains, lakes, love unextinguishable, thoughts unutterable, and the nightmare of my own delinquencies I should, many a good day, have blown my brains out." Shelley found "pinnacles of snow intolerably bright . . . the immensity of these summits excited . . . a sentiment of ecstatic wonder not unallied to madness".

The Alpine fastnesses of Switzerland were "the end of the line", in one way, for the Romantic: a stark, elemental laying bare. Another line led in the opposite direction: to the sunny south, where the animal man flourished. While the countries of the Grand Tour were cut off by the Napoleonic Wars, the Romantic tourist could travel direct to Greece and the Near East by boat.

Like the late-twentieth-century package tourist in that part of the world, the Romantic was attracted by warmth, in both the caloric and the temperamental senses. The ancient cultures were nearly untouched by the refinements and equivocations of modern Europe. The exuberant, essential man could get free.

Following the Byronic route, the traveller made a brief journey through Portugal and Spain and then took ship from Gibraltar via Malta for Byzantium: Albania, Turkey, Greece, and the islands. He disembarked on the Dalmatian coast and came shortly to Yanina in Albania – dazzling, with soldiers and slaves in full dress, minarets and mosques, rhythmic kettledrums. The Albanians had never heard of tourism, and the rare visitor was greeted as something of a celebrity. The Ali Pasha was hospitable, especially if the tourist was graced with aristocratic looks – curly hair, small ears, and little white hands – like Byron, whom the pasha was certain had noble blood. When anyone was made a guest at the pasha's palace, he was shown to a room hung with embroidered tapestries and furnished with silk sofas. The pasha pampered him hourly with almonds, sherbets, fruits and sweetmeats, and if the tourist had an aesthetic penchant for little boys – one of the unwritten but profound attractions of the Near East – he also appreciated the grandsons of Ali Pasha with their artificially rouged cheeks and enormous black eyes, "the prettiest little animals I ever saw", declared Byron, whom they kissed. It was wise to stay on the right side of the eunuchs at court. The Englishmen Dodwell, Atkins, and Gell, in Albania in 1801, displeased one, who then denounced them as conniving Frenchmen.

Albania was not the place to incur displeasure, especially for the tourist. He'd heard how in the mountains brigands made a practice of capturing foreigners; they'd cut off their victim's nose and ears and pull his teeth, then send them one by one to his friends like ransom notes. On the outskirts of Yanina, Byron and Hobhouse saw, surreally juxtaposed, a human arm hanging from a tree in a bright citrus grove.

The landscape of Albania had a rough beauty that was unsurpassed. For hours on end Byron would "gaze with an air distrait and dreamy upon the distant mountains". Only occasionally was his sight drawn downwards by one of those mishaps that has perpetually disrupted the romance of tourism. Once, for instance, he got caught in a lightning storm and his baggage fell into a ravine. Byron went into a fury and fired off his pistols, to the general dismay of the party. But the *milordi* (as the English tourists were called – for "my lord") were permitted their temper tantrums. A special pleasure for the traveller in primitive or half-feudal societies was the opportunity to exercise fully the privilege of his class.

The milordi had little choice but to rough it. Some nights the tourist found himself camping out with a band of soldiers in the mountains. For supper a whole goat was roasted, then washed down with that "ardent spirit" *raki*, made from grape husks and barley. A huge bonfire was built, and the soldiers danced round the blaze, whirling like dervishes and singing of their exploits in crime – all had once been bandits. *This* was what the tourist had come looking for; he couldn't be happier.

Less romantically, on busier roads the English stayed at a *khan*, the country travellers' hostel that served also as an animal shelter. The *khan* was a large, stone-walled, lead-roofed structure with a narrow raised platform running along the walls, and several fireplaces spaced at intervals. Horses, cows, goats, and pigs lodged on the ground floor, their masters on the platform above them, each party with a chimney for cooking. The traveller's repose was somewhat marred by animal noises at night and animal smells in the morning. Nor did the *khan* provide a staff of servants; the tourist had to rely on his own, who were unlikely to be graced in local arts. Byron's valet Fletcher took ages figuring out how to delouse his master's shirt, he cowered in fear of storms, bandits, and famine, he disliked the Albanians, and he sighed perpetually for his wife and his pint of ale.

From Albania the route continued across the Bosphorus to Constantinople. Lady Craven arrived there by sea on a frigate, songbirds in tow. Like the milordi, she was treated royally by the local dignitaries. When she met the pasha – who reposed on a silver sofa, dyed his hair black, and kept a pet lion that terrified his entourage – he told her solemnly that she was the first great lady to visit his city since Iphigenia. Accompanied by four janizaries in enormous fur hats, Lady Craven was carried about in a gilt and varnish sedan chair, a luxury tainted only by her constant fear of being dropped.

On other occasions Lady Craven could be Romantically intrepid. She was the first woman to descend the grotto of Antiparos, sliding on her hands and feet. She was also duly taken to the baths; she found the nudity distasteful, especially when it exposed the "fat and disgusting" bodies of the older women. For her own part, Lady Craven kept covered up, since a friend had warned her that "the encomiums and flattery a fine young woman would meet with in these baths would be astonishing". She was, however, much taken with feminine clothing in Turkey. Concealed from top to toe in veils, she reasoned, women had the liberty of total anonymity: "I never saw a country where women could enjoy so much freedom as here." As noted earlier, Arnold von Harff made the same observation three hundred years before, but without the same approval.

Lady Stanhope also felt free in Constantinople: she was the first female ever, it was said, to ride alone through the streets on horseback. (Later, despite warnings, she did the same in Damascus; the people were honoured, and expressed their respect by pouring coffee on the road before her horse.) In her masculine garb, she felt completely at home. Only her maidservant could not get used to the place: to make it seem more like England, she called Lady Stanhope's boy Phillipaki by the name Philip Parker instead. But Lady Stanhope was proud of her British nationality, too. When she went riding into the desert in search of a buried cache of money, she wanted to prove that she wasn't the disreputable sort of Briton who plundered Arabia for its antiquities – so, when she came upon an ancient statue, she conspicuously smashed it on the ground rather than profit from it.

For Byron, Turkey was a rugged masculine idyll. On the ancient battlefields of Troy, while Hobhouse read Pausanias, Byron went snipe shooting. He topped his swimming record by crossing the wide, hazardous Hellespont against the current from Sestos to Abydos, as Leander had done in ancient times to prove his love for Hero. Byron bragged that the only words he knew in Turkish, besides "bread" and "water", were "pimp" and some horrible oath, and he added, "I smoke, and stare at mountains, and twirl my moustachios very independently."

From Turkey, one could sail across the Aegean, past the islands to the mainland of Greece. The islands quite struck the Romantic imagination: the Frenchman Louis Martin du Tyrac saw them as "dried flowers strewn upon the sea". Another French Romantic in the Greek islands was the poet Lamartine, who extravagantly leased a 250-ton boat with a crew of sixteen just for himself, his wife and his daughter; also on board was a library of five hundred books and an arsenal. His cruise was a kind of homage to the Romantic penchant for living in the imagination: Lamartine was so carried away by his mental pictures of the places on his itinerary that he often described his entire visit to an island before he even landed there.

The traveller by merchant ship or other less elegantly appointed vessel, however, found the Romantic atmosphere somewhat dispelled by the crew. "As the men began to be heated with rowing, we found ourselves almost overpowered with the nauseous smell of garlic, which they exuded from every pore," complained Dodwell.

On the mainland, remembrances of classical antiquity were everywhere. Almost nobody had visited them since Roman times. Scholarly tourists scrambled busily over rocks and through streams, to the natives' incredulity, but it was not certifiable or quantifiable culture that the genuine Romantic wanted to experience. Shortly before the classicist Hobhouse and Byron parted company, the poet wrote,

Hobhouse and I wrangled every day. . . . He would potter with
map and compass at the foot of Pindus, Parnes and Parnassus. . . .
I rode my mule up them. They had haunted my dreams since
boyhood. . . . I gazed at the stars and ruminated; took no notes,
asked no questions.

More elementally, the Romantic visitor to Greece also took
pleasure in his food. Pure and simple, it was part of getting back to
nature. He might even become vegetarian while he was there – how
agreeable to sit in a garden of fig trees and turtle doves eating melon,
cabbage, and cauliflower, with pure honeycomb for dessert! Besides
its aesthetic appeal, several tourists ignorantly conceived of
vegetarianism as a remedy for having drunk the local water. For
picnics, olives and caviare travelled well and satisfied the craving for
meat, but *feta* cheese was too salty. It was more Romantic to swill
wine out of a goatskin than to sip it from a goblet. More elaborate *al
fresco* repasts were also attempted, although it proved annoying to
drag an entire roast lamb up a mountain.

Most tourists loved looking at the country people, too: Greek men
wore socks with red silk, tassels, multicoloured leggings, purple
tunics with gold buttons the size of hens' eggs, and red or yellow
leather shoes (although they needed the Turks' permission to wear
yellow). The women's black braids were hung with foreign coins
and reached to the ground. Some natives preferred the exotic fashion
– such as young Eustathius of Patras, who dressed in a scanty toga of
the ancient style with long sausage curls hanging down his back and
a parasol to protect his complexion. He and Byron struck up a
sentimental friendship, and he resolved to follow his English lord to
the ends of the earth, with "as many kisses as would have sufficed for
a boarding school and embraces enough to have ruined the character
of a county in England".

Reaching Delphi, site of the ancient oracle, the traveller was
disappointed: nothing but mud huts. Athens, though, had more life,
and required an extended stay. There were rooms available at the
Capuchin convent; no longer used by nuns, it was now inhabited by
a troop of sylph-like Athenian youths. Like the latter-day tourist
who goes abroad to spend all his time by the hotel, the nineteenth-
century visitor might be tempted to hang out all day at the convent,
for the youths spent their days drinking skinsful of Zean wine,
bawdily clowning, tenderly flirting, and swearing undying love for

their new friend. Byron declared himself "vastly happy and childish" there.

Yet the tourist must bestir himself and see the antiquities. Obligatorily he went to the Parthenon – though to Byron it resembled nothing so much as London's Mansion House. Then there were day-trips out of town: to the grotto of Mount Hymettos, where Hobhouse got lost; when he came out, he vented his frustration by badly thrashing the guide, in the true spirit of one of the milordi. Byron visited the Temple of Poseidon at Sounion, on the southern tip of Attica, where he left his mark by carving his name on one of the pillars. For contemporary culture, there were the winehouses of Galata, where for the tourist's delectation the boys performed women's dances that even Byron pronounced to be "highly unsavoury".

There were also essential social calls to make at Athens. Every British tourist paid visits to the British diplomatic community: the gossip was all about the Elgin marbles, the greatest archaeological find to date. If Lady Stanhope were in town she also invited her compatriot to stop by for a sorbet, a hookah, and a chat: she told him what she thought of tourists (not a lot), and he thought her unconventional behaviour unfetching in a woman (Byron and Lady Stanhope were very much unimpressed with each other). But the English Romantic, unlike his predecessors, had not come abroad to meet others of his countrymen. Romantic tourism has to do with getting away from the familiar, and the Athens expatriate community was confiningly small.

Invitations were forthcoming from prominent Greeks, too. One sat in the parlour and chatted politely with their daughters about flowers or social events, while casting a would-be connoisseur's eye over their feminine attributes. The Athens society girl, wrote Dodwell, had fine white teeth and big dark eyes but too much flesh and not enough conversation. She could be well born and well dressed yet illiterate. So if she wanted to write to her lover she used a system of hieroglyphics, little drawings of fruits and flowers each with a codified meaning. The tourist might get a message from his Athenian sweetheart in the form of a coin with a hole in it, a piece of charcoal, and a scrap of silk: just the sort of poetically inscrutable gesture that has made romance with a "native girl" so appealing throughout the annals of tourism.

The most popular young women in Athens were the three Macri

sisters, daughters of the British consul. Byron frequented their drawing room and became violently infatuated with twelve-year-old Theresa and once shot off his pistols in a fit of passion over her; she was the spirit behind his "Maid of Athens". Thereafter, until the sisters were thirty, every young British tourist visited the Macris and fell in love with one of them.

Otherwise, the tourist could "slip into something more comfortable" and see another side of Athens. John Bacon Sawry Morritt, who was there in 1795, enjoyed going about town in a Maniote lady's costume sometimes; other days, he favoured long robes, an ermine pelisse, and a large turban made by winding his sister's shawl round his head. On evenings when Byron wasn't courting Theresa Macri, he sometimes amused himself by staying "home" at the convent, in one of the Greek lady's dresses he'd bought.

To carry back to England at the end of it all, besides his Romantic memories, the visitor could pick up a unique collection of souvenirs in Greece at the turn of the nineteenth century; the treasures of antiquity were just beginning to be unearthed. Many tourists came especially to acquire, by purchase or by looting, a few choice pieces of marble, to be sold later, combining business and pleasure: the perfect mode for minor adventurers. Byron's collection of souvenirs was exemplary: marble, human skulls, a phial of Attic hemlock (commemorating Socrates, who used hemlock to commit suicide), four tortoises, and a greyhound – though the dog didn't survive the return trip.

Greece represented one extremity of Romantic tourism; Switzerland another. But the ripest place to visit, where feelings swelled to operatic heights, was Italy – north of one, south of the other. Italy had everything the Romantic was looking for: a blithe southern innocence, artistic refinement, dark-eyed passionate lovers, "beautiful crimes" and voluptuous death. There, the Romantic circle closed.

For the traveller arriving from Switzerland, Italy was very easy to reach after 1805. Napoleon had blasted out a wide, well-paved road through the mountains and across the Simplon Pass. The project took four years and required 175,000 pounds of gunpowder, but it enabled one to go from Brig on the Swiss side to Domodossola in Italy in a single day if one were up and away by five in the morning.

About a day's drive down from Domodossola was Milan, the first major stop. The tourist was most looking forward to La Scala Opera House, as much for the amorous intrigues pursued there as for the music. The institution of the *cisisbeo* – which separated love from the unromantic trammels of property relations that went with marriage – appealed strongly to the Romantic, at least in theory. It was especially favourable for the tourist, who necessarily preferred brief intensity over duration.

Milan was known as the school of love, where the amorous arts were most refined. Promiscuously adulterous liaisons were approached as an exquisite discipline of sensibility and spirit, performed with all the graces of dress, language, comportment. The theatre of operations was La Scala, where all could see and be seen, and precise etiquette governed every detail of the proceedings. The Grand Tourist had had instructions on taking the Italian chambermaid to bed, but he'd been awkward with his first *contessa*. Now, the Comte de Stendhal's guidebook came forward with tips for those wishing to make the right first impression:

About the middle of the evening the *cavaliere servente* has ices brought into the box, and handed about. There is commonly some wager going forwards, which is always sherbet. The sherbets here are divine; they are of three sorts, the *gelati*, the *crêpe*, and *pezzi-duri*; this is an useful piece of information for strangers.

(From there on, Stendhal was silent: the tourist had to improvise.) After his night at the opera, to meditate further on the exigencies of love, the tourist visited the Ambrosian Library, where the love letters of Lucrezia Borgia and a lock of her hair were on display; Byron stole "one shining strand".

The Romantic's itinerary next took him across the perennially lovely countryside of Lombardy, towards Venice on the Adriatic coast. Tourists had always been charmed by those landscapes; the Romantics took an even deeper pleasure in them. It was cultivated, sweetly ordered nature that the Renaissance and neo-classical Grand Tourists had loved: for the Romantic, the artful human touch set off the beauty of wild nature. He loved the elements of nature,

the green earth and transparent sea, and the mighty ruins of ancient time, and aerial mountains, and the warm and radiant atmosphere which is interfused through all things . . . the most sublime and lovely contemplation that can be conceived by the imagination of man . . .

wrote Shelley.

Then – in the mode of high contrast, which gave everything added intensity – the golden abundance of the countryside was set off by the dark dangers of the roads, where *banditi* might lurk. Stendhal greatly admired the *banditi*, especially those pure nihilists who would rob or even kill just for a few pennies or from a momentary rage: "beautiful crimes". He said, "When I am waylaid by highwaymen who fire at me, I always feel a great anger at the government, and at the local curé. As for the bandit, I like him because he is energetic and amusing."

Arrived in Venice, the Romantic inhaled deeply, sating his *nostalgie de la boue* – a longing for decay, darkness, voluptuous filth. The canals made silvery reflections and gave a watery evanescence to everything, suggesting languour, surrender, sorrow, death, giving off a provocative effluvium of slime.

Like Beckford, the tourist wanted to prowl those alleyways, get a feeling for the street life of Venice. Stendhal had advice for getting to know what made a city tick: seek out, he counselled, the most hated man, the most beautiful woman, and the richest man. (Stendhal's style of touring, with its emphasis on the feeling of places, discovered through intimate details of daily life, made a strong impact when his travel books were published. The first English translation appeared in 1818.)

The Romantic visited Venice's usual attractions, too. But he dwelt more on their unconscious mood than on their formal qualities. Beckford delighted in a day spent rowing out to one of the little islands, with a picnic and a mandolin, to discover an old pagan temple festooned with sculptures "more devilish, more Egyptian than any I ever beheld". When he was taken to see the opulent Doge's Palace, Beckford could think only of the horrible tortures that had transpired in its dungeons. That evening he couldn't eat supper, "but snatching my pencil, I drew chasms and subterraneous hollows, the domain of fear and torture, with chains, racks, wheels, and dreadful engines, in the style of Piranesi".

As Milan was the "school of love", Venice was the city for conspiring lovers. In the web of narrow alleys and passages near St Mark's Square, one could rent a flat for secret trysts that no jealous spouse could hope to discover. The revels lasted all night. As Beckford saw from his hotel window, each dawn the floating fruit market on the canal was thronged with noblemen purchasing a final repast of grapes, peaches and melons to enjoy before going home to sleep.

The tourist looked forward to an erotic liaison of his own in Casanova's city. Young Beckford caused the two Cornaro sisters to fall violently in love with him – while he in fact preferred their brother. Even the shy Rousseau had a romance in Venice; he was "frozen and transported" by the lady, but she suggested he stick to mathematics. The only one who had no taste for Italian ladies was the fastidious Shelley, who exclaimed in disgust, "Young women of rank actually eat – you will never guess what – garlic!"

Carnival was still the emblematic festival of erotic intrigue. Amongst the spangled performers and the clowns wandered figures in enormous dead-white masks like birds' heads, surmounted by a black tricorne hat that held in place a large black cloak. The rest of the figure was covered in a black cape; the sex of the wearer could be determined only if a skirt showed below the hem, and even that was not always a sure sign. Thus disguised, high-born ladies could have unspeakable adventures. Men could even sneak into the convents. The unfortunate Byron got caught out when his mistress Margarita Cogni, in a fit of jealous rage, snatched the mask off his companion – it turned out to be her sister.

To achieve the maximum high contrast, the Romantic tourist next must proceed to Naples: earthy and sunny, *dolce far niente*. There, he delighted in another new world of sensations. Under a canopy of "skies like light-blue taffeta", in the words of Goethe, who made his *Italian Journey* in the 1780s, there were bright red gilded carts drawn by horses wearing artificial flowers, plumes, crimson tassels and tinsel. Fruit stalls were piled high with rosy pomegranates, purple grapes, green figs, peaches, lemons and oranges – even the butchers' suspended joints of meat wore gold frills. From little carts hung with paper lanterns, street vendors sold fried fish, hot macaroni, lemonade and watermelon, and the Romantic enthusiasm for the texture of daily life was fully satisfied.

The Neapolitan people were vivid also. The strict hold of the Church, reflected Stendhal, had paradoxically rendered the populace hopeless, will-less, and pleasure-mad: very attractive to the northern Romantic. Men and women gorged themselves on food, cheap wine, and sex. Goethe, whose sexual initiation took place in Italy, had a wonderful time in Naples with a prettily eccentric princess dressed all in striped silks. After just a few minutes' acquaintance, she invited him to supper, where she sat close beside him heaping his plate with the choicest morsels; she agreeably shocked him with her salacious and scatalogical jokes (most titillating when aimed at supper guests from the clergy), and then invited him to have an affair with her. (He was flattered but demurred on that occasion.)

Then there were the excursions on the Bay of Naples, most notably to Vesuvius. The best time to see it was at night, as Shelley did. He wrote,

We were as it were surrounded by streams of a red and radiant fire, and in the midst from the column of bituminous smoke shot up into the sky, fell the vast masses of rock white with the light of their intense heat, leaving behind them through the dark vapour, trails of splendour.

The eerie drama was enhanced by the guides:

complete Savages. You have no idea of the horrible cries which they suddenly utter, no-one knows why. . . . Nothing however can be more picturesque than the features and physiognomies of these savage people. And when in the darkness of night they unexpectedly begin to sing in chorus some fragment of their wild . . . but sweet national music, the effect is exceedingly fine.

The culmination, the Eternal City, was Rome. Unromantically, the city was full of tourists. As soon as the Napoleonic Wars ceased, they reappeared, more of them than ever, particularly the English. They swarmed about the Spanish Steps so thickly that the neighbourhood became known as *il ghetto degli Inglese*. English-speaking servants congregated there to solicit patrons. Rome was much cheaper than London: a large, well-appointed house could be rented monthly for the equivalent of about £200 today.

The tourist set down his bags and then took himself to a café, a good place to watch life flow by. The favourite haunt of foreigners, particularly Romantics, was the Café Greco, frequented by Goethe and later by Stendhal, where the visitor might catch the dark eye of an Italian beauty. Stendhal observed in Rome that

Timid persons, who have been deeply smitten with the soft passion, know that a long conversation may be carried on by no other-medium than the eyes; there are indeed shadings of sentiment, if not the sentiment itself, that the eyes alone can give. Perhaps this is only true in Italy.

In Rome, the tourist would look at formal works of art too. The great Renaissance collections, vibrant with homage to everyday life, were a joy to the Romantic. He read Vasari's *Lives of the Artists* but eschewed the dry classicism of Winckelmann. With its humble themes and reverent realism, Goethe pronounced Italian art much finer than the "Gothic junk" of the north. Mary Shelley especially exulted over the work of Raphael, "the God of painting (I mean a heathen God, not a bungling modern divinity)". Tears in his eyes, the Romantic might be seen standing for hours before a beloved work while more prosaic tourists briskly made the rounds of the gallery.

In Rome, too, one could contemplate violence and even death – the touchstone of Romanticism, without which life lost its poignant exigence. The Shelleys demurred, but most Romantic tourists felt exhilarated amongst a "hotblooded" race who followed their impulses to the limits. The public guillotinings had an antique nobility, so much finer than the antiseptic executions of England. Byron took his opera glass and noted

the masqued priests; the half-naked executioners; the bandaged criminals; the black Christ and his banner; the scaffold; the soldiery; the slow procession, and the quick rattle and heavy fall of the axe; the splash of the blood and the ghastliness of the exposed heads.

Afterwards he needed a drink, but by the third execution he found himself unmoved.

Rome also held the death of classical antiquity. The Romantic tourist went round the ruins without an antiquarian scholar: he stood in the Coliseum and let time, and then timelessness, wash over him. Shelley wrote,

It has been changed by time into the image of an amphitheatre of rocky hills overgrown by the wild-olive and the myrtle and the fig tree, and threaded by little paths which wind among its ruined stairs and immeasurable galleries; the copse wood overshadows you as you wander through its labyrinths and the wild weeds of this climate of flowers bloom under your feet. . . . The interior is all ruin. I can scarcely believe that when encrusted with Dorian marble and ornamented by columns of Egyptian granite its effect could have been so sublime and so impressive as in its present state. . . . Rome is a city of the dead, or rather of those who cannot die, and who survive the puny generations which inhabit and pass over the spot which they have made sacred to eternity.

The circle was closed.

The most unromantic aspect of tourism is returning home. The Romantic travellers were so deeply imbued with what they saw in Europe that they stayed away for a long time, for years on end. Stendhal and Beckford became perpetual travellers. Byron and Shelley died abroad, but it is most likely that they would have remained there, rather than return to England, had they lived.

If he had to return, the Romantic was more "distrait and dreamy" than ever. The bittersweet denouement of transcendence is memory, fixing one's soul on the doomed perfection that was, longing after the past like a broken-hearted lover. Nothing suited the Romantic so well as looking back. Affectingly listless, Beckford declared upon coming home from his first trip, "I fear I shall never be half so sapient, nor good for anything in this world but composing airs, building towers, forming gardens, collecting old Japans and writing a journal to China or the moon." Byron wrote to his mother on the homeward steamer from Greece after his first trip, "I hope on my return to lead a quiet, recluse life" – above all, he promised, he had given up the vainglorious vice of writing. Within a year, however, he had published the first cantos of *Childe Harold's Pilgrimage* and become the most popular poet in Europe.

The Romantic anti-hero Childe Harold himself was a tourist. He roamed about Europe

> To meditate amongst decay and stand,
> A ruin amidst ruin . . .

– wandering for the sake of wandering. A hundred and fifty years later, hordes of anti-heroes from America and Europe were to travel the Orient in much the same spirit: though few of them knew of Childe Harold, they were nonetheless his descendants. But the sentimental Victorians loved *Childe Harold*. On steamboats and railway trains, in organized masses, they followed to have an earnest look at the scenes Byron described. Soon the desolate places were filled with tourists, Romantic refuges no longer.

CHAPTER SIX

The Victorian

The year is 1849 and the place, once again, is St Mark's Square in Venice. The ambience is as colourful and lively as ever, but seedier: market stalls are ignominiously established in the cathedral arches, vagrant children sleep on its steps while older ones scrounge cigar butts, and old ladies scurry mechanically in and out of the church to perform their rituals. In the midst of the activity, a lone figure, clad in modest black frock coat, trousers, and cravat, is singular for its focused stillness. Penetrating the degraded vivacity of the present scene, his attention is "struck back to obedience and lovely order", back to that exalted age when the cathedral took form: the high Gothic era. With passionate deliberateness, his gaze zooms in and travels upward, from the porphyry, jasper, "and deep-green serpentine spotted with flakes of snow, and marbles, that half refuse and half yield to the sunshine, Cleopatra-like, their 'bluest veins to kiss'", to the mystically foliated capitals, up to the archivolts crowded with men and angels, to the golden Greek horses and the triumphant lion "until at last, as if in ecstasy, the crests of the arches break into a marble foam, and toss themselves far into the blue sky in flashes and wreaths of sculptured spray". Thereupon the observer – John Ruskin – is carried off in a transcendent epiphany as well.

Two years later, Ruskin's thoughts and impressions were to be published in *The Stones of Venice*; he himself was to become the great arbiter of aesthetics in England for the next several decades. One must, he wrote, fix one's attention ever upon the divine inspiration in the work of man; and one must *work* at doing so. Few travellers might reach Ruskin's contemplative heights, but he sounded the clarion note for the high Victorian tourist, who earnestly endeavoured to ascend in his footsteps.

As soon as the Napoleonic Wars were over, tourism returned to Europe with renewed vigour: 150,000 British visitors per year now made the trip. The notion of the Grand Tour had become so appealing that now the whole family wanted to go; along with the young man and his tutor came mother, father, and several sisters (there always seemed to be several sisters). The tutor served more as a courier – all-purpose travel agent – than in his original role.

As in the days of the Grand Tour, mid-nineteenth-century continental travel served as a means of social advancement, with the ranks of the upwardly mobile swelling all the time as prosperity spread. In England, everybody knew "who one was"; class lines were clearly drawn, not to be crossed. But on the Continent – on a cruise boat down the Rhine, at a fine hotel, and most especially at the gaming tables – elusive social contacts could be achieved much more easily. If nobody from home showed up, one might pass oneself off as one of one's "betters". Arrived in Paris, Mrs Roberts has her card printed up as Mrs de Roberts, and Mrs McCarthy makes herself known as Mrs M'Carthy. The ladies invest liberally in French frocks for themselves and their daughters and then in lavish champagne soirées where they can be displayed, no doubt attracting the attention of a mysterious but marriageable count. Meanwhile, young James is quietly draining the bank account from the other end at the gaming tables. The next stop will be Baden-Baden; the count is wooing his dainty English peeress with whispered lines from *Childe Harold*, James is running up more debts, and the head of the family is making his gout much worse with cream sauces and more champagne. A wedding is planned, but at the last minute count and peeress discover each other's pedigrees to be false, whereupon a Romantic duel is only just avoided. Then the family repairs to a villa on Lake Como to recuperate; and thence to Rome for a last, desperate try. Of course it fails, and they return to the shires where they belong, sadder but wiser.

The scenario was definitive. Several indignant novels appeared in the mid-1800s to let the world know that the English had identified the culprits and weren't "all like that", and to caution other Britons who might have it in mind to try the same tricks. Two very popular works were Frances Trollope's *The Robertses on Their Travels* and Charles Lever's *The Dodd Family Abroad*.

There were, however, genuine "great ladies" who didn't quite fit in in London but toured the Continent like royalty. Chief among them was Lady Marguerite Blessington. Her early life read like a Gothic novel: a proud young beauty, she had been sold into marriage to a profligate soldier at the age of fifteen; ran away from him to live under the questionable protection of a Captain Jenkins; and was then presented for £10,000 to the jovial Lord Blessington, who made an "honest woman" of her. But still she found Britain uncomfortable, so they took themselves to foreign parts.

No expense was spared on their travels. In Paris, they leased a fashionable flat, all silver-edged mirrors and satin-canopied beds, decorated with little trinkets Lady Blessington picked up on her antiquing jaunts there: Mme de Maintenon's pincushion, Mme de Sévigné's perfume flagon, a handkerchief box once belonging to Ninon de Lenclos, the scissors of Mme du Deffand, and – the ultimate prize – an amber vase of the Empress Josephine. Sighing with Romantic melancholia over the vanities of this world, Lady Blessington submitted to the tyranny of fashion and bought some new things, too. Monsieur Herbault, he of the "fairy fingers", was Paris's most modish hatter: Lady Blessington had a crêpe hat with flowers at 320 francs (£200 in 1980) and a negligée morning-cap for about £60 – impossible to duplicate in London. She lingered at the Louvre and loved to go sightseeing in the Latin Quarter, haunt of artists, scholars, and bohemians. With the men in rusty threadbare black, the women pale and thoughtful, it was melancholic and picturesque.

Leaving Paris for Italy, the Blessington party suffered no such picturesque poverty: though the mood was Romantic, the mode derived from the high Grand Tour. The Blessington equipage was enormous, with coach after coach packed with the accessories to the good life, not omitting several copper soufflé moulds. They passed through Genoa, where they presented themselves to Lord Byron, by then a portly, dispirited, out-of-date dandy, much to Lady Blessington's disappointment; through Verona, where there was another disillusionment: the tomb of Juliet Capulet, standing in a vineyard and strewn with vegetable fragments, so it looked like a pig's trough, as Lady Blessington complained to the tomb's proprietor; and to Venice and Rome. Their ultimate destination was Naples, "the appropriate locality for an elysium that was to last for ever, and for any sojourn of English tourists of *haut ton*". The

Blessingtons moved into a *palazzo* overlooking the bay, replete with marble fountains, alabaster columns, and perfumed gardens, whence they could overlook the vivid life of the city with selected British houseguests. *Ton* was maintained when they went sightseeing: a trip to Pompeii featuring a picnic lunch of anchovy salad, cold lobster, and champagne; and a hike up Vesuvius where "the wit and drollery of some of the persons of the party contributed to render this visit one of the merriest, perhaps, that was ever made to a volcano" (a singular distinction in the annals of travel).

Lady Blessington told all in her *Idler in Italy*, published in 1837. As the title suggests, it expressed a mood of perfect leisure, the mark of the aristocrat, since "leisure" was only for those who could command their own time. During the same period in England, however, a new social class was tasting leisure for the first time, as the paid holiday came into wide practice. With the Industrial Revolution, which had truly taken hold, many workers were no longer tied to the land, so they were free to get away sometimes. The Industrial Revolution also provided a means for doing so, with the invention of the railway.

The railway burst upon the nineteenth century much as space travel hit the twentieth century: it revolutionized ideas about where and how humanity could travel. It opened up great vistas on one hand, and assaulted cherished ways on the other. Thundering, massive, belching smoke and hurtling along at unprecedented speeds, the train was a monstrous apparition across the gentle green hills of England. It drowned out the church bells, terrified the livestock, polluted the air. Surely it was committing even worse outrages on the fools who were actually inside – their lungs were getting too much air; the vibrations were interfering with their brain functions (in the early days, it was universally recommended to travel with a foot cushion); and what if they fell out? Equally devastating, to the minds of some critics, was the railway's effect on the traveller's sensibility. He could no longer smell the air, feel the breeze, experience the terrain's undulation. The landscape was reduced to a streak, and the traveller utterly isolated within an enclosed projectile. John Ruskin pronounced that travel by train was like being sent somewhere in a parcel, or concentrating one's dinner into a pill. Gone was the intimacy of discovery, the exultation at the end of a day's journeying when one came silently upon the lights of a village, the reward from the work that travel (*travail*, originally) had always been. The more developed one's sensitivity, the more one would want to linger over the landscape. "A fool wants to shorten space and time; a wise man wants to lengthen both," Ruskin wrote. "All travelling becomes dull in exact proportion to its rapidity."

Others, however, exulted at man's triumph over space and time. Moreover, as an essentially British invention, the train was a star jewel in the crown of Britain's industrial achievement. Queen Victoria, who took her first ride in 1842, gave it the ultimate mark of *ton*. And if the train oppressed cows with its noise, it had taken a load off horses: "the power of steam has at last emancipated those noble quadrupeds from toil", wrote one enthusiast, who found nothing more gratifying than to watch horses grazing in peace as he streaked past them on the train. Noblest of all its virtues, the train provided inexpensive and rapid transportation for the multitudes: a factory worker could now travel anywhere as quickly, and essentially as comfortably, as a duke. The train was an agent of democracy. The masses could see the great world, or more of it, and the great world could receive them; each profited by it. Travel need no longer be the privilege of the élite: "God's green earth in all its fullness is for the people." So declared the man who would put it all together: Thomas Cook, inventor of the modern tourist industry.

The germ of the idea came to him one morning in the summer of 1841, as he walked along the fifteen miles of railway line between Harborough and Leicester on his way to a temperance meeting. "What a glorious thing it would be," he thought suddenly, pausing exactly midway between the two towns, "if the newly developed powers of railways and locomotion could be made subservient to the promotion of temperance!" – a perfect Victorian conjunction of virtue and industrial strength. When Cook got to the end of the line, he went without hesitation to the stationmaster and proposed chartering a train from Leicester to Loughborough for the next meeting. The idea was approved, and Thomas Cook's first excursion was launched. At a reduced group rate of one shilling apiece, 570 people purchased tickets, and with a brass band for a send-off they crowded into the open carriages "to crush the monster Intemperance". Cook saw to it that there were hams, loaves, and tea for everybody; later, there was dancing and cricket in between exhortations. But Cook's most remarkable ability was his knack for crowd control. As one observer later noted,

Crowds obeyed his instructions implicitly, and certainly regarded him as an infallible authority. Frantic and agitated females such as are always to be found on railway platforms, even those obey Mr Cook, and their minds are at peace.

(Curiously, it was also in 1841 that Henry Wells, founder of American Express, got started in the travel business by making his first cross-country freight shipment.)

Cook's first meeting succeeded so well that he was urged to organize others. His amateur efforts reached a peak in 1843, when 3000 schoolchildren were transported to Derby for tea so that they would be out of Leicester while the horseraces were exerting their pernicious moral influence on that town. "We must have RAILWAYS FOR THE MILLIONS", Cook proclaimed in 1844, in the name of virtue. By the same token, in the name of shrewd business, millions were needed by the railways if the railways were to utilize their capacity. Group travel exemplified the utilitarian principle: the greatest good for the greatest number. It was merely following the natural order of things when, in 1845, Cook organized his first pleasure excursion, fourteen shillings return from Leicester to Liverpool, and became a professional. Besides putting together a package ticket, so that the excursionist didn't have to sort through bewildering railway timetables on his own, Cook checked the hotels *en route* and also compiled a guide to recommended shops and places of historic interest.

During the next ten years, Cook organized pleasure trips. throughout the British Isles. Very popular were excursions to Scotland, scene of the Romantic legends of Sir Walter Scott, to wild ancient places where "the strongest sensibilities of your natures shall be awakened". Then in 1855 there was the great Paris Exposition. Cook organized a five-day visit: 17s 6d return fare, 8s 6d per day accommodation. With that, his career on the Continent was launched. He was soon conducting tourists to the Rhineland, Switzerland, and Italy – and then well beyond. There might be "purse-proud younglings who affect to treat with disdain those who occupy a lower social sphere than themselves and . . . think that places of rare interest should be excluded from the gaze of the common people", Cook wrote indignantly:

But it is too late in this day of progress to talk such exclusive nonsense . . . railways and steamboats are the results of the common light of science, and are for the people. . . . The best of men, and the noblest of minds, rejoice to see the people follow in their foretrod routes of pleasure.

The quick Paris jaunts were so economical, and fitted so neatly into a workman's schedule, that a truly "uncommon element" appeared in that city; even Cockneys could afford to go (the Mmes de Roberts and M'Carthy were very unnerved to see them). Those who took longer holidays with Cook were also hitherto uncommon among the ranks of travellers: Charles Dickens observed that "the July and August excursionists [were] ushers and governesses, practical people from the provinces, representatives of the better style of the London mercantile community . . . many of them carry books of reference and nearly all take notes" – earnest, vigorous, self-improving types, respectful of their "betters" but eager to better themselves, too.

The older ones were often in couples, but the younger ones were frequently single; women significantly outnumbered men. For the Victorian woman, deeply imbued with a sense of duty and of her proper station in life, a trip abroad was a bold step: upwards, by means of cultural self-improvement, and outwards, into realms of danger and freedom, one of the most liberating things she could do. She had heard about such intrepid characters as Ida Pfeiffer, a German woman who went all around the world on her own in 1846, via the Amazonian jungles where she beat off a cannibal attacker with her parasol, telling him, in pidgin, that she was a tough old bird anyway, and wouldn't be very succulent; Tahiti, where she wore trousers and hauled herself up the vines to a perilously high waterfall; and China, where angry mobs outraged at "the boldness of European women" followed her to the temple of the sacred swine, the opium den, and other points of interest. The Chinese were interesting, said Pfeiffer, but they made terrible tea. In 1872 there had been Marianne North, who, on her own, catalogued the world's insects in delicate watercolours from the tropics. And, as Chapter 5 relates, there had been Lady Stanhope, who went too far, of course, but still spurred the imagination. The average woman tourist was not immodest enough to dream of following those examples, but if some ventured to the ends of the earth, could not middle-aged maidens undertake a short tour of western Europe? Three who did wrote,

Many of our friends thought us too independent and adventurous to leave the shores of England and thus plunge into foreign countries not beneath Victoria's sway, with no protecting relatives, but we can only say that we hope this will not be our last excursion of this kind. We could venture anywhere with such a guide and guardian as Mr Cook for there was not one of his party but felt perfectly safe when under his care.

In turn, Thomas Cook held his charges in no less esteem. He wrote of the female tourists,

as to their energy, bravery, and endurance of toil . . . they are fully equal to those of the opposite sex, while many of them frequently put to shame the "masculine" effeminates. . . . The trappings of prevailing fashion may sometimes perplex them in climbing over precipices [but they] push their way through all difficulties and acquire the perfection of tourist character.

The female element introduced a fresh imperative into the business of travel. There was so much more at risk now: "pre-eminent in modesty, purity, refinement, and self-respect", the Englishwoman must be protected by all means from continental perils and vulgarities. Industry responded to the call, and a whole new range of travel goods appeared on the market. Besides the anti-vibratory foot cushion, the lady traveller would want to pack an etna to boil water, a hot-water bottle, a luminous matchbox, a wedge for the door, and an emergency rope-and-pulley fire escape. There were handsome (but expensive – £10 in 1888, or £200 in 1980) carrying cases for the smaller necessities: a silver-clasped handbag of crocodile leather which included two silver-topped scent bottles; ivory clothes- and hair-brushes; glove stretcher and paper knife also of ivory; tortoiseshell comb; Russia writing case; and miniature sewing kit. At least one practical guidebook was mandatory – Murray, Baedeker, or Bradshaw – but several travellers brought all three. Barrett & Sons of Piccadilly sold a portable bath, enamelled in olive or claret, in a wicker case, for approximately £1 10s in 1888. For other health needs there were Keating's Powders to repel bugs and beetles, Seymour's Patent Magnetic Amyterion for seasickness, Bunter's Nervene, Henry's India Liniment and, for quick energy, cocoa lozenges (hard to find, but there was an address in Derby). Miss Davidson's *Hints to Lady Travellers* listed twenty-eight mandatory medicaments (lucky for those "of the homeopathic persuasion", whose pills were smaller). Finally, to avoid the unpleasantness of having "to meet and glide by the moustached foreigner . . . with his waistcoat unbuttoned, cigar in his mouth, and his hands fumbling at his braces in the corridor" *en route* from the train lavatory compartment – or worse, actually sitting inside it with the door open, for foreigners were unbelievably immodest – to avoid that, there was a portable, mahogany-rimmed chamberpot disguised as a bonnet box, on sale from Fyfe's Repository of Scientific Inventions for Sanitary Purposes, 46 Leicester Square.

The keynote in dress for the adventurous lady traveller, however, was spare to the point of austerity. Petticoats were to be kept at a minimum, and "all flowers, bright ribbons, feathers, etc., are in the worst possible taste and should be avoided". Simple shoes with a minimum of laces, and a grey flannel dress and jacket, constituted the ideal garb. As Miss Davidson put it, "to have to struggle into a gown of complex construction as the breakfast bell is ringing . . . is an experience calculated to make one look with a friendly eye upon the simple feminine toilets of the savage races". On the other hand, simplicity did not rule out elegance: there was no reason to go about in "antique mackintoshes, side elastic boots, and mushroom hats", remonstrated Miss Davidson, adding pointedly that "deerstalker caps are affected by many women in travel, but suit very few". The single most important piece of equipment on Miss Davidson's list was "a cultivated mind . . . trained to the right perception of the true and the beautiful".

Whether she was going to romantic Switzerland for nature, or to classic Italy for culture, the tourist usually began in Paris. She went to Cook's office in Ludgate Circus, London, and secured a rail ticket and hotel coupon for that city, where she made her way on her own, and she met the tour group at the Gare de Lyon next day.

In the 1860s, the return fare to Paris, with three days' room and board, came to £5 7s (£90 in 1980). Certain parvenus in the travel business purported to do it for less, but Cook scoffed,

We are often amused at the pretensions of some bustling upstarts who seem as though they would kick the world like a ball . . . and it is especially laughable to see their puffery. Some make a feat about taking visitors to Paris, keeping them and bringing them back to London for £5. These presentations are all bosh to those who know anything about Continental travel.

Sure of embarking on the right path, though still concerned over the safety of her suitcase, the tourist made her way to Victoria Station well ahead of departure time. If this were her first trip, she had a maximum of hand baggage: shawls, hatboxes (one concealing the chamberpot), picnic basket, medicaments, umbrella; but if there was a man with her – a kindly nephew or a protective elder brother, if not a husband – he would take charge of these particulars. Thus they were off to Dieppe.

On the boat, to ward off seasickness, she "gave herself over to lively speculation" about her fellow travellers. That clergyman, had he suffered in his youth? Those elderly sisters, were they retired governesses? Or gentlefolk come down in the world? Most important, which of them were on her tour, and what would befall them together? Then, six hours after leaving London, she was at Dieppe, setting foot on the Continent for the first time.

The usual crowd of cabbies and hotel touts awaited the docking of the ferry. Tourists of the old guard sniffed, identified the odours of stale tobacco and raw onions, and wished themselves in the capital. But the new Victorian tourist judged the effect quite "rembrandtic". Unwrapping a packet of Aunt Sarah's Yorkshire tarts, she repaired to a local café and ordered tea, which she discreetly pronounced to be "peculiar". One couldn't blame the poor foreigners for lacking English graces. Rather than wait around at the railway station where, as French rules forbade waiting on the platform, one would be confined in a stuffy waiting-room, she set off at a brisk pace to examine the town, Murray at the ready.

There was little to see at Dieppe. She liked the flowerboxes in the windows, which "spoke in unmistakable language that Nature's gifts were appreciated by the good people of Dieppe"; though the sewage running in the gutters was a disgrace. Still, what could one expect from people who employed no board of health? Apart from those details, she was most impressed with the clear French light, with its instantaneously transcendent effect. As Miss Davidson had promised, there was "everything to take the mind off itself and obliterate the keen memory of the past". Next, the tourist boarded the train with alacrity, bowled across flat Normandy, and made it to Paris in another four hours, whereupon she was installed in her hotel.

Luckily it was one recommended by Cook's: French hotels, she knew, could be full of unpleasant surprises. Viator Verax's *Cautions for the First Tour* had warned her to inspect the floor panels for peepholes, double-check the locks, and briskly pull back the curtains to dislodge the insects; and to ask whether there were "foreigners" in the next room, and whether they smoked. She knew she could not expect to find clothes pegs or washbasins; and even if there was a basin there wouldn't be any soap, as many tourists had discovered too late, when their faces were already wet. Nor was there a convenient chamberpot – though French women had been known to use bureau drawers for the same purpose, Verax assured her. Then, at table, things wouldn't improve. To the usual English complaints about French food – all frills and no substance – Verax added, his chivalry outraged, that the men took all the best bits and left the scraps and bones for the women, and that the noise of young children cracking walnuts with the fruit course was annoying in the extreme. But he went on to say that the cuisine had suffered largely in response to English tourism; the French presented measly roasts and sodden vegetables because they thought foreigners liked them that way. However, Cook had spared the tourist those indignities. She ate well, and then went out to see night-time Paris.

Unchaperoned in Paris by night! Yet the central city was warmly illuminated with gaslight everywhere, and if she followed Cook's counsel, she'd be safe. His literature instructed her that "Ladies may without impropriety visit the best cafés or sit at the tables outside. Ladies should, however, on no account enter the cafés on the north side of the boulevards between the Grand Opera and the Rue St Denis." Turning to Murray, the lady visitor read that "some cafés have a splendour of glass and gilding quite dazzling", even to his judicious eye. As she sat over an ice while Paris paraded before her, had she ever been more the woman of the world?

Later, she might even venture into one of the dance halls: the Jardin Mabille along the Champs-Elysées, or the Closerie des Lilas in the Latin Quarter – respectable ladies did so now. Set amidst flowerbeds, lit every colour of the rainbow by gas jets, they were modernist fantasias, worth looking at if nothing else. The dancing began at eleven p.m., and admission for men was the modern equivalent of £4.50, free for women. There the tourist would find herself among the notorious *grisettes* and bohemian students of the Latin Quarter, those who, in Murray's words, led "a life of gaiety and freedom from restraint which is hardly to be understood by an Englishman". They were doing the waltz, that daring new dance wherein a lady actually permitted herself to be clasped around the waist by a stranger. "Nevertheless, aside from the impropriety inherent in the very nature of waltzing, there was not a word, look, or gesture of immorality or impropriety," avowed the emancipated Mrs Stowe (an American, it was true), adding that the atmosphere of a Paris *palais de danse* was much more wholesome than that prevailing at a London gin palace.

There was also the notorious cancan. Mark Twain, who saw it in Paris in the 1860s, explained:

The idea is to dance as wildly, as noisily, as furiously as you can; expose yourself as much as possible if you are a woman; and kick as high as you can. . . . I suppose French morality is not of that straitlaced description which is shocked at trifles.

In his opinion, "Nothing like it has been seen on earth since trembling Tam O'Shanter saw the devil and the witches at their orgies that stormy night." In later years, Thomas Cook – perhaps using his talent for crowd control with a bit of reverse psychology – played the whole thing down:

The majority of these establishments, though presenting some attraction to the visitor on account of the "fast" reputation which they formerly had, are now of the most dreary description. The "can-can" is danced by paid performers, and is altogether of an unnatural and forced abandon. Nine-tenths of the company consists of men, attracted by simple curiosity.

For the travelling Englishwoman, it had been an interesting evening, but it was high time she got to bed. She had to be up before dawn tomorrow, in time for the early train to Geneva.

Ahead of time as usual, she easily found her fellow travellers; in those early days of railways, there would have been few others of their appearance about, especially at that hour, on the station platform. They took each other's measure with eager interest. There would be contention – the earnest young lady and the elderly wag, the headstrong student and the cautious matron, were bound to disagree – but it would be of a friendly, stimulating sort; and on the great adventure of travel, transcendence was the mode. Besides, Thomas Cook had presumably screened out the sourpusses: his brochures frequently contained the proviso that no one was welcome "who cannot accompany us with a genial, sociable, and confiding spirit". The train would get them to Geneva by midnight. Then, shortly, they would embark on the great post-Romantic pilgrimage through Switzerland.

A walking tour of eleven days, with supplementary transport by rail, carriage, or mule for the difficult or tedious places, would take the tourist from Geneva to Chamonix and the Mer de Glace, past Mont Blanc, up to Interlaken via the Wengenalp, Gemmi Pass and Grindelwald, to the Rigi Kulm in time for sunrise and then back down to Lucerne, thence by train to Neuchâtel and Paris: just right for a sixteen-day vacation, at a total cost of twenty-one guineas (£375 in 1980).

The tourist and her party spent a day in Geneva. How fine if it were the sabbath, there in the haven of Protestantism! Next day, up well before the servants, she appeared in the hotel foyer, radically attired in her knickerbockers – wrote Miss Morrell,

it is amusing to find Mr Ball . . . writing in his guidebook that "knickerbockers are undoubtedly preferable to ordinary trousers, but most persons will wait until this dress is more generally known before they carry it on a Continental tour." Whilst this was being written at home, some of [us], despising the refinements, so called, of modern civilization, were actually doing what had been thus timidly suggested.

When finally, with the sun, the servants awoke, the party set off for their walk.

The Englishwoman and her companions found themselves in a landscape of unspoiled beauty, all smiling: "limpid lakes, green hills and valleys, majestic mountains and milky cataracts dancing down the steeps and gleaming in the sun", wrote Mark Twain in 1867: pure, but not pagan – more like a scene from a fairytale to the Victorian eye. Delighted, the tourist gathered a spray for her hat and paused to take some floral likenesses in her sketchbook. These flowers, thrilled Mrs Stowe, stood pre-eminently for "earth's raptures and aspirations, her better moments, her lucid intervals". The tourist had not yet reached sufficient elevation to find the Swiss national flower, the edelweiss, which had a "noble and distant way of confining itself to the high altitudes", wrote Twain, adding, "but that is probably on account of its looks"; since, despite its reputation, "the fuzzy blossom is the color of bad cigar ashes and appears to be made of a cheap quality of grey plush".

Was she hungry? There was a little old woman selling cherries. The tourist purchased some, gratifying her sense of charity as well as her appetite. Thirsty? A quartet of charming Alpine maidens proffered spring water. She bought some of that, too – it was pricey, but excellent – only to come upon the spring itself a few paces farther on; but she and her companions merely laughed good-naturedly. Next time, though, a gallant male tour-member made them promise, they must wait and let him fetch them water from his "drinking shoe", an excellent contraption he was anxious to try.

The path was not by any means empty of people. But then, the Victorian traveller, unlike her Romantic predecessor, was not at all anti-social: she took a lively interest in these encounters. It was to be observed that the Germans wore knee breeches, knitted socks, and hobnailed boots, "and the intent and determined look of men who were walking for a wager", Twain reported. They must have been trying to beat Baedeker's estimate of how long it took to cover a given distance. They always tipped their hats to those coming the other way, unlike the more reserved English and Americans (there were few Mediterranean tourists; evidently they preferred less strenuous holidays). One young German woman wanted to chat at length with the young Englishwomen in Cook's party: How had they managed to get away on holiday without their parents? Then there were the little Swiss urchins begging for coins; her heart full, the tourist obliged them. There were also the yodellers. Suddenly, out of nowhere, one heard a "lul . . . l . . . l . . . lul-lul-*lah*ee-o-o-o pealing joyously. . . . Now the yodeler appeared – a shepherd boy of sixteen – and in our gladness and gratitude we gave him a franc to yodel some more. He generously yodeled us out of sight," reported Twain.

This joyous noise contrasted regrettably with another: at one franc per shot, a man in the hamlet of Cluse would fire his cannon, causing massive reverberations throughout the mountains. The tourist clapped her hands over her ears and called upon all her cheerful forbearance of those who preferred "a less unique grandeur brought home to the senses through cast iron". At any rate, she was glad the gentleman from Birmingham found *something* to enjoy. As for herself, by the end of the day she had walked no less than seventeen miles; and tomorrow, from Chamonix to Montanvert, would accrue still more to her virtue, for it was much steeper.

For that, some special preparations were in order. The tourist supplied herself with an *alpenstock*, the emblematic walking stick of Switzerland, and then had her name branded on to it. Later, each peak she scaled and each glacier she forded would be commemorated with a brand on the alpenstock, too; so she mustn't tarry in getting one, lest her record of achievement be incomplete. She was likely to be overcharged in Chamonix: two and a half or even three francs (£2 in 1980) for what should have cost only one. The party required a local guide; it was hard to choose one from the line-up at the hotel, because few were fluent in English. But a guide might endear himself to the whole group with a respectful gallantry to one of its older spinster members: it was taken quite innocently, and everyone appreciated the power of positive thinking. Thus armed, they set off to ascend the Montanvert, their first true Alpine assault; and beyond that, the Mer de Glace, their first glacier.

Up they went, zigzagging along the slopes. How singular to see everything at a slant! The chalets seemed almost perpendicular to the mountainside. What would happen, wondered Twain, if you happened to slip on an orange peel in the front yard? And Mrs Stowe, at one such high place, "by a very natural impulse . . . exclaimed, 'What does become of the little children there? I should think they would all fall over the precipice.'" (The guide assured her that, on the contrary, Switzerland was quite a wholesome place to grow up.)

At the summit, the tourist stepped from nature into super-nature: at the top of Montanvert was the great glacier known as Mer de Glace, Sea of Ice, like a heaving blue ocean suddenly frozen solid. Deferring to natural law, she accepted the hand outstretched by one of her male companions and stepped gingerly on to the ice, over frozen swales and billows which rose and then dipped into crystalline blue crevasses. It was thrillingly dangerous going. There were, it was true, men who, for about one franc per step, would hack little ledges into the ice for the tourist to step on; but Twain reported that the steps were about the right size to accommodate a cat. With women in billowing skirts and men in bowler hats, hand in hand sliding carefully about, the Mer de Glace reminded Twain of a skating rink. However, the greatest challenge was yet to come: the descent via the Mauvais Pas (Bad Path), a bare ledge along the side of the glacier, with a 100-foot sheer drop above a treacherous stony moraine, protected only by a thin iron railing; and it could be negotiated only by crawling. The tourist arrived back in Chamonix that evening in the highest elation, after her great conquest.

Later, she and her friends trooped down to the evening meal in a whimsical assortment of costumes, whatever could be salvaged from their overnight bags (the bulk of the luggage awaited them farther on, in time for Sunday) that was neither muddy nor snow-soaked. Some of the women amused themselves by draping their garments *à la grèque*, or fashioning monkish cowls. Were they not free spirits and world citizens, at liberty to comport themselves playfully, fancy restaurant or no? Restaurant dining for the many was a recent innovation, another consequence of a solvent urban middle class, but this surpassed what they had seen in England. A typical menu included soup, salmon in cream sauce, roast, sweet-breads, two kinds of fowl, artichokes and six desserts. Not that the Victorian Englishwoman was uncritical: though newly acquainted with the good life, she was ready to discourse on the relative merits of local wines, and would not meekly swallow a plate of vinegared chamois, even if it were the national animal. When the food was good, she was not too stuck-up to say so.

The other diners were interesting, too. It was noted with amuse-ment that some tourists brought their alpenstocks with them to the table, lest their achievement be underestimated. The diners were an assortment of types, and the lady traveller was full of lively specula-tion about all of them.

Others in the dining room were less enchanted. "I do not rejoice," wrote the former actress Fanny Kemble, on holiday in 1877, when she was already in her sixties, "in the increase of the pleasure of travelling for the million." Miss Kemble thought tourism was ruining Switzerland; she was only grateful she had had a chance to see the Alps in her younger days. The mammoth new hotels were forcing smaller places out of business; several closed every year. The service had become ungracious: they chased one out of one's room first thing in the morning to make room for new customers, and everything was geared to fast turnover and tourists who came and went in haste:

The present mode of travelling detracts much from its pleasure, in consequence of the vast crowds of people one meets in every direction. The inns or hotels, begging their pardons, are all like palaces (gin palaces, I think I ought to say), magnificent, flaring, glaring, showy, luxurious in all their public apartments but noisy, disorderly, dirty and quite deficient in comfortable *private* accom-

modation. . . . To the attractions of these huge houses of entertainment are added musical bands, illuminations, fireworks, fire
balloons, spectacles of every kind, *besides* that of the sweet, solemn,
and sublime natural features of the beautiful scenery – all which
seems to me very *vulgar*– bread and butter, and pâté de foie gras, and
marmalade and jam, and caviare, one on top of the other.

Another purist among the diners was Sir Leslie Stephen, eminent
in Victorian public affairs and letters, and father of Virginia Woolf;
he deplored the "cockney-ridden" tourist centres. After a meal
involuntarily shared with fellow Londoners, who edified him about
his bad choice of wine and quoted Murray chapter and verse, he was
very grateful to get out into the mountain air. But at least, Sir
Stephen reflected, the Cockneys and Cookites and Americans
tended to cluster in a few places: Chamonix, Interlaken, St Moritz,
which, rather like fly paper, "do not indeed diminish the swarm
of intrusive insects, but profess at least to confine them to one
spot".

The offending tourists in question, happily for them, were too
busy looking onwards and upwards to notice. After dinner they too
went out to take the air, and to look at the mountains by moonlight.
The sight was unbelievable:

Presently the moon rose up behind some of those sky-piercing
fingers or pinnacles of bare rock. . . . She would show the glittering arch of her upper third occasionally, and scrape it along behind
the comb-like row: sometimes a pinnacle stood straight up, like a
statuette of ebony, against that glittering white shield, then seemed
to glide out of it . . . and become a dim spectre, whilst the next
pinnacle glided into its place and blotted the spotless disk with the
black exclamation point of its presence. . . . But when the moon,
having passed the line of pinnacles, was hidden behind the
stupendous white swell of Mont Blanc, the masterpiece of the
evening was flung on the canvas. A rich greenish radiance sprang
into the sky from behind the mountain, and in this some airy shreds
and ribbons of vapor floated about, and being flushed with that
strange tint, went waving to and fro like pale green flames. After
awhile, radiating bars – vast broadening fan-shaped shadows – grew
up and stretched away to the zenith from behind the mountain. It
was a spectacle to take one's breath, for the wonder of it, and the
sublimity.

So wrote Twain of the view from Chamonix by night.

The next day, the Victorian lady and her party set off towards Martigny, and on to the northeast. They were now in a region especially noted by John Ruskin for its formalistic beauty: "ever-varying curvature in the most subtle and subdued transitions . . . the utmost possible stability of precipitousness attained with materials of imperfect and variable character". He wrote at length about the Alps as architectural forms, God being the consummate architect. Then, a day beyond Chamonix found the tourist traversing the Col de Forclaz, "a pure and uninterrupted fulness of mountain characters of the highest order. . . . The paths which lead to it . . . rising at first in steep circles . . . like winding stairs among the pillars of a Gothic tower", as Ruskin said. The soaring, transcendental Gothic style which came back into fashion with the Victorian resurgence of faith comprised a new appreciation of the Alps as well.

Not everything the visitor encountered was so sublime. The tourist industry was virulent. Every "humble chalet" offered meals of strawberries and fresh milk: delicious but expensive. There were more innocent maidens selling water at a high price, but water was cheaper than another national beverage: "they called it beer, but I knew by the price that it was dissolved jewelry", Twain averred. There were also poor old ladies selling cherries; the cry of "twenty centimes" echoed so continually along the path that the tourist was tempted to give some poor old lady a piece of her mind. Those cries were in turn drowned out by the ubiquitous yodellers, now appearing once every ten minutes. Reported Twain,

We gave the first one eight cents, the second one six cents, the third one four cents, the fourth one a penny, contributed nothing to numbers five, six, and seven, and during the remainder of the day hired the rest of the yodelers, at a franc apiece, not to yodel anymore.

But the tourist kept up her spirits. To avoid having to buy so much water, she sucked on a pebble to moisten her throat (a new tip); and she beat time with her alpenstock to maintain the walking pace.

In these first days in the mountains, she had a continuous view of the majestic white mass of Mont Blanc. To have climbed Mont Blanc would have made a glorious mark on her alpenstock; and the Chamonix Guild of Guides awarded diplomas to those who completed the three-day trek; Twain reported that, by 1878, 685 people had received the honour. Yet the tourist was not quite ready to attempt such a feat, despite her admiration for the men (it was almost always men) who did.

High mountains were, historically speaking, an acquired taste: from the medieval revulsion to the eighteenth-century agreeable shuddering, through the soul-shattering experience of the Romantics on the peaks. By the mid-nineteenth century, everybody liked looking at the Alps from a distance, but Murray himself wrote, in pre-1850 guidebooks, that "only those of unsound mind" would actually want to climb them. By 1857, when the Alpine Club was formed, however, high-adventure tourism was beginning to be a tradition in Switzerland. Sir Leslie Stephen, an avid mountaineer, described the stratification: English Alpinists on top; Germans next; under them, adventurous ladies; and at the bottom, "domestic sightseers".

The spirit of the high summits, in true Byronic tradition, was heroically, ruggedly *masculine*. Sir Leslie compared the view from the top to "the repose of a soldier resting in the midst of a battle – not that of a stolid farmer smoking his evening pipe after a supper of fat bacon". Even Rousseau was now deemed too sentimental. But it was not, Stephen reported to those down below, the misanthropic spirit of Byronic nihilism – matter over spirit – that prevailed in the high places. What one felt, he said, was "an awestruck humility", an affirmation of creation and spiritual supremacy.

(Mark Twain, though male, did not avail himself of his sexual prerogative to make the ascent. However, with a good telescope, a splendid novelty that added much to Swiss travel, he followed the steps of one party that did, so closely that he felt he, too, had completed the climb. The Chamonix Guild of Guides refused him a diploma.)

After five days' trekking, the tourist reached the Gemmi, from which vantage point she beheld another legendary mountain, the Matterhorn. It was impossible not to recognize, because "latterly we had been moving through a steadily thickening double row of pictures of it, done in oil, water, chromo, wood, steel, copper, crayon and photography", Twain explained. Sir Leslie Stephen found it so annoying that he very nearly turned away from the Matterhorn: with all the reproductions, he fumed, such a famous view "strikes me as little better than a plagiarism". But Twain continued to stare, and then he wrote, "Its strange form, its august isolation, and its majestic unkinship with its own kind" – the

Matterhorn was not snowy white but appeared black – "make it, so to speak, the Napoleon of the mountain world": an extra Romantic resonance.

Three days on from there, on the Wengenalp, the tourist beheld the awesome line-up of the Eiger Munch, the Jungfrau, the Silberhorn, and the Schreckhorn – Twain spotted the Dinnerhorn, the Saddlehorn, and the Powderhorn also – unforgettable sights. More than the spectacle of beauty, it was the immersion in pure air and comradeship that refreshed the tourist's soul. She revelled in a sense of surpassing well-being. Declared Miss Morrell,

Our lives needed no other romance than was afforded by the perfect freedom we enjoyed. It was an entire change; the usual routine of life was gone . . . we lived only in the enjoyment of the present. We all felt that the recollection of these pleasant days would form a precious possession for the rest of our life.

In Twain's words, "The great spirit of the mountain breathed his own peace upon their hurt minds and sore hearts and healed them; they could not think base thoughts or do mean and sordid things here, before the visible throne of God."

At the end of ten days' trekking, the tourist and her party got to Lucerne, whence they took the steamer across the lake to Weggis. Gripping their alpenstocks, they began the climb to the summit of the Rigi. It was night when they got to the top, and after a quickly devoured supper they got straight into bed, but not for long. At three a.m. a great Alpine horn sounded through the corridors of the hotel, summoning everybody to the slope of the Kulm to see the celebrated sunrise.

A crowd of two hundred struggled out of bed, the ladies with their hair still in plaits, the men hastily buttoned into their mackintoshes, some, like Red Indians, wrapped in the hotel's scarlet-and-black blankets; one or two souvenir sellers, with handworked needlecases, circulated among them as well. The view spanned almost 300 miles, a sea of clouds with mountain peaks rising out and a dozen silvery lakes gleaming through. From the first "maiden's blush" of dawn through all the colours of fire until the sun rose fully "like a shield of Jehova", as Mrs Stowe exulted, the spectacle lasted four hours: a crowning record to brand into the alpenstock, signalling that the Swiss tour was completed. At seven, the tourist went back into the hotel for a last, lingering Alpine breakfast, before heading down and home.

While one party of Cook's tourists was following the Romantic route from Paris to Switzerland, another was bound in the footsteps of the Grand Tourists, to Italy. Like the Grand Tourist, the Victorian traveller looked to Italy as her cultural heritage; but on the back of that great English beast, the railway, she could see all the major cities in about a tenth of the time it had taken him, at a total cost of about £50 (£850 today) for a month's round trip. "Certain of our friendly critics have supposed that it contains too much to be accomplished," Cook wrote, with a smile, but the tourist put her faith in Cook's. She, too, knew the value of time, as she knew the value of money; nor was she prey to those unwholesome distractions that had delayed the Grand Tourist; much could be accomplished in a month.

To see everything so fast, the railway had to be used extensively. It was in flagrant violation of Ruskin's precepts: for him, just to hear the whistle of that "screaming tea-kettle" as one stood in contemplation of the Doge's Palace was a high abomination. All the Victorian lady could do was supply herself with some good novels (Tauschnitz's English Editions, published on the Continent and ridiculously cheap, were recommended) to help while away the hours profitably.

The first part of the journey was alarming, as the train hurtled through the high pass at Mont Cenis. Despite herself, the tourist clutched the arm of the gentleman beside her. She knew it was silly, but then even the intrepid Miss Davidson admitted "It is so much an instinct with the stronger sex to protect and look after the weaker." Soon the train descended reassuringly into Italy. The gentleman politely detached his arm and went to enjoy a cigar in the smoker, and the Englishwoman settled back into her book till they reached Turin, for a quick look at her first Italian paintings and *palazzi*.

That city dispatched, the tour switched east to Milan, where everybody loved the Duomo: it was in the exalted high Gothic style, and it was a prodigious piece of industry, doubly rewarding to the Victorian soul. The tourist thought about that while she was travelling south on the train to Genoa, all decaying splendour and ancient marble. She remarked with sorrow and distaste that their party was dogged by vagrants who scrounged the gentlemen's cigar butts. (Ruskin, a virulent anti-smoker, had pointed out that tobacco juice causes permanent damage to marble, among its many unpleasant properties.) She was even more indignant at the Chapel of St John when she was refused admission on account of her sex, the rationale being that a woman was responsible for the death of the saint. The tourist was not *so* sad to leave Genoa at the end of the day. The men stocked up on more cigars, and they were off to Pisa and thence to Rome, the first extended stop: three days.

With Cook's at the helm, the usual tedium of entering that city was reduced to the presentation of a passport – unnecessary in most other places, but the prudent tourist had supplied herself with one at Cook's offices for just such an eventuality – and the payment of a five-franc fee. Though summer was the usual time for the Victorian holiday, if the tourist were going to Rome it was ideal to make the trip in spring, so she could be there for the ceremonies of Holy Week.

Cook's had found her excellent private accommodation, the inns being all booked up for the festivities. Having settled into her lodgings, she and her companions made their way over to St Peter's, where the main events took place.

Trust the papists! The great church was got up with green carpets, vermillion curtains, yellow sashes and gold lace ornaments so that, as Charles Dickens put it when he was there, "the whole concern looked like a stupendous Bon-Bon". Pursing her lips, the tourist marshalled her energies to make her way forward in the crowd, and pitched her portable camp stool where she could get a good view of the impending ceremony, a re-enactment of the Last Supper. Was that a mustard-pot and vinegar-cruet on the table? She never found out. Once the show began, the crowd surged around her so powerfully that she saw and heard nothing. Several times she was almost swept from her stool. One large Italian matron, she could have sworn, even tried to dislodge her from her seat with a hatpin. It was all very well, reflected the Victorian lady ironically, for those who had the "penitential urge", but she was a Protestant, thank you very much.

After that, the Englishwoman went round the antiquities and thanked Providence for her station yet again. The Coliseum was impressive, especially by moonlight; one always went after dark for a second look. But she was too much of a realist not to consider what her fate would have been as an ancient Roman: there would have been no banqueting on pearls and peacocks' tongues for one in her station, well she knew. Unlike the Grand Tourists and the Romantics, who shuddered at the modern usages of the ancient places, the Victorian was glad to see them put to some more wholesome employment. She was especially pleased to see the crude wooden crucifixes at the bottom of the Coliseum, where old ladies went to say the Stations of the Cross. On her way out, she said to herself, as Dickens had, "God be thanked it's a ruin!"

The next phase of the Roman tour included the art treasures of the Renaissance, endlessly displayed in the *palazzi*, more thickly concentrated at the Villa Borghese, and bursting the seams of the Vatican. It was even more numbing to the Victorian than it had been for her eighteenth-century predecessor, since she took it in so much faster; and, perhaps more significant, there had been another century of travel writing and the consequent great expectations laid on since the days of the Grand Tour. She valiantly endeavoured to suppress such thoughts; after all, Florence and Venice were yet to come.

First, though, there were Naples and the bay: *haut ton* and *dolce far niente*. These were unfamiliar styles to the modest and earnest Victorian, yet had she not earned her vacation? She emerged from Naples railway station with eyes wide. Indeed, she saw, the sky had never been bluer, the sun never warmer, fruit wagons never more tempting. But what poverty! The delightful character eating grapes by the kerb turned out, on close inspection, to be in rags, and the grapes were probably his only nourishment all day. And so many beggars! She was grateful for Cook's courier, who kept them at bay. Whenever she and her group stopped at a "charming" trattoria, she was surrounded by smiling importunings for her pennies. Mark Twain expostulated in fury:

They seize a lady's shawl from a chair and hand it to her and charge a penny . . . volunteer all information, such as that mules will arrive presently, two cents – warm day, sir – two cents . . . the concentrated essence of the soulless, dust-licking, scum of the earth the lower classes of the whole nation are! Anything for money!

The Victorian lady wouldn't go that far; they couldn't help themselves, after all. But as for the high contrast of opulence and degradation, she did not love it at all. Her sentiments were altogether with Dickens, who wrote from Naples:

Painting and poetizing for ever if you will the beauties of this most beautiful and lovely spot of earth, let us, as our duty, try to associate a new picturesque with some faint recognition of man's destiny and capabilities; more hopeful, I believe, among the ice and snow of the North Pole than in the sun and bloom of Naples.

As to the surrounding attractions, such barbaric spectacles as the Grotto del Cane were beneath mention; and the tourist was glad to hear that an English company was draining the Lago d'Agnano. Pompeii, on the other hand, was fascinating, if saddening: what was mortality, after all? And Vesuvius was very edifying; despite the discomforts, the tourist peered so closely over the top that she nearly set her shawl on fire, and she giggled watching the men fashion tapers to light their cigars from the hot fissures. Nature, she reflected, was always worthwhile. But now she was back on the train for Florence, city of art.

From Ruskin she knew she was to admire Tintoretto but not Veronese or Titian; the latter artists, he pointed out, made worldly figures more beautiful than saintly ones, in the faithless spirit of the Renaissance. Privately, she did not like to see the early religious paintings that showed martyrs stuck full of arrows but smiling in tranquillity. Ruskin had told her that the finest works were always the dark little sketches in the back rooms of the art treasuries "which now and then an exploring traveller causes to be unlocked by their tottering custode, looks hastily round, and retreats from in a weary satisfaction in her accomplished duty". The Englishwoman suspected guiltily that she was one of those wearily dutiful travellers who couldn't see the finer things. In her heart of hearts she much preferred the brightly restored works to the originals, which age had rendered "ghastly nightmares done in lampblack and lightning", as Mark Twain saw them. On the other hand, Twain went on to point out relentlessly, if one liked the patina of age then one wasn't really admiring the old master, because the patina of age wasn't there when he'd originally painted it. It was just as well that reproductions of the old masters were all she could afford to buy – and a hundred years later, her great-grandchildren thought so too, when they resold the reproductions to Italian art collectors.

Ultimately there was Venice. The tourist's favourite view of it was by moonlight, when its blemishes were softened, everything became pearly and ghostly and the great spirits of the past walked the quiet streets; she thought of Desdemona. But by day she had the most serious sightseeing to do, for Ruskin said the key to European history was here: "Since the first dominion of men was asserted over the ocean, three thrones of mark beyond all the others have been set upon its sands: the thrones of Tyre, Venice, and England." Here lay the lesson of power and corruption, in the fine distinction between the spiritual Gothic and the worldly Renaissance modes of art. She must learn well the difference between the exaltation of St Mark's and the subtle degradation of the Palladian *palazzi* which celebrated human vanity. "In Venice only . . . effectual blows can be struck at this pestilential art of the Renaissance," declared Ruskin; for contemporary England was menaced by the same downfall. "Let this be the object of our ambition . . . and the London of the nineteenth century may yet become as Venice without her despotism and Florence without her dispeace." It was a tall order for two days; but if the tourist got nothing else from Ruskin, she knew at least that art was serious business.

After scrupulously analysing moral character, Ruskin concluded that the British were superior; the Victorian tourist agreed with him. The Italians also had a high regard for the British, for altogether different reasons. To the Italians, anyone English was an aristocrat. They did not guess that Cook's patrons were mostly middle-class semi-professionals; like the Grand Tourists before them, they must be Milord and Milady. Dickens met one waiter who couldn't see an Englishman without seeing Lord Byron. When Dickens admired the floormat,

he immediately replied that Milor Beeron had been much attached to that kind of matting. Observing . . . that I took no milk, he exclaimed with enthusiasm that Milor Beeron had never touched it. . . . The big bed itself was the very model of his. . . . When I left the inn, he coupled with his final bow . . . a parting assurance that the road by which I was going had been Milor Beeron's favourite ride; and before the horse's feet had well begun to clatter on the pavement, he ran briskly upstairs again, I daresay to tell some other Englishman in some other solitary room that the guest who had just departed was Lord Beeron's living image.

If innkeepers and souvenir sellers were ready to take a tradesman and a schoolmistress for Milord and Milady Inglesi, the *real* Milord and Milady Inglesi were by no means ready to cede pride of place to "i Cucchi". Genteel English expatriate colonies had existed in Italy for centuries, never more flourishing than in the Victorian era, when a steady income from home enabled families to lease or buy a villa in town or in the *campagna*. Italy was a place to pursue idle pleasures with an aristocratic ease much more difficult to achieve amidst the chilly exactions of Britain. When these gentlefolk repaired to the afternoon *corso* and there encountered "tribes of unlettered Britons . . . whose great unmeaning looks of wonder and stolidity one meets at every corner", they were not pleased to see them. The champion of the indignant expatriates was the journalist and consul of Trieste, Charles Lever, who also wrote the cautionary *Dodd Family Abroad.* Lever launched an all-out attack on Cook and "i Cucchi" in *Blackwood's Magazine.* He prodded them from every angle: Where was their British spirit of independence to be led about so? Did they realize how they looked,

forty or fifty in number, passing along the street with their director – now in front, now at the rear, circling round them like a sheepdog – and really the process is as like herding as may be . . . anything so uncouth I never saw before, the men mostly elderly, dreary, sad looking; the women somewhat younger, travel-tossed but intensely lively, wide-awake and facetious.

Then Lever attacked the sheep for their arrogance:

They deride our church ceremonies, they ridicule our cookery, they criticize our dress, they barbarize our language. . . . Take my word for it, if these excursionists go on, nothing short of another war and another Wellington will ever place us where we once were in the opinion of Europe.

Far from retreating, the package tourist was on the verge of further forward thrusts. In 1867, Cook's led their first excursion to the USA; two years later, they guided a tour through the Holy Land and Egypt, the ancient and perennial exotic vacation-land. There was no touristic "infrastructure". Cook created it as he went along – romantically rough and Orientally sumptuous by turns. Yet the price was modest: in 1873, three months across Palestine and up the Nile through Lower Egypt cost £120 (£2000 today).

The first part of the journey, through Palestine, was quintessentially Cookian in conception. What finer thing than to combine piety with commerce by leading tourists through the Holy Land? The general resurgence of religious faith, along with a renewed interest in Bible study and the first-ever views of the Holy Land by David Roberts recently circulated, made it especially timely. Armed with stout Christian principles, tempered with an emancipated tolerance for "those less fortunate than herself", the traveller to the Middle

East (somewhat wealthier and more solidly upper-middle-class than her cousin on the European tour – as the greater cost and time of this trip required her to be) set out in a spirit of exalted high adventure. On the ship from Marseilles to Palestine, she might enjoy a harmless flirtation, but her family need not fear, for she would soon be safe in the saddle with Cook's.

She landed, like her ancestor the pilgrim, at Jaffa. Unlike *his* forebear Agosto Contarini, however, Cook made the proviso with his clients that *they* would have to bear the cost of unexpected delays or extra tolls incurred in case of quarantine; but usually Cook's implacable handling of the local sheikh made that unnecessary. There was as always a crowd of robed and turbaned onlookers, staring at the exotic Europeans and importuning them for baksheesh; and then, the dromedaries and domes and spires, the troubling perfumes of the Orient. The tourist was supposed to be shocked, she knew, but in fact she was fascinated. Yet she couldn't tarry, for the pilgrimage was about to begin.

One wore one's usual clothes. Cook had particularly praised his female desert clientele for their "marked absence of all silly extravagance in dress". The only addition to a dark dress with tight bodice and voluminous skirt was, pinned to her hat, a "thin gossamer veil of brown, blue or green. . . an immense comfort and great protection against sand, dust, or glare" – while the men wrapped their bowlers in muslin – and perhaps a pair of green-tinted wrap-around sun-spectacles. A "sensible and enduring little horse", one guaranteed to "climb with remarkable discretion and safety", Cook promised, was chosen for her. She opened her large white umbrella and the party set off: 56 muleteers, 3 dragomans, 18 camp servants, 65 saddle horses, 87 pack horses, 28 asses, several mules, 5 watchdogs, and 60 tourists "knees well up and stiff, elbows flapping like a rooster that is going to crow, and the long file of umbrellas popping convulsively up and down", as Twain saw them.

It was a formidable cavalcade, but not *that* formidable: the deserts were still ruled by unscrupulous sheikhs and unspeakable bandits. They eagerly entered into protection agreements with Cook, but one couldn't trust them. There were, of course, the native dragomans accompanying the party: fearsome types, swarthy and moustachioed, swathed in multicoloured tassled rags, gleaming with scimitars and firearms of several vintages. Murray's *Egypt* advised all male tourists in the Middle East to carry pistols nonetheless. Warning shots were fired whenever the party passed through Bedouin country; and to keep alert, the men engaged in a bit of spontaneous target practice as they rode along, just in case. The Victorian lady flinched at first, but then she got used to it, a significant desensitization in learning to deal with the natives.

Mostly, though, the tourist absorbed herself in the barren loveliness of the sands, all pale, shimmering pastel colours. From time to time they passed a caravan of Arabs and dromedaries: "One cannot help being struck by the patriarchal simplicity of the incident," wrote Miss Edwards. The tourist was transported back to the days of the Old Testament – for her, the most exciting journey. Then there was just the wasteland again.

Once in a while these dreamlike passages were punctuated when the party passed through an Arab village. Many villages boasted Biblical ruins, ancient tombs where saints lay buried, spots where Jesus had stopped to rest, the same places the pilgrims had seen half a millennium before. However, it would have required the imaginative power of Ruskin to recreate the original events: all that remained in most places was a heap of stones, which diminished with the passage of each tourist party, for the nineteenth-century pilgrim was as zealous as his predecessor in collecting relics. As to the rest of the village, it too hearkened back to the Old Testament, but not "picturesquely": mean alleys and small windowless houses like dry-goods boxes frescoed with discs of fresh camel dung set out to dry for fuel. The streets swarmed with life – men at work, women doing the laundry, children running about like dogs and cats, dogs and cats on every doorstep, ledge, and rooftop – to a degree that positively constituted indecent exposure. The tourist was open-minded, but she had her limits. Still, one did not wish to bury one's head in the sand: one was resolved to see everything on the programme. Cook's tours often included a visit to a slave market, for instance. Sipping sweet coffee, the tourists sat at ease inspecting the goods, presented the proprietor with the customary tribute, and then "left the dirty den with our hatred of Eastern abominations very much intensified". The lady might do some private exploring of the town, too. Gathering her skirts in closer, she ventured for a stroll through the streets, preferably on the arm of a male member of the party. At every turn they were besieged by beggars: malnourished children, tattooed tribeswomen, men missing limbs and crawling with vermin, all crying, "Baksheesh, howajji!" The tourist and her escort flung some coins on the ground and watched the wretches scrabble for them – such abjection! But one walked away feeling better for having "helped".

The squalor of the natives' living arrangements was in maximum contrast with the tourist's own, a contrast which emphasized the luxury of the latter. At the end of each day, her party arrived at their halting place to find camp already pitched: twenty-one handsome blue sailcloth sleeping tents, three large tents for dining, the Union Jack flying jauntily from each. In the dining tent, there would be camp chairs, candles, and linen napery (one had the same numbered napkin every night), and a generous meal to rival the best *table d'hôte*: roast mutton, goose, chicken, fried potatoes, tea, pudding, and fruit. The sleeping tents – three ladies per tent – were arabesqued with Oriental patterns, floored with Turkish carpets, and had real beds with iron bedsteads. After a sleep sweetened by the sounds of the desert, the six o'clock bell sounded, and an attendant provided a bathtub with hot and cold water. At breakfast, featuring tea, coffee, milk, eggs, fresh bread, chicken, and cutlets, the sides of the dining tent were rolled up so one could watch the desert turning rosy and golden; and four or five hours later, after an exhilarating morning ride, lunch would be served on carpets under a palm grove, followed by a siesta. Domestic help was plentiful at home, but the tourist had never been so sumptuously outnumbered by servants as this; she felt like royalty.

The starred attractions were Bethlehem, the Dead Sea, Jericho, and ultimately the Holy City of Jerusalem. With his customary flair for orchestration, Cook knew just how to impress the sublimity of the scene upon his charges: "My plan," he confided, "was to let as little of [Jerusalem] on the west side be seen as possible until the glorious sight of walls, domes, minarets, flat and dome roofed houses burst at one view on the astonished beholder." The tourist was moved – perhaps no less than Margery Kempe before her – but she expressed her feelings by solemn silence instead, sublimity being singularly incongruous with hysterics, to her way of seeing things.

Inside the city, the Church of the Holy Sepulchre was still rife with paradox. The courtyard was mobbed with beggars, and the age-old conflict between the different sects still prevailed within, each deriding the others: the tourist remarked sorrowfully that few had attained the transcendent Christian spirit. Then, too, the austere

Victorian sensibility was "scandalized by trumpery, gewgaws and tawdry ornamentation", in Twain's words, that festooned the sepulchre itself. However, in the enlightened spirit of contemporary Christianity, Cook organized "a lovely Sabbath, the worship of the Anglo-Prussian church being most highly appreciated. Prayers were read morning and evening by the famous traveller and Eastern explorer, just escaped from a brigand shiek [sic] in the land of Moab, Dr Tristram". With that affirmation of her own faith, the Victorian lady was ready to step back farther still, to before its beginnings, into the pagan mysteries of ancient Egypt.

The Egyptian vogue in Britain began with the turn of the nineteenth century; since Napoleon's Egyptian campaign in 1798, Egyptology had gripped the popular imagination. The Obelisk of Luxor had stood in the Place de la Concorde in Paris since 1830, and for nearly half a century Londoners had been examining mummies, lion-headed goddesses, sheets of papyri and hieroglyphics at the Egyptian Hall in Piccadilly. Arcane sciences appealed to the general thirst for knowledge that went with a belief in human perfectability. Also, for the female Victorian especially, there was a pull towards the proud, full-lipped, silent goddesses, those powerful images of woman, particularly at a time when her own powers were emerging.

Tourism in Egypt had been in existence for some time. Throughout the nineteenth century, small parties of travellers had secured themselves a dragoman and ventured into the desert or up the Nile. Especially favoured was the Nile cruise, in a small, elegantly fitted cabin boat called a dahabeah, much in the style of Roman tourism in antiquity. Genteelly intrepid English ladies with an interest in sketching found it particularly felicitous. But for those without the time or the initiative to organize such a trip on their own – for those who wanted to be sure – there was Cook to tie up the package.

The great foregathering place in Egypt was Shepheard's Hotel in Cairo. Half the 300 guests there were bound for the Nile, reported Miss Edwards in 1873, and of that half, nine-tenths were English or American.

When the tourist made her first appearance in the dining room, all eyes were upon her; for the travellers felt themselves to be a little community, however temporary. Their paths would cross and re-cross all the way up the Nile, and by the time they got to Thebes they'd probably all have met. The tourist herself was very curious. From Murray's reading list, she had chosen the *Nile Novel*, or another of the genre of new romantic fiction set in Egypt. And even though it was silly, she couldn't help imagining that the virile-but-brooding crocodile hunter, or the worldweary-but-sensitive antiquarian, might find, in her, his destiny, under the shadow of Sekhmet.

However, there were surer and more edifying attractions in Cairo, too, that "strange combination of ancient Orientalism with Parisian innovations", as Cook tantalizingly put it. Not one to sit about languishing, despite whatever dark memory may have prompted her trip, the tourist set off on a walk forthwith.

Though the streets were "regrettably" narrow, lamented Murray, that circumstance was compensated by their exotic atmosphere. Everywhere one saw characters from the Arabian Nights, slipping quietly past on donkeys with the fantastic insouciance of figures in a dream. Aiming at the heart of what the visitor was after, Miss Edwards counselled,

In order to enjoy an overwhelming, ineffaceable first impression of Oriental out-of-doors life, one should begin in Cairo with a day in the native bazaars; neither buying nor sketching nor seeking information, but just taking in scene after scene with its manifold combinations of light and shade, colour, costume, and architectural detail.

There were spices and shimmering fabrics and artefacts all in filigree; people of every shade from ebony to saffron, some all veiled and some nearly naked; strange music; a dozen languages. Was life not a dream? the tourist mused. She herself could enjoy considerable liberty in Cairo. Since the days of Lady Stanhope, it barely caused comment in that cosmopolitan city if two English ladies went strolling on their own: they were but one rarity among many. As usual, the tourist hadn't time to linger: Cook's excursionists "did" Egypt in little over three weeks. She must launch into the antiquities, beginning with the Pyramids of Giza and the Sphinx.

The party started out early in the morning from Shepheard's Hotel. Refastening her veil and mounting her donkey – which, though diminutive, "collided with camels, dervishes, effendis, asses, beggars, and everything else that offered . . . a chance for collision", Twain reported – the tourist had another, less unhurried view of Cairo. (And if the donkey-boy could discreetly nudge the lady off her donkey, there could be baksheesh in it for him when he helped her back on.)

Forthwith, she came to the riverbank, where tourists and beasts crowded together on a small sailboat, taking care not to tread on each other's toes. They cruised along the Nile to Giza, where they disembarked, remounted, and rode towards the great shapes in the distance, shimmering like mirages in the heat.

Her first impression, on reaching the Pyramids, was that they were rather small. The tourist remembered reading that to remedy the effect she must stand right against the wall and look straight up. But there was little opportunity to stand still and stare, with the insistent activity surrounding her: she was besieged. There was a mob of souvenir sellers, offering everything from scraps of mummy bandage to "antique jewellery". The mummy bandage probably was genuine and made a harmless enough memento, Murray reckoned. But the visitor should on no account buy the jewellery: "When the Pyramid Arabs have got a good thing, they do not offer it first hand to the European sightseer," he reasoned cannily. There was also a mob of guides vying for the privilege of hauling the tourist up to the Pyramid's summit. Presumably, Cook's had arranged a group fee with the sheikh of Giza; the going rate was four shillings per person (£3.50 in 1980), for two Arabs to hoist the tourist up by the arms and one to support her from below. Murray counselled that it was smart to slip some extra baksheesh to one of these assistants for fending off the rest.

Knotting her skirts securely, the Victorian lady prepared for the ascent. It was an Alpine achievement, each step being, according to Twain, as high as a dinner table. Perspiring but proud, after forty-five minutes she attained the peak. There she caught her breath and looked around her, out across the Plain of Pyramids: a magical vision, with the golden Pyramid of Maydoom standing out like a colossal wedge of Double Gloucester cheese. The Arabs, ever hopeful of inspiring a small donation, sang their version of "God Save the Queen" for the British and "Yankee Doodle" for the Americans; French visitors were offered a small speech praising Napoleon. Or, for a dollar, an Arab would descend Cheops, cut over to the Pyramid of Cephren, ascend and descend its glassy sides and be back at the top of Cheops in nine minutes. Smiling to herself at these native antics, the tourist made her polite but firm refusal – an

American tourist would no doubt pay for the display anyway – and braced herself for the downwards trip.

Now, if she chose, the tourist could go inside the pyramid and look at the tomb. It was dark, dusty, and close in there, and the passageway had apparently been used as a latrine for centuries. Miss Martineau averred that, while there was really nothing to fear, "It is a dreadful place to be seized with a panic, and no woman should go who cannot trust herself to put down panic by reason." So the tourist chose to wait for a more wholesome tomb upriver. It was time for lunch, anyway; and then, over the sands to the Sphinx.

The Sphinx was the enigmatic emblem of the secrets of Egypt. The tourist looked up from Murray's facts and figures to let her thoughts wander back and beyond. Murray himself even conceded that there was no objective view of the Sphinx:

The mutilated state of the face renders it impossible to trace the outline of the features with any accuracy, and the traveller must draw on his fancy and imagination to decide whether they be sublimely beautiful or sweetly smiling, calmly benevolent or awe-inspiring, typical of a solemn majesty or debased idolatry.

Thus Mr Stanley thought of pharaonic grandeur; Mr Loftie was reminded of Charlotte Brontë's Heathcliff; the implacable Miss Edwards saw a watchdog gazing towards a yet-unrisen dawn; the American democrat Twain saw a sorrowful witness to aeons of human oppression; and the Frenchman Monsieur Lenoir saw an ancient Egyptian soubrette: feminine beatitude spiced with a hint of irony. Squinting for a closer look, Twain also spotted a wart on the Sphinx's jaw; but it turned out to be a tourist, trying to chip off a souvenir. So, under the Sphinx's inscrutable regard, the Victorian visitor passed between the portals to ancient "Nilotic" Egypt.

While the old-guard tourists looked on from the decks of their dahabeah, "i Cookii" travelled up the river on a brand-new steamer, a floating hotel with all European amenities. (Historically, it was a significant passage in more ways than one: the Khedive of Egypt was so impressed that in 1870 he appointed Cook official government agent for Nile passenger travel; and by 1880 Cook had exclusive control of the traffic on the Nile. A luxury hotel was built at Luxor by Cook in 1887. Increasingly, what the tourist inhabited was not so much Egypt as a world created by Cook.) From that comfortable vantage, the tourist watched an ancient landscape unfurl: palm groves; water buffalo, whose milk, advised Murray, could be made into an excellent facsimile of Devonshire cream; women filling earthen jugs with water; and, as usual, "beggars importuning each newly arrived European stranger with the odious word *baksheesh*". At Gebel Aboofayda, the tourist might spot her first crocodile. Murray reassured her that they were clumsy, timid beasts who rarely pursued humans, although it was not recommended to go wading with them. Then there were special points of interest:

Gebel-el-Dayr, on top of which stands a Coptic convent whose inmates plunge into the river as soon as a boat is in sight and swimming towards it with great dexterity catch hold of the small boat in tow, get into it, and climb on deck to ask for baksheesh. Ladies had better retire to the saloon for the visit.

Also, the sugar refinery called El Baboor (the Arab word for "vapour", because it was steam driven); and then, the colony of dancing girls, or *ghawazee*, at Keneh: Murray declared firmly,

Many travellers have raved about the beauty of these ghawazee and the gracefulness of their dance; but the real truth is that nine-tenths of them are ugly and repulsive and their dance inelegant when kept within the bounds of outward decency and disgusting when allowed full swing.

The tourist had a look herself, and heartily concurred about those

damsels in gaudy garments of emerald green, bright rose, and flaming yellow. . . . They showed their teeth and laughed familiarly in our faces. Their eyebrows were painted to meet on the bridge of the nose; their eyes were blackened round with kohl; their cheeks were extravagantly rouged; their hair was gummed, greased, and festooned upon their foreheads and plaited all over with innumerable tails. Never before had we seen anything in female form so hideous

as Miss Edwards concluded. Principally, though, there were the ancient temples, grottoes, and tombs, culminating with those at Thebes, the world's grandest ruin.

Every tourist stopped there: the riverbanks were thronged with *dahabeah* flying flags from other countries, who greeted "i Cookii" as they dismounted. At the entry points, there were the ubiquitous souvenirs: Thebes specialities included scarabei, little porcelain gods, sealed alabaster vases of ointment, strings of pale blue beads, and the shrivelled brown hands and feet of mummies. But the tourist soon turned from such ephemera, to contemplate the enormity before her. Here was Memnon, now forever silent, and here were the colossal gates to the city: veritably "an ancient London", as Miss Edwards put it. Yet the vastness was only a façade: behind the portals was squalid ruination. As per the *Nile Novel*, "Man defied Nature, but his work today is hers, not his"; the lady traveller recalled the line with a curious, faintly melancholic pleasure.

Beyond, there were wonders to behold. The tourist examined worlds of carved friezes and painted temples in her customary lively manner. Murray to hand, she was gratified to pick out the figure of Amun Nicrotis, a female figure in male dress. Then, too, having conscientiously looked into Lepsius, she had her own pet theory of Egyptology, to be disputed with the other tour members as they went over the evidence; and she also had "her own" taste in art. A penchant for the earliest art was the mark of the élitist (often disliked by other tour members, who were made to feel common); whereas, as Miss Edwards noted, "the fleshiness of the feature and the intolerable simper are common to every head of the Ptolemaic period"; but the Pharaonic period was very agreeable. Since she liked content best, the Englishwoman was riveted by all the scenes of daily life festooned on the temple walls: eating, hunting, scything, worshipping, and some very *risqué* soirées, too. Also, like her Roman predecessor, she appreciated the decorative effects. What the Victorians saw in Egypt, and what they brought back, was later influential at home: Egyptian motifs recurred in the work of such "decadent" artists as Gustave Moreau, Oscar Wilde, Aubrey Beardsley, even though they themselves had never been to Egypt.

After such a full morning, a lunch break was welcome, amidst the handsome broken pillars of the Ramasseum. The claret was brought out, and cigars for the gentlemen. Now, fortified, the tourist must descend into one of the tombs.

Each had a personal candle and slid bravely along the narrow underground passageway, which was well greased with centuries of dripped wax. When all had gathered inside the vault, the guide lit a magnesium flare. Startled, white lizards scattered in all directions, and in a flash of illumination the tourist saw the weird denizens of the Egyptian netherworld – hawk-headed men, catwomen, reptile deities – and had a thrill of the horrors. There, too, was the full-lipped goddess with her mournful smile. Magnetized, the Victorian lady stood by her. She lingered behind the group for a moment of solitary communion – her candle went out, and she fancied she heard . . . .

Soon she was back in the light again, and on her way to the richest treasury of all: the temple complex of Karnak, with its endless avenues of sculpture, its hieroglyphics still full of colour. It was breathtaking. Yet, strong in her social conscience, the tourist reflected that "Every breath that wanders down the painted aisles of Karnak seems to echo back the sighs of those who perished in the quarry, at the oar, and under the chariot-wheels of the conqueror," as Miss Edwards put it. The tourist spent all day there; and she must come back and see it again by moonlight, when the eerie laughter of hyenas echoed away in the distance. Leaving Thebes at last, she "rode back across the plain, silent and bewildered. Have I not said that it was like a dream?" asked Miss Edwards's words.

Her imagination brimming, the tourist regained the steamer, for the last leg of the voyage to Aswan and the first cataract of the Nile. The dahabeah-folk had their boat hauled over the cataract, a nominally perilous but exciting operation, especially with the antics of the native boatmen; steamer passengers, of course, could only look on. Instead, for their final thrill, "i Cookii" went camel riding at Aswan. Now it was the dahabeah travellers who looked on, rather scornfully: Miss Edwards compared a camel ride at Aswan to a half-hour on the Mer de Glace in Switzerland. Buffeted between the humps of the tassled animal, which evidently shared Miss Edwards's contempt for tourists, and snarled, the Victorian lady was guided through the necropolis and thence to the granite quarry where the monoliths had originally been hewn from the earth. This afforded another meditation upon the source, and a poetic climax to the journey.

From there, it was summarily back to Cairo, where one picked up whatever souvenirs one still wanted: a funerary statuette, an amulet of Isis, an "antique" scarab (though some, the tourist knew, achieved their venerable appearance by passing through the digestive system of a turkey, whereupon the merchant picked the scarab out of the bolus; others, it was rumoured, originated in Manchester), and perhaps another genuine *anteeka*. Then one boarded the ship for Europe.

The trip had been broadening in more ways than one. The Victorian tourist had braved a measure of hardship; she had peered deep into the past; and she had sampled contemporary life beyond Christendom. She could not have failed, for instance, to notice the native women, those disturbing creatures of the senses. Some veiled their faces but bared their breasts, of all things. The gentlemen in the party, she couldn't help but notice too, also looked. She wondered whether, when they stole away from the group to examine the native quarter at closer range, the men weren't practising a trick described by a certain masculine travel writer who suggested to the male tourist that he walk down the street calling "Fatima": since that was the name of half the women in Egypt, they'd all come to the window. The Englishwoman had her eyes open, and she knew what she knew.

Maybe the men wandered even farther away. Gustave Flaubert, who was in Egypt during the Victorian period, described the prostitutes' quarter:

The Negresses had dresses of sky blue; others were in yellow, in white, in red – loose garments fluttering in the hot wind. Odours of spices. On their bare breasts long necklaces of gold piastres, so that when they move they rattle like carts. They call after you in drawling voices: "Cawadja, Cawadja", their white teeth gleaming between their red or black lips, their metallic eyes rolling like wheels. I walked through those streets and walked through them again, giving baksheesh to all the women, letting them call me and catch hold of me; they took me around the waist and tried to pull me into their houses – think of all that, with the sun blazing down on it!

Flaubert continued:

She was wearing a large tarboosh topped with a gold plaque containing a green stone, and with a loose tassel falling to her shoulders; her front hair was plaited in thin braids that were drawn back and tied together; the lower part of her body was hidden in immense pink trousers; her torso was entirely naked under purple gauze. . . . She began by perfuming our hands with rose water. Her bosom gave off a smell of sweetened turpentine, and on it she wore a three-stranded gold necklace. Musicians were sent for and she danced. . . . That night we visited her again. There were four women dancers and singers, *almehs* (the word almeh means "learned woman", "bluestocking", but has come to signify "whore" – which goes to show, Monsieur, that in all countries literary ladies . . . !!!). The party lasted from six to half-past ten, with intermissions for fucking. Two rebec players sitting on the floor made continual shrill music. When Kuchuk undressed to dance, a fold of their turbans was lowered over their eyes, to prevent their seeing anything. This modesty gave a shocking effect. . . . When it came time to leave, I didn't. . . . I went downstairs with Kuchuk to her room. We lay down on her bed, made of palm branches. A wick was burning in an antique-style lamp hanging on the wall. . . . My night was one long, infinitely intense reverie. . . . I thought of her, of her dance, of her voice as she sang songs that were for me without meaning and even without distinguishable words. . . . As for the *coups*, they were good – the third especially was ferocious, and the last tender – we told each other many sweet things – towards the end there was something sad and loving in the way we embraced. At seven in the morning we left. I went shooting with one of the sailors in a cotton field, under palm trees and *gazis*.

These things the tourist did not see, but she could not fail to scent them. While they were, of course, unspeakable to her, still she had stared at the face of Cleopatra, and stood by the monoliths of pagan mystery. She didn't speak of these things, but she had been to Egypt.

The pleasures she had tasted broadened the tourist. They certainly broadened her appetite. Cook's in Egypt signalled the beginning of an epoch: luxury travel for the middle classes, against a backdrop of native poverty – for how else could it be so effectively achieved? On the Continent, the tourist had been conscious of her "betters"; but here, as a white English lady, she had no "betters". The natives existed to serve, and if they failed one did what a pharaoh would have done. It was the way of things: if you let them get out of hand, they'd overwhelm you like beasts. Cudgellings were endemic. No wonder the ladies were sent into the cabin at Gebel-el-Dayr: on deck, they'd have seen the whole crew turned out with sticks, ropes and obscene curses to drive the beggars away. When Flaubert passed, he found the "proliferation of beatings" hilarious, but John Mason Cook himself, annoyed with one of the native steamboat captains, took the fellow by the shoulders and heaved him into the Nile: the most efficient way to deal with bad help. Milord Howajji was alive and well in Egypt – and now the middle-class package tourist could assume that privileged title, too. Mass pleasure tourism was about to come into its own.

CHAPTER SEVEN

The *Belle Epoque* Sojourner:
An Interlude

The year is 1928, and the place is a town on the French Riviera. Along the seafront there are handsome white hotels, outrageously cupolaed and flanked by tropical palms, pepper trees, and flowering mimosa: an exotic assemblage like nothing nature ever put together, but delicious. Various well-heeled northern European types in white linen suits and Panama hats – plus a few stylish Americans in striped jerseys and espadrilles – are gathered on the terraces, cool drinks at the ready, watching the other foreigners. Has anyone worth knowing arrived? They quickly dismiss the sightseeing party of female Midwestern American schoolteachers who suddenly straggle into the foreground: obviously no fun. These women have probably been to see the Roman antiquities or one of the perched villages dating back to Saracen times; something "improving", at any rate. Now they are out of breath from trying to keep up with their guide, a "facetious and contemptuous" individual who doesn't seem to think much of them either. One tourist, however, a passenger on a cruise ship that has docked here for the day, appears to sympathize with their "haggard and uncomprehending eyes, mildly resentful, like those of animals in pain, eloquent of that world-weariness we all feel at the dead weight of European culture . . . poor scraps of humanity . . . trapped and mangled in the machinery of uplift"; they are the direct descendants of the early Victorian Cookites.

The one who is watching them (Evelyn Waugh), and the ones who are ignoring them constitute a new development in the species. While earlier tourists tried to move about as much as possible, this new type tends to remain seated; whatever he requires will be brought by the waiter. In fact, he has been relaxing since he left home, for he is carried in the lap of luxury: via luxury liner, or the Train Bleu. The only real difference when he disembarks at the Riviera is that there the pleasure dome is stationary; for effortless pleasure is the single object of the trip. At its apex, it is achieved in a glamorous modern mode which, as Waugh wrote, could evolve only in an age of "Negro rhythms and psychoanalysis, mechanical invention and decaying industry", a post-Victorian, pre-cybernetic spree for the last of the "good old days".

As one who bestirs himself little, this "tourist" is a departure from the type as heretofore characterized. But he is a vital link with the next mutation in the species, who busied himself all over the globe, and so it seems worthwhile to stop awhile with him – a small sorbet between two heavy courses.

When the Romans stopped going on *peregrinatio* to their Riviera nearly two thousand years before, pleasure travel to the seaside fell out of fashion. But the tradition of "taking the waters" was a venerable one. Originally conceived as a spiritual cure, the sacred spring turned into a health spa as the Middle Ages waned. The facilities then began expanding to include other restorative and relaxing amenities, like elegant promenades, fancy inns and gambling casinos. The health resort became more and more a pleasure resort; and the pleasure seeker had an excellent alibi for being there. By the same progression, holy days turned into holidays.

It was not until the eighteenth century that the English took to *salt*-water bathing for health's sake. Medically speaking, the best time to go was said to be in November: one went to Brighton and took one's place in an enclosed wooden cart mounted on large wheels, which was drawn into the ocean by a horse, whereupon a sturdy individual called the "dipper" would hold one in the icy water for hours at a time – the women in big, tentlike bathing dresses, the men naked, quite out of each other's sight, of course. The clientele was irreproachable, but the procedure was hardly a pleasure. Inevitably, diversions were developed to take the chill off when the bather came out of the water. By the 1780s, all the pleasures of London high life were at hand: opulent dwellings, champagne soirées, fancy walkways, and fancy ladies. In that era, too, there sprang up the Brighton Pavilion, that pastel folly of onion domes and minarets, Chinese interiors and Mogul cupolas, a structure singularly out of time and place, an emblem of extravagant escapism. It was built at the behest of the Prince of Wales, whose patronage conferred the ultimate *ton* on Brighton, but the *ton* was soon to be brought low by that great leveller, the railway. By the 1820s Brighton had become accessible to middle-class "day trippers": the long amusement pier, laid out in 1824, serves as emblem of their patronage. The "best people" had to look further for a suitable seaside resort.

At the same time, if only in a small way, a refined colony was establishing itself along the Mediterranean coast of France. The first Englishman to discover and record the charms of the French Riviera was the exacting Tobias Smollett, who stopped off at Nice during his Grand Tour. He found that the sea air "being dry, pure, heavy and elastic must be agreeable to the constitution of those who labour under disorders arising from weak nerves, relaxed obstruction, perspiration fibres, a viscidity of lymph and languid circulations". Smollett also found Mediterranean sea bathing to be salutary, but except for a few Swiss officers garrisoned in Nice at the time, almost nobody followed his example in that for years to come. While he deplored the lazy domestic servants and the absence of English newspapers, Smollett was delighted with the fresh anchovies, the watermelon, and the profusion of flowers. These observations were widely circulated with the publication of his *Travels through France and Italy*.

In the century that followed, more and more Britons came to sample the felicities of the Riviera. Most of them came – at least ostensibly – for their health; if they survived the journey, they were almost sure to start feeling better. By the 1820s a hundred English families were wintering at Nice, most of them in the English quarter, known as Newborough. Then in 1834 Lord Brougham discovered Cannes as well; and ten years later that town boasted a Protestant church, tennis courts, croquet lawns, and gooseberries in the market. The roads were still "as bumpy as a bridal bed" and plagued with brigands, and the general landscape was hardly to English tastes. Algernon Swinburne inveighed,

a calcined, scalped, tasped, scraped, flayed, broiled, powdered, leprous, blotched, mangy, grimy, parboiled country WITHOUT trees, water, grass, fields, – WITH blank beastly senseless olive & orange trees like a mad cabbage gone indigestible; it is infinitely liker hell than earth & one looks for tails among the people. And such females with hunched bodies and crooked necks carrying tons on their heads & looking like Death taken seasick.

Nonetheless, the English came.

By 1863 the railway had got as far as Cannes. The journey took about thirty hours, so it meant sitting up for an entire night: not luxurious, but endurable. At the same time, local lobbies pressed for a relaxation of passport requirements, a further incentive to tourism. Then, in 1868, there appeared something that really glittered along the shores: the Casino Royal at Monte Carlo.

In the 1850s the small nation of Monaco had been virtually bankrupt after Menton and Roquebrune revolted against its olive oil tax. Prince Grimaldi had the idea of developing his country as a winter health resort, with the added attraction of gambling. Various concessionaires took on the project, but without success, until 1868 when François Blanc, whose gaming rooms at Baden-Baden were so successful, took over the casino. In short order, Blanc hired Charles Garnier, architect of the Paris Opera House, to re-design the casino. He also rebuilt and landscaped the Hôtel de Paris, improved the roads, had the railway line extended, and in general provided the infrastructure that such an establishment required. The new casino was soon a vast success: its profits were so high that taxes on the citizens of Monaco could be entirely eliminated, and that country became the first "underdeveloped" nation to solve its economic problems through tourism.

In the 1880s another essential element of luxury infrastructure was added: the Train Bleu from Paris, sumptuously appointed with sleeping compartments. Now the Riviera journey could be executed in royal style too.

Royal tourists poured in. Queen Victoria conferred her patronage on the Riviera several times during the 1890s. She arrived in a private seven-carriage train at Nice station, where the platform and waiting room were entirely carpeted in blue violets in her honour. Treading lightly so as to crush as few as possible, the Queen repaired to the Riviera Palace Hotel. Her retinue included, among many others, several ladies-in-waiting; a bodyguard of turbaned Hindus (though the Aga Khan, who was watching, said they were only second-class servants by Indian standards); two kilted Highland valets; and Jocko the donkey. The Queen did not frequent the gambling establishments, but she enjoyed sampling the local colour on promenades in her landau, drawn by Jocko. Among her favourite sights were cemeteries and funerals.

Perhaps more in the spirit of place were the visits of her son Edward VII. His favourite town was Cannes, where he had extensive apartments at the Cercle Nautique yachting club. He spent his time boating, trading racy stories with Frank Harris, gourmandizing and womanizing. The last two functions came apocryphally together one night at a Riviera café when a waiter accidentally set alight some liqueur-flavoured crêpes the Prince had ordered. They proved surprisingly delicious, and the waiter proposed naming the new dish *crêpes Prince de Galles*; but the Prince decreed instead that they be named after his companion of the evening: *crêpes Suzette*.

Then came the Russian nobility. First was the Czar, who travelled with one hundred retainers. Next, a series of flamboyant grand dukes whose sybaritic extravagances fully equalled those of their Roman predecessors on Riviera holidays. One of them ordered a kilo of strawberries for breakfast each morning, even though it was winter, crushed them lightly with a fork, merely inhaled their perfume, and threw them away. Another employed forty-eight gardeners to transplant and reposition each flower in his vast garden every day, so he wouldn't get bored with the view. Fortunes changed hands at the roulette tables with an equal insouciance. The grand dukes were losers on an imperial scale; never, apparently, more in their element than when they were throwing wealth away – the ultimate act of conspicuous consumption. The Aga Khan wrote with approval of their pearls, rubies, emeralds and diamonds, dazzling in the Mediterranean sunlight.

There was also a complement of eccentric American millionaires – like James Gordon Bennett, scion of the *Herald Tribune*. One lunchtime, finding his favourite table at a Monte Carlo restaurant occupied, Bennett bought the entire restaurant so he could sit where he chose, finished his lamb chops, and gave the deed to the restaurant as a tip to the waiter, Ciro: thus, Ciro's of Monte Carlo. There were also eager maharajahs, notorious French courtesans, nefarious middle Europeans, and others of the "beautiful but damned" to stock several Mills & Boon novels – which did, in fact, make use of them during the period.

At the heart of it all was the Monte Carlo casino, that "large house of sin blazing with gas lamps by night, flaming and shining by the shore like pandemonium or the habitation of some romantic witch", as John Addington Symonds incanted. The witch had driven so many desperate gamblers to suicide, it was alleged, that the casino's foundations were stuffed with corpses.

Publicity like that was bound to attract tourists in numbers. The Riviera became a prime destination for upper-middle-class winter vacationers, especially British ones, throughout the *belle époque*. It was expensive; for the very wealthiest, it cost as much at the turn of the century as it cost in 1980 (while the pound sterling in that period decreased in value by 2000 per cent). Yet the ranks of the prosperous had never been fuller, and there was no shortage of those who could afford a sleeper on the Train Bleu, a hotel room at the Palace or the Paris or the Negresco, and a modest portion of champagne and caviare. And if the place was immoral, it was nonetheless genteel and therefore respectable, for the "new Romans" of the British Empire. *Queen* magazine assured its readers that

The cheap Brighton tripper is not felt. The cheap tripper in France again does not proclaim his caste loudly from the third-class window of the train, or in his straggling gait, as up the Queens Road, Brighton, penniless on his return.

High life on the Riviera continued to flourish up until the First World War. During the 1913–14 winter, 50,000 tourists spent fifty million gold francs there. Then, with the Great War, came the Russian Revolution. The aristocracy – and the idea of aristocracy – were never the same again.

When the war was over, prosperous people were even more eager than before to travel for pleasure. The long confinement had made them restless. The dark mood of war swung inevitably to one of optimism, and the exchange rate was excellent: the English pound bought 244 French francs, the US dollar bought 50.

Now, too, Americans in numbers confidently joined the ranks of luxury travellers. With the demise of the aristocratic ideal, the *nouveaux riches* needed no longer hesitate before the elegant portals of the Old World; they were as good as anyone, if not better. The First World War had also provided the infrastructure to take them there in style. The exigencies of transatlantic troop transport had produced the modern ocean liner.

It wasn't altogether a new thing. Fine passenger ships, or "floating hotels", had been around since the 1840s, when P&O took the builders of empire across the seas to the Orient. Thomas Cook was carrying excursionists around the world by sea in the 1870s; and by the 1890s, sea travel could be truly opulent, with velvet-draped, gilded saloons, dancing on the promenade deck, and the late-Victorian multi-course *grande bouffe* at mealtimes. However, nothing before the war could quite equal the liners that crossed the Atlantic in the 1920s: several blocks long, up to 100 feet deep, with a capacity reaching 50,000 tons, but sleek and swift, cutting through the seas at up to twenty-five knots. Though there were many prestigious lines, Cunard perhaps possessed the ultimate cachet; and of the great Cunard ships, most favoured of all was the *Aquitania*. To cross the Atlantic from New York to London in summer on the *Aquitania* ($286 return, slightly less in winter – just under £1000 in 1980); then to connect with the Golden Arrow train from London to Paris; and then the Train Bleu to the Riviera, constituted the ideal international tour – though it was really more like a series of fancy still-lifes.

The earnest, intrepid, cheerful Victorian Cookite would have no scope for her virtues on such a trip, and its pleasures would have made her uncomfortable. Typical passengers on the *Aquitania*, wrote Cunard's copywriters,

tend slightly towards Burke and Debrett . . . the people who cross in her are people you might meet at an important Thursday to Monday, where blood and achievement both count. . . . If you like to pack your simplest jumper and your heaviest boots alongside of your most explicitly chic evening gowns and slippers and go down to Surrey or Berkshire or "Bucks" to weekend in some Elizabethan house that shows how beauty may multiply with the years, you will like . . . the six-day crossing on the *Aquitania*, the aristocrat of the sea.

In fact, confided Basil Woon, in his guidebook *The Frantic Atlantic*, some of these "society people" might turn out to be gigolos who used to be masseurs, heiresses who used to be fan-dancers, and tycoons who had made their fortunes in the Brooklyn rag trade. But the "beautiful people" – genuine peers and movie stars – would turn up too, Woon promised. Knowing the difference – with a smile, of course – would show his fellow passengers what the tourist himself*

---

*As explained earlier, for simplicity's sake I have employed the masculine singular pronoun; but from this point forward, women toured as much as men.

was made of. As in every epoch, tourism enhanced status if one did it properly. The new secret was knowing how to party.

When the smokestacks let off the first puffs and the whistle hooted, the tourist was ready to take off. Eager, but looking cool, he jumped into a cab for New York harbour, dressed in his dinner jacket if it were an evening departure. Arrived at the port, advised the *Aquitania* publicity brochure, he'd find

Turmoil, hubbub, flurry! Taxis chugging . . . Rolls-Royces emitting Wall Street-y gentlemen . . . tall, slim-hipped young men recently at the Racquet Club . . . hypothetical debutantes . . . and proverbial cinema stars. . . . Orchids . . . gardenias . . . photographers . . . flashlights . . . trunks . . . trunks . . . trunks

(some individuals brought as many as twenty). A brass band would be playing: every passenger could play at being a celebrity. It sounded tongue-in-cheek, but the tourist was meant to take it seriously despite himself.

Having seen and been seen, the voyager repaired to his stateroom, panelled in wood, its furnishings, typically, of walnut covered in *petit-point*: "dignity", expounded Cunard's brochure, "united with exquisite taste and severe simplicity. Indeed we are reminded of John Ruskin's maxim that no architecture is so haughty as that which is simple." Perhaps, then, it didn't matter so much that the tourist planned to miss the stones of Venice. The true art lover – or wealthy art lover – could travel to Europe in the constant presence of high art, for there were eight "artist's suites" on the *Aquitania*, each decorated entirely in originals by a master: Holbein, Velasquez, Van Dyck, Rembrandt, Reynolds, Gainsborough, Romney and Raeburn. Remember, the brochure continued, "the saying of Schiller that 'Life is earnest, art is lofty'". The *Aquitania* not only brought the tourist to Old World culture, it *was* Old World culture, and the plumbing was impeccable.

Came the dawn, or, more likely, eleven a.m., the tourist climbed into his white flannels, buttoned on his dark blue blazer, and adjusted his cravat (while she belted her crêpe *pyjamas de bâteau*, or smoothed her Chanel jersey) and set out for another reconnaissance of the social terrain. The "beautiful people", Woon warned, tend to surface unexpectedly, so you couldn't depend on finding them right away or all at once. Meantime, there was all of the past – or rather, the past perfect – to look at, for the *Aquitania* supplied ambience from every

great age in history. Flanked with antique-style pillars, the swimming pool was done in an ancient Egyptian motif. The early Middle
Ages were evoked in the Carolingian smoking room. Then there
was the Elizabethan grill, replete with hogskin settees. Commemorating the Renaissance was the illustrious Palladian lounge:
white Ionic columns, frescoed and mirrored walls, ceilings inlaid
with gilt, pure marble hearth, mouldings inspired by Christopher
Wren, oak floor, plum damask curtains, and the carpet an exact copy
of a Savonerrie. Representing the neo-classical period was the Adam
library where, according to the brochure, the tourist must surely
reflect,

There was no more beautiful or powerful woman in London during the era of the brothers Adam than Georgiana, Duchess of
Devonshire . . . a sympathizer with the aspirations of the American
colonists. It is fitting, therefore, that a fine mezzotint of the Duchess
should be included among those which adorn these walls.

The voyager was not likely to be caught expressing such sentiments
himself – it wouldn't make him popular around the pool – but he was
glad somebody else had set the tone by doing so.

The *Aquitania* provided the best of both worlds: classy antique
setting, jazzy modern script. In the Egyptian swimming pool, the
women wore newly abbreviated bathing suits, and playing around
by the pool with a "bright young thing" was a great way to make
friends; it was not long ago, after all, that the beaches of Brighton
had been sexually segregated, with ladies in costumes that came to
their ankles. Then in the Elizabethan grill the tourist could *drink*.
America was in the grips of Prohibition, so that was a major
attraction of foreign travel in the 1920s; the bar opened twelve
miles outside New York harbour. In the smoking room, against a
backdrop evocative of Charlemagne, there was gambling. A number of games were unique to ocean liners: the Hat Pool, where ten
players bet on what would be the last digit in the ship's run; the
Eddystone Sweep, with sixty players gambling on which minute in
the hour it would be when the Eddystone Lights were sighted; most
complex was the Auction Pool in which, within a range of twenty
miles per day, twenty guesses on the number of miles the ship
covered would be auctioned off to players. The auctioneer was often
a celebrity, and winnings could go as high as $5000 (almost £180,000
today): the tourist just might turn into the tycoon he was trying to

look like. In between, there were all kinds of dice and card games: watch out, warned Woon, for the proverbial "mild-mannered gent", who was always the sharpie. And from time to time there were big games like the ship-wide treasure hunts, wherein one risked one's whites by searching in the coal scuttle – but not too often, because it wasn't glamorous to be too silly.

The most exigent event in the daily round was mealtime. Lunch lasted two hours, and then there was dinner, where things were laid on to the maximum.

The tourist had already changed from blazer and cravat to plus-fours (or a different Chanel jersey) three times in the course of the day. Now it was time to strike a different note. The promotional literature had promised "By night a sudden increase of tempo . . . a blaze of jewels . . . the gleam of ivory shoulders . . . gowns, rose, gold, green." On the other hand, Emily Post stated in no uncertain terms that those appearing in ball gowns were

in the worst possible taste . . . like overdressing in public places [it] indicates that they have no other place to show off their finery. People of position never put on formal evening dress on a steamer, not even in the à la carte restaurant. No gentleman wears a tailcoat on shipboard under any circumstances whatever.

Dismayed, the tourist surveyed his overflowing wardrobe – and usually, uncoolly, put on his best after all.

The dining room suggested unlimited opulence: all ivory and gold in the manner of Louis XIV, seating 700 first-class passengers, with eighty-seven items to choose from on the menu. But again, the parvenu must restrain himself. There were those like Emily Post's apocryphal "Richan Vulgar", who invited innocent celebrities to share his table in hopes of meeting other "fashionables" in that way. Meet them he did, "but the question of what he gets out of it is puzzling since with each hour the really well-bred people dislike him more and more intensely". The waiter, at least, flattered him by answering his questions in French. He could always console himself with the food. A typical meal started with bluepoint oysters, followed by bisque of lobster Americaine, Dover sole, rare roast beef cut from a gargantuan joint, or even a slice of roast antelope with foie gras, four vegetables, chipolatas, and a wedge from a two-foot-tall soufflé, with appropriate wines – once again, an international selection representing the best from all possible worlds.

Following that, there would be dancing. At the end of the night, if he'd done things properly, Woon promised some "Great Moments with the young thing in crêpe-marocain on the lee of the starboard ventilator". In a setting like the *Aquitania*, the voyager would not need to provide too much dialogue; the romance was already laid on.

After a week, the boat docked in England. Some of the American passengers would stop there awhile, latter-day Grand Tourists in search of their heritage. Like their predecessors, they acquired as many cultural treasures as they could. Some surpassed even Lord Burlington: he had merely *copied* a Palladian mansion; American tourists in the 1920s brought back and reconstructed, stone by stone, two original houses, Great Lodge from Essex and Agecroft Hall from Lancashire. But the new Jazz Age traveller imposed no such obligations upon himself. When he got off the boat, he simply had himself transferred to another pleasure dome, the Golden Arrow train.

Since the days when the Victorian tourist had sat up all night in a second-class carriage for culture's sake, railway travel had progressed from a means to an end for the vacationer: a sumptuous experience in itself. With the introduction of the *wagon-lit* (sleeping carriage) by Georges Nagelmacker, the first-class train became a hotel-on-wheels, and no pleasure was spared. Everyone knew about the Orient Express, set in motion in 1883, with its silk-walled, Turkish-carpeted drawing rooms; its mosaic-tiled bathrooms with hot showers; and its dining car of Cordoba leather and Gobelins tapestries, with eighteenth-century-style waiters in silk breeches and powdered wigs. In the forty-odd years since, railway luxury had been further enriched. Now, a cab took the tourist from the London docks to Victoria Station in time for the morning departure of the Golden Arrow for Paris: brown trimmed with gleaming gold on the outside, inside all fitted out with carpets, soft lighting and deep armchairs, and a white-jacketed steward to escort the tourist to his place and serve him a pre-lunch refreshment of coffee, brandy and smoked salmon sandwiches. There was a *haute cuisine* meal on the Channel crossing, and at the other end the tourist boarded the cream-and-brown Flèche d'Or. In Paris he was routed round from the Gare du Nord to the Gare de Lyon (no ignominious scrambling with baggage across the city), and thence the Train Bleu transported him to the Riviera in a manner befitting his aspirations. There was nothing he lacked on the journey – except, perhaps, white peacocks:

since one passenger, Mrs Henry Clews, wife of the American sculptor, had repeatedly let hers loose on the tracks, a special ruling forbade their presence on the train.

Arrived next morning at the Riviera, one beheld the showpieces of the *belle époque*, the great wedding-cake hotels surrounded by their unnaturally English-green lawns, the rows of boutiques selling Parisian frocks and expensive cigarette-cases. The archetypal grand hotel of Cannes was the Carlton: its twin domes, spiked with nipple-like spires, were supposed to commemorate the breasts of la Belle Otero, one of the legendary Edwardian courtesans who augmented her fortunes on the Riviera. It was said that once, to show up her great rival Liane de Pougy, la Belle Otero had gone to the Monte Carlo casino wearing all her jewels, scintillating from head to foot; in revenge, the following night Liane de Pougy showed up in no jewels at all, but with her small terrier covered in them. Of course, one had to go up to Monte for a "flutter" at the casino, too.

The beauties of the *belle époque* had vanished. There were no beribboned Russian grand dukes – only a few Russian *emigré* waiters, though Diaghilev's Ballets Russes now had their summer head-quarters at Monte Carlo, which would never have transpired had it not been for tourism. There were no courtesans in emeralds and satin; they had been replaced by the "casino girls", some of them old enough to have grey hair, down-and-out female gamblers who stood by the tables begging small tips from the winning players. Terriers might still be in evidence, in the possession of elderly English ladies who waited for their young Latin gigolos. But gone were the glamorous gangsters, the monocled intriguers or the high rollers smoking gold-tipped cigarettes in diamond holders. The new player was, typically, a spinster or a certified public accountant who repeatedly bet the same number at the lowest possible stake. Or else, wrote Peter de Polnay, they were

portly men in grey flannel suits, men with grey moustaches accompanied by dowdy, jewel-studded wives. . . . Their faces were red, for they sunbathed. . . . They were cautious people, and sat down two or three together believing in the safety of numbers.

If the *belle époque* wedding cake had gone stale, there were fresher pleasures to be sampled just a short way along the beach. Turning away from the casino, the knowing tourist had his room reserved at the Grand Hôtel du Cap, at Antibes. In the late 1920s it was the height of Riviera chic; for it was there, a few years earlier, that a new style of recreation, a sophisticatedly simple "return to nature" under the summer sun, had been created by the newest wave of the touristic avante-garde.

When the First World War was over, the original *beau monde* of the winter Riviera – what was left of them – had begun wintering instead on the Normandy coast, at Deauville and Trouville. Without the Russians, the Riviera wasn't the same. Winter on the Riviera had become *passé*; and summer was as usual out of the question, too savagely hot. Then in 1922 the American lyricist Cole Porter, well off the beaten track, happened to rent a château for the summer at Cap d'Antibes, east of Cannes. His friends the Gerald Murphys, an American painter and his wife, were fashionably installed on the Normandy coast at the time, but they found it too damp and chilly; so when Porter invited them south to visit they gladly accepted. A year later, the Murphys were still there, into their second summer, converting a Provençal house into a villa. Friends had joined them: Scott and Zelda Fitzgerald, Gertrude Stein and Alice B. Toklas, Rudolf Valentino, Fernand and Mme Léger, Picasso, the Heming-ways. In that imaginative company, they amused themselves art-fully with small things: fantasias made from seashells, costume parties on the beach, impromptu dramas for the children, with toy soldiers and sand castles. At local restaurants they discovered the Provençal cuisine: *crudités*, grilled fish, *bouillabaisse*, instead of the rich Parisian hotel fare.

They lay on the beach turning dark gold; they set off their tanned skin with loose, light clothing in the fashion of sailors and Provençal peasants; they swam in the sea for pleasure. There were just enough of them for the perfect party, and to house all the guests the Hôtel du Cap stayed open past the beginning of May for the first time. In those days it was a modest little place, faded-rose colour, "Deferential palms cool its flushed façade, and before it stretches a short, dazzling beach," wrote Fitzgerald in *Tender is the Night*, where those first summers are described. Stripping away the opulent encumbrances of the *belle époque*, the summer Riviera scene constituted a new romanticism, "natural" and "free"; but like earlier forms of roman-ticism, it was really an art. Its time, like jazz and "primitive" painting, had come.

In the next summers, additional discerning vacationers joined the party on the Riviera: artists, film stars, socialites and tycoons.

Shortly, the Hôtel du Cap became the Grand Hôtel du Cap, and Frank Jay Gould opened the Hôtel Provençal at Juan-les-Pins. The perfect circle of the Murphys – their "desperate bargain with the gods", in Fitzgerald's phrase, to retain the childlike purity and artful simplicity of their pleasures – was broken. The paying tourist had arrived in his perpetual hope of a good time.

He checked his bags at the hotel and then went into town for the right clothes, the one element of the ambience he had to supply himself. Following Gerald Murphy's lead, he bought workman's cap, sailor's striped jersey, white ducks, espadrilles (while she got cotton sundresses and a big straw hat), copying the fisherman and the peasant, and leaving the body free to move. Murphy had got his in the back streets of Nice, but by now the fashionable Paris houses also ran a line of beach clothes.

Then, removing most of them, the tourist rubbed his body with coconut oil and stretched out on the beach for a tan, another recent innovation. Since the days when the Romans on the Riviera sat drinking wine under the plane trees, leisure and pleasure had been associated with shade. Pale skin was always the mark of aristocratic beauty, while the suntan was the coarse coloration of the labourer. Now, when more and more "labourers" sat constrained in offices, the suntan became the golden emblem of beauty and freedom. Also, tanned skin suggested the beauty of the black races, whose sexually syncopated jazz rhythms set the beat of the times. Warmed by the summer sun, cooled by the bright blue sea, everybody taking their clothes off together, "Body and Soul" playing somewhere in the background: all the basics of happiness were provided – sea, sun, and sex; sand, slightly uncomfortable but inevitable, was sprinkled in with the package too. And *was* that Mary Pickford paddling out among the waves? For she was here somewhere; everyone was. The tourist raised his head for a moment to look, took a sip of his cool drink, lay back down. All he had to do was nothing.

The evening might be livelier. A well-off bachelor would try to get hold of a fast car and a "bright young thing" and go whipping round the curves of the Corniche to some "little place": for the new romanticism of "little places" where "real people" ate had its beginning amidst the luxuries of the Riviera now – though once the tourists started arriving in numbers, the real people could no longer afford the little places. Later still, anything could happen. Strolling by the harbour under the stars, the tourist and his date might cross paths with a pair of society ladies disguised as sailors, roaring drunk and trying to pick up unknowing local girls (as at the end of *Tender is the Night*). The Riviera vacation was after all about a kind of abandonment, and some people's idea of that was sordid. But the tourist was often intoxicated himself by that hour (he was still escaping Prohibition). Besides, he'd heard of Freud, and what the hell? And so, at last, to bed – perhaps not alone, for the "young thing" had also heard of Freud, and was also far from home, amongst these "sophisticated" Europeans.

Sailing home on the *Aquitania* a few weeks later, the tourist had a golden tan, a slight tarnish of sophistication that was very becoming, and a lot more clothes, though it was hoped that he, and especially she, would refrain from showing them off at dinner. He was a satisfied customer. Modern American technology had combined with European "gracious living" to give him the best of both worlds, in a perfect bubble which admitted no disagreeable realities. Though the ensemble was touristic, all the elements were authentic, from the Gainsboroughs on the *Aquitania* to the Mediterranean bouillabaisse. All you needed to have these good things was to know how to make money.

Later, he would be glad he had gone when the going was good: for the Great Depression was imminent, and then the Second World War. As always, war would raze one version of the "good life"; and at the same time, it would create the infrastructure whereby more tourists than ever could get to where the fortunate few had been before them.

CHAPTER EIGHT

The Tourist Explosion

The year is 1967: International Tourist Year, as designated by the United Nations General Assembly. The place is . . . indeterminate, but somewhere in the Old World: in the neighbourhood there are historic cathedrals, museums of art and restaurants that serve wine with the meal. The man in the picture has had his money's worth and seen all of them; at least, the tour guide says he's seen them. He himself is looking very un-continental, in his straw hat, loud Hawaiian shirt, and Bermuda shorts. Armed for action, he has a camera slung round his neck and a wad of bills in his pocket. But, like a newborn chick to its mother hen, he stays close to the big bus. Nobody knows his name, but everybody calls him "Homer" and his wife "Mabel". He is, significantly, only a cartoon character, so he has only one unforgettable line: staggering off the bus in yet another quaintly imposing *grande place*, he has no way to identify where he is except by dazedly scrutinizing his itinerary – blinking, he utters the familiar caption, "If it's Tuesday, this must be Belgium." Borne aloft on a gargantuan infrastructure, target of the world's biggest growth industry, "compleat consumer" (since he only brings money *in* to foreign countries, and he has to buy everything he needs from the natives), universally "distasteful" but every marketer's favourite dish, he's simply and starkly the tourist. Everybody has been one, nobody wants to be called one. All he is trying to do is to find something of value in the wide world that makes it worth working forty-nine weeks a year.

Though the exclusive bubble of pleasure burst at around the time of the Great Depression, letting in the pollutants of vulgarity, overdevelopment, and overcrowding, tourism continued to grow.

The Riviera, for instance, may have been lost, but it was not forgotten. Holidays with pay became mandatory in France and Britain in the 1930s, and the summer Riviera was more popular than ever with middle-class vacationers. Beverly Nichols wrote of them, "Ye Gods, the people! Drunken, debauched, heartless, of an incredible vulgarity – swooping, screaming, racketing." Of the picturesque locals, Cyril Connolly remarked that "elderly peasants and shopkeepers . . . seemed to have acquired an air of licentiousness from their customers". At the same time, the idealistic strain of tourism as exemplified by Thomas Cook's paragon continued to flourish. With cars, trains, and ships at his disposal, the earnest student of culture and ethnography could visit more places than ever, thinking to spread international understanding and goodwill; it was a particularly popular mode amongst German tourists.

Then came the Second World War, and travel for pleasure came nearly to a halt. But when the war was over, tourism experienced its typical resurgence. Prosperity and optimism bloomed; the mobile middle class was bigger than ever. Most important, there was a revolutionary infrastructure set out across the globe: planes and airfields, now lying idle, ready for new passengers.

The passenger air travel industry had its very beginnings sometime earlier. Though the masses did not take flight for pleasure until after 1950, a small number of privileged travellers had been going by air since the end of the First World War. In 1919, apprehensive but exhilarated trippers bought tickets for a brief aerial tour of Blackpool, operated by ex-RAF pilots. And by 1920 there was a regular run from London to Paris out of Croydon, a three-hour flight that took off inside the hangar itself. Box lunches were sold at the airport, but passengers had to bring their own drinks, plus a heavy overcoat, as there was no heating and the windows were opened for ventilation, and cotton wool to stop up their ears against the deafening noise of the engine, which was such that if you wanted to communicate with your fellow passengers, you might pass a note. Amenities were rapidly added, and the flight soon acquired a reputation for luxury, efficiency and chic. One advertisement told women that

it is much easier to look charming after an air journey than by any other form of travel . . . your complexion will not suffer . . . the child travels free from dust and dirt, and there is such a lot to interest them that they never have time to cry.

High up, "the chops of the Channel will be like ripples to you"; and flying overland your view would not be obstructed by houses and trees. Airborne lavatories were first launched by the British in 1922, and by the end of the 1920s Imperial Airways was serving a seven-course meal on the London–Paris flight. Then in 1930, America's United Airlines pioneered the first stewardess. Stewardesses were required to be registered nurses, and they wore the nurse's uniform during the flight service.

The airborne equivalent of the transatlantic luxury liner was the flying ship, a German innovation which came into being in the mid-1920s and reached its high point with the Zeppelin Hindenburg in 1936. The Hindenburg had an upholstered dining room with white linen, fresh flowers, and fine china and silver; a lounge, library, and reading room; two spacious promenade decks with big windows; cabins featuring an automatic pushbutton cocktail-server; and a Bluthner baby grand piano made of aluminium for lightness and covered in yellow pigskin. However, susceptible as they were to fire and high winds, the large, fragile airships had a short life; at the end of the 1930s they were almost extinct.

While the Zeppelins were going down, long-distance flights by aeroplane were up and coming. The Dutch airline KLM pioneered the field, offering a service from Amsterdam to Djakarta in 1929; though there were neither maps, radios, night lights, nor hangars at most of the places where the plane touched down (over two dozen times in twelve days). By 1935, Imperial Airways had extended that route to circle the globe, via Australia. Passengers prepared as they would for a cruise: women were advised to pack jumpers and tweeds, a leather coat and a fur, a felt hat, gumboots for wet aerodromes, a black lace evening dress and a Shetland dressing gown; though passenger and suitcase put together might not exceed 221 lb. The trip combined adventure – over Africa, you could see wild game close enough to get good photographs – and luxury, with a landing for the midday meal, another for supper and a night at a hotel. Some stops were primitive: in Cambodia, baggage was carried from the airstrip to the inn on elephant-back; and at Lombok Island guest house, passengers were obliged to sleep three to a bed. Every effort was made to provide a familiar cuisine: in Indonesia, at noon in temperatures nearing 100°F, the meal consisted of hot omelettes and macaroni, hot peas and salmon, tinned fruit and mineral water. Then, on board, there were frequent beef teas and other snacks, often prepared by the mechanic (one passenger noted a preponderance of smoked eel when the mechanic was Scandinavian). But eccentricities just added charm to the trip. Long-distance air travel was cheaper than going first class by sea, and more comfortable than going by train: on a train, the windows were dirtier, the seats didn't recline, and you were more likely to spill your tea and be late in arriving. Planes were also glamorous, exotic and faster than anything. By the end of the 1930s many of the world's future airline empires, including Air France, Pan Am and TWA (under its former designation of Transcontinental Air Transport), besides those already named, had tried their wings.

Such fledgling flights, however, were nothing like the surge that appeared after the Second World War. Aeronautics developed rapidly, producing aircraft that were successively bigger, faster and more fuel-efficient; a new type appeared roughly once every five years in the years 1950–75. Since demand always lags behind supply until the public can be well informed of the new facility, the new planes were further promoted by "price wars" between competing airlines. In 1952 the first transatlantic "tourist class fare" was introduced; and by 1957, when the jumbo jet (initiated with the Boeing 707) had been flying for two years, more passengers were crossing the Atlantic by air than by sea. Then in the early 1960s airline fare wars were intensified when the marketing concept of the charter flight was introduced, whereby a bulk of tickets was sold at a reduced rate to a group of travellers – allegedly, to comply with regulations, a bona fide society that had pre-existed for at least six months and was travelling for a specific purpose. Thomas Cook, it might be surmised, would have rejoiced to see the masses set even more free to taste the fruits of God's green earth through the benignity of science and the healthy play of the marketplace.

For the producer to profit from this new resource, the large planes had to be filled. The airline operates at a loss unless the plane is 60 per cent full; the charter company loses unless 90 per cent of its tickets are sold. The investment requires a high guarantee of return – not to mention the investment of developing countries in enlarged airports to receive the jumbo jets; in water, sewage, transportation, and communication systems to serve the airport; in huge tourist hotels to justify the outlay in all that "primary infrastructure"; and then increased and specific agricultural production to supply the hotels with food, plus housing for the construction workers and then the service workers on all these projects. Everything has to be large-scale, especially in newly developing destinations. Then, to ensure that it is all utilized, a few selected destinations must be targeted for the tourist. His tastes need to be standardized so he won't call for anything off the menu: the best way to ensure that is to give him what he's used to getting – steak and chips. The whole economic proposition becomes most viable with the air-inclusive package tour: pioneered in 1950 when Horizon offered two weeks at a Corsican tent camp; widely adapted, expanded and elaborated in the following decades.

Tourism developed steadily along this model. From 1960 until 1974 it experienced a consistent growth of over 10 per cent per annum; by 1974 tourists spent $29 billion per year, 6 per cent of total international trade, widely reckoned the world's fastest-growing industry. Thereafter, the upward growth was somewhat less steady; but it has persisted.

As such an important economic figure, the tourist in turn became the subject of intensive anthropological and statistical investigation – statistical profiles being another postwar phenomenon. He was well known by how many nights he spent at his hotel, what quantity of chips he consumed, the number of trips he made to museums as against trips to the beach. He was, wherever possible, intercepted and questioned as to his age, occupation and marital status: the norm was a single, upper-white-collar worker under forty-five years old. In the 1950s and 1960s the far-ranging international tourist was especially American. Then in 1970 the British travel-allowance restrictions were removed and the Americans were joined in numbers by the British; and then again by the Japanese, who had even more cameras and even more yen; affluent Germans, too, were prominent among the ranks.

His hosts were very interested in the "typical tourist", though they knew him only as the person inside the package – and it was *they* who had created the package. It was also known that everybody travelled, from the super-rich to the working classes, from the octogenarian to the infant, from the conservative to the bohemian (the 1960s saw the creation of the "hippie trail" over the Middle East, through Afghanistan, across India to Southeast Asia): the class of tourists comprised nearly everyone in modern Western urban society.

So the tourist's desiderata ran the gamut as well, from a complete survey of high culture in history, to the latest in modern art and style, through remote exotica and high adventure, to a place on a hot beach with a cold beer within access and the proverbial bikinied blonde within view: venerability, beauty, knowledge, nature, romance, pleasure, all that tourists ever wanted in the past and all that the workaday world, in an age of "alienated labour", lacked. In the era of the "lifestyle", one expressed oneself more at leisure than at work; by one's hobbies, one's possessions, one's tastes. The tour represented all of them. Or, as the anthropologists saw it, the tour was the "sacred journey" to a plane which gave meaning to ordinary life. Even on the non-sacred plane, not travelling was as bad as not having a car or a TV: going away was a necessary rite of social status. Hoping for much and secure in his prosperity that he would get it, the tourist went to see his travel agent, whereupon he crossed the threshold into "the system".

Travel agents first came into being, in any appreciable numbers, with the airlines. Before that, tickets could be bought direct from the railway and shipping companies, who had offices in the city; tour operators, like Cook, Lunn, and Frame, were relatively few. But when the airlines first started, most could not afford to maintain offices in town, so the travel agent came on the scene, augmenting his air ticket business with other assorted travel commodities. By the 1970s, the travel agent was often associated with a much larger concern – part of that process whereby one big entity replaces many small ones, with the attendant gains and losses. British Petroleum and the National Cash Register Company have holdings in retail travel agencies. Thomas Cook & Son Ltd have long been under the auspices of larger ownership: in 1928 they were acquired by the Compagnie Internationale des Wagons-Lits; the UK government reclaimed them in the Second World War; and in the 1970s they were bought by a consortium of the Midland Bank, Trust House Forte and the Automobile Association.

The travel agent was equally businesslike: his job was to assess his client's demographic and socioeconomic status and then choose the holiday to match it, up- or down-market. In accord with the principles of standardization, while the travel agent carried many packages there were only a limited number of "images" for sale, with all the packages grouped under a few categories. It was more cost-efficient to develop a few images thoroughly than to work on several: printing full-colour brochures is expensive.

Seated on the travel agent's leather banquette, however, the tourist was grateful for advice. With all the fare "deals", the mechanics of savings were bewildering: the price of a ticket varied according to when and where the tourist bought it; who was going with him; how long they would be away; the month, day of the week and hour of the day they would be going and coming; how old they were. For example, the cheapest way to get from London to Calcutta was sometimes via Bangkok. Unpopular destinations were discouraged by higher fares even if they were not far away. Despite the advent of computers, which cut out all the work of poring over timetables and so forth, individual arrangements were made to seem as difficult as possible. Pan Am "Travel Planners" warned the tourist that if he did not take one of their inclusive tours, he would lose a whole day on arrival and departure procedures each time he moved from one place to another. As the vice-president of the Common Market Travel Association put it in 1972, "The individual traveller could be described as 'the idiot who has not moulded himself into groups'." Everything was done to encourage the tourist to buy a package.

Though there might be something subtly the same about all of them, what a panoply of variety the packages presented. Tourist attractions seemed to be everywhere, and in all combinations. Most of all, there was the beach with the blonde, which could be found on the hotter shores of many continents, in countries that could for all intents and purposes remain nameless, their national identity being extraneous to the product. But there were also far-ranging tours for such special people as dog lovers, horse lovers, antique collectors, tennis fans, sexual adventurers, sportsmen of every type, Arctic naturalists, readers of Sherlock Holmes, French-food gourmets, gays, and – simply – "singles".

If he could do all that, why could the tourist not do more, and go all the way around the world? As the tour connotes a circle, so that was the greatest circle, an apt figure for the epoch when tourism was everywhere. Most expansively, there was a round-the-world fishing safari on offer: $33,000 for thirty-three weeks. At the other end of the spectrum, for $2093 the tourist could go around the world in eighty hours from Dayton Ohio, via London and Moscow, with time for an overnight stop in Tokyo, whereupon he became a member of a round-the-world club established by Alan Wilgus of AAA World Travel, Dayton. An "average" round-the-world tour of forty days with Thomas Cook's, however, cost £760 without extras in the early 1970s (about £3000 in 1980): going from London via India, the Far East, California and New York City, it followed an abbreviated version of the route that the fictional Phineas Fogg took nearly a hundred years earlier in Jules Verne's *Around the World in Eighty Days*. By stretching the circle southward to include Kenya, Bali, and a South Sea island instead of the Middle East and India, one might construct a trip that took in all the major categories of attraction: Old World culture in London, high adventure on safari in Kenya, ancient tradition in Bali, an island paradise in the Pacific, the other side of the world in Japan, and something from Walt Disney in the USA. To be sure nobody rained on his parade, the tourist might also be persuaded to pick up a weather insurance policy: offered by the American Home Assurance Company in 1971, it guaranteed that three out of four vacation days would be fine; one paid from $1 to $4 per day, for a return of $25 to $100 in case of rain. Patting his pocket confidently, Homer went to tell Mabel the good news.

Britain made a good starting place for the tour. It was America's direct cultural ancestor, the genuine Old World; its people were universally reputed to be "polite and reserved" and indeed this was one of its chief attractions, an aspect of its quaintness; and the visitor had little to fear from muggers or tropical diseases there – he could even drink the water. Throughout the 1970s, London's Heathrow was the busiest international airport in the world: in 1974 it handled 217,000 international flights and almost seventeen million passengers. London itself accommodated about six million foreign visitors annually in those years; among its other venerable distinctions, it became known as "one of the world's biggest tourist resorts". So the tour must stop there for three whole days to do it justice.

Arrived in London jet-lagged but determined, Homer and Mabel were launched without pause into their itinerary. Day one was for the "must-see" attractions. Heading the list was Trafalgar Square: 93 per cent of London's visitors saw that spot, as per the precise statistics of the early 1970s. Trafalgar Square was one of the places the bus wouldn't stop: the tourists had to content themselves with looking out of the window. Mostly what they saw was other tourists. And there were the hippies – almost all of them foreign tourists as well – wading in the fountain if it was summer, and climbing over the statuary. Those would make good shots, thought Homer, if the bus window hadn't been too dirty to shoot through;

he liked the juxtaposition of "Historic London" with "Swinging London". But what he liked even more was recognizing Trafalgar Square by name.

Next came Westminster Abbey, visited by 85 per cent of tourists, another gratifyingly familiar name. There, the tourists got out for a closer look, if the bus could find a parking place. (Homer recognized *that* modern headache; but it was a pain to be stuck in traffic when you'd paid good money for this trip.) At last one was found, and the tourists filed out behind their leader; they would be able to find the leader amidst the crowd in the Abbey because he would be the one with the yellow flag, as opposed to the red plastic cubes or pink stuffed bunnies that other tour leaders would hold aloft. Crowd control was a major problem in the Abbey, though it was better since a one-way system had been introduced, despite the anachronistic effect.

Shuffling slowly along with the mob but rapidly taking in names and dates, the tourists moved respectfully among the great men of the past: all of them "white male supremacists", as one college-aged daughter, dragged unwillingly along, pointed out to her mother. But she was quickly hushed, lest some of the guide's spiel be missed.

Westminster Abbey served as a kind of Grand Tour in miniature. But the original Grand Tourist in Italy had been closer to his classical and Renaissance ancestors: he still took them as cultural models, and at any rate he was previously acquainted with them through his studies. Homer, the 1970s tourist, rarely referred to the past, especially the past as characterized by Westminster Abbey, in his daily doings. "Reality", one of his favourite words, had little to do with the lofty sentiments of bygone heroes: though, safe in the past, those heroes watched over him in some vague way. When they seemed so unreal it was hard to keep your mind on the guide's lecture. Still, you had to see it if you came to London.

Soon, however, he was back in the light; the group had to be at Buckingham Palace by eleven-thirty for the Changing of the Guard, which had the distinction of being London's fastest-*growing* attraction, with 20 per cent more visitors each year. "Oh!" exclaimed one tour member as the bus drew alongside it, "I thought this was the Houses of Parliament": on her last trip to London, apparently, she had toured the city with an unlicensed guide – maybe an out-of-work actor with a drinking problem, typical of those found at the bottom of that profession. Homer himself put her right, feeling most enjoyably knowing. Then he checked his camera strap and patted his money belt in preparation for the spectacle.

Parking the bus proved to be a problem again: the lot was made to accommodate only 92 coaches, while in high season at least 200 vied for places. Seeing the Changing of the Guard was even more difficult: 3500 people could see comfortably, but as many as 15,000 were likely to show up. The experts had suggested moving the ceremony to more spacious grounds – Horse Guards Parade, perhaps – or performing it more frequently. But the guardsmen replied that they were soldiers, not actors (perhaps they could have done with a briefing from an anthropologist as to their true social function). Homer and Mabel stood on their toes and craned their necks to little avail. Gone was the hope of getting a shot of Mabel shaking hands with a soldier in a big fur hat. But Homer didn't protest, not even inwardly. After all, the Changing of the Guard was something "great".

Hope of fulfilment sprang again, though, at the prospect of eating: now for their first quaint London pub. Authentically "quaint" pubs abounded in London: quiet, smoky places with Victorian-glass windows, or fine old panelling, or some former habitué's antique clay-pipe collection on display. Travelling in numbers, the tourists were more likely to go somewhere that knew they were coming and had been recently made or remade for the occasion, the kind of place with "oak beams" made of polystyrene. The wait was interminable, but the food, if slightly stale, was good: Homer had never tasted a pork pie, nor even heard of a Scotch egg, before. The beer, unfortunately, was too warm for him; luckily Mabel stopped him in time from asking for ice cubes. The only ones discontented with pub food were the Japanese tourists; they were taken whenever possible to a Chinese restaurant instead.

After that, it was back "home" to the bus, for a long ride through the nether regions of London to Hampton Court Palace, another kind of view of the past. At Westminster Abbey, the departed great men had seemed so *remote*: not real people who had ever lived and struggled, but more like abstractions of virtue or genius. But at Hampton Court, in the beamed halls, in the enormous kitchen where oxen had been roasted whole, a tourist could evoke a bygone golden age that seemed *super*-real compared with the pallid sensations of the present. Though in real life he categorically preferred central heating and electric range to the open fire, and strove to equip himself always with "the latest", at Hampton Court Homer found himself suffused with bittersweet nostalgia for a past he had never known. And since, as per prototype, he did not submit the fantasy to political analysis either, he automatically identified with the banqueting princes rather than with the kitchen staff.

There was a last royal relic in store on the way back to the hotel that evening, when the tour bus passed the Albert Memorial. Mabel was about to exclaim that (like all antiques) it was "beautiful" and "fascinating" until the guide remarked that the Albert Memorial was a particularly appalling bit of Victoriana. Mabel wrinkled her brow, and was glad to get back to the hotel. Exhausted, she and Homer went out for a pizza, then straight to bed.

Next day, however, came something that could not be missed. The first stop was London's other most popular attraction, the Tower: action-packed, with something for the whole family. Though its history was grim, the Tower of London was billed as an entertainment: it might be part of the programme to swoon a little, like William Beckford, over the charms of Hampton Court, but not to go all morbid at the Tower as he had done at the Doge's Palace in remembering the atrocities that had taken place there. The brisk pace and the crowds helped to keep the tourists from any such disturbingly vivid impressions.

Then, in the afternoon, a bit of contemporary London. First, there was Hyde Park Corner, a showplace for the renowned British "tolerance". There, as one American guidebook put it, the tourists would hear speakers who "would be locked up in almost any other country of the world as either mad or politically dangerous". Next, the bus continued down Piccadilly past the fabulous Ritz – now rather unremarkable, surrounded by other equally imposing buildings. Was it true, asked the misguided lady – the same one who had mistaken Buckingham Palace for Parliament – that they had once flooded the lobby of the Ritz for a royal visit? (Evidently, the guide on her first trip had been recovering from a really wild night.) And from the Ritz, for a view of Swinging London, to Carnaby Street: shades of Twiggy and the Beatles. By the 1970s, Carnaby Street was long passé: the King's Road would have been more appropriate. But Carnaby Street was all set up for tourists, with its pedestrian mall and cheap souvenir shops; and it was a safe bet that Homer and Mabel wouldn't know any better.

Day three was a free day. Most of the party went shopping: the Japanese, typically, came away with Yorkshire woollens, cigarette lighters and raincoats. Those who wanted to do more formal touring, especially for something *really* different, might come upon all kinds of things: one firm, See Britain, offered a tour of Victorian and Edwardian lavatories, with architectural and historic commentary (cost 25p in 1970). As to the tourist in search of London Future – very much out of step, since London was for the past – he just had to raise his eyes: there was the 600-foot-high NatWest Bank, blocking out St Paul's; the Vickers office tower and the Shell Tower diminishing the Houses of Parliament, Westminster Abbey and Big Ben (now, more appropriately, Little Ben). The ultimate irony was the Hilton Hotel: made for tourists and brutalizing their favourite view along Kensington Gardens and the Serpentine. But few visitors took that view of things. Homer and Mabel would have loved a room at the Hilton; they found their London room cramped, and the towels much too small – though the breakfast was a real buy. Still, it was great to have seen London at last.

On day four, London was "done": off, now, to Kenya. As a group, the tour members had to check in earlier than most airline passengers; they were at Heathrow hours in advance of the flight. Homer always got the creeps going through the metal scanner and the magneto-meter: but then, he figured, it was a small price to pay to cut down the risk of hijacking, which was at a maximum in those years. Once through, there was a long wait in the departure lounge. The Japanese tourists weren't bored: they kept regrouping themselves in front of the flight-information screen and taking snapshots – a good thing, too, that they had their cameras with them, because baggage loaders at Heathrow had been known to rifle valises tagged from Japan for expensive photographic equipment. Homer and Mabel kept busy by frequently patting their pockets and checking the straps of their money belts: international airports were notorious for pickpockets, especially on the lookout for credit cards and traveller's cheques, which they then exploited to the maximum in the duty-free shop. Then, too, the tourists re-examined the safari brochure, with all its high-colour images. The safari was an "extra" on their tour, costing from £100 to £200 for a week's trip (£300–£600 in 1980's value), depending on the amenities. For that, Homer and Mabel would have a "holiday only the rich could afford" up until recently; "an escapist's hideaway", the brochure announced shamelessly; "Hemingway country", "timeless, tranquil, elemental"; at the close of day, "blood-red sunsets"; then "black velvety night".

Safari holidays in the early 1970s were Kenya's major export: sixty-five safari companies operated from Nairobi in 1972. Homer and Mabel might thus enjoy feeling that they were contributing to the wealth of the Third World with their holiday, but in fact only one of the companies was wholly African-owned. The rest of the proprietors were old colonialists, Great White Hunters, former soldiers who had originally come to fight the Mau Mau, or foreign investors who had never lived in Kenya at all: one way and another, 40 per cent of the money generated by tourists in Kenya left the country. Most of the drivers and guides, however, were black, so Homer and Mabel could forget about the colonialist and anti-Mau-Mau proprietors, and just plunge into the "peaceable kingdom", where man and beast wandered free.

Safari appealed to everybody. There were even men with beards and long hair (or longish hair, for the government was vigilant) who might otherwise eschew the label of "tourist". Young and old, "hip" and "straight" alike bought new bush jackets for the occasion – the ceremonious Japanese had been known to wear pith helmets as well – and state-of-the-art photo equipment. Thus armed, they took their seats in the minibus (down-market tours featured buses painted with big black-and-white zebra stripes; the more expensive tours used discreetly elegant plain ones, as befitted Hemingway country) and headed into the bush: Amboseli, Ngorongoro, Serengeti, Tsavo.

The day began at dawn, when everything was freshest and most beautiful. A Kikuyu servant boy brought hot tea and milk to the tent, salaaming as he said good morning – some tourists found such servility disturbing, especially with its racist overtones; if the political underpinnings of the dream vacation were too apparent, one might be forced to wake up. Then, after breakfast there was a morning tour in the minibus, to see what animals were about.

The guide's skill lay in finding them. He watched the skies for vultures: their appearance signalled a recent kill. He scanned the terrain for droppings, which he identified precisely. A herd of minibuses in one spot was the surest sign of something to see.

There were often birds, strange and brightly coloured. Gazelle or wildebeest or zebra were very exciting. But the tourists were most especially on the lookout for what the brochures billed as "the big five": the rhinoceros, the elephant, the buffalo, the leopard, and–the biggest thrill of all – the lion.

The bus could roll along for hours without a sighting. Then, suddenly, the grasses stirred and a cheetah appeared. Instantly the driver veered towards it and drove along on its trail, as close as possible, while the cameras sprang to the ready for some "action shots". On this kind of safari, the gun had been replaced by the camera, the new instrument of capture and possession. The others sat rapt, looking and looking.

It was a curious reversal of the ancient bond between man and the "savage beast". Men had always joined together to kill dangerous wild animals: the hunt was, among other things, a ritual of human solidarity against raw nature, and man drew power from it as well as vital sustenance. Later, the white man came to Africa and performed the essential ritual just for his pleasure, profaning its spirit while retaining its form. Now things had gone full circle: the savage beast had become one to be protected, admired and almost revered: one of the few sources of authenticity and vitality in a stale world. Strangulated by always having to be in the "driver's seat" of civilization, the tourists enjoyed this feeling of being one with wild beasts, even as if vulnerable to them.

However, the humans were still the ones on wheels, and with the best intentions they caused a profound disturbance. Minibuses had run animals over; cheetahs had died of heart attack from being chased. But Homer and Mabel, and certainly the British tourists as well, loved animals: they would never have done it on purpose.

Obediently, they stayed inside the bus (it was in fact required by law) while the animals ranged round them; it made a kind of anti-zoo, with the spectators the ones in the cage. Viewed always through the bus window, the animal spectacle was rather like a nature programme on colour TV, Mabel thought sometimes.

At the driver's discretion, exceptions could be made and the tourists allowed out. Mabel's favourite moment of all was when she fed a monkey the grapes left over from her packed lunch, while Homer got it all down on film. But it was absolutely forbidden to feed bigger animals, like elephants. There were stories of elephants that had become addicted to bananas because of tourists and had then wrecked minibuses to get at the fruit. Somebody somewhere had been trampled to death when he tried to feed an elephant a croissant.

Another high moment was watching the love-play of the lions: the male's repeated, awkward advances, the female lazily pushing him off. "Aren't they *sweet?*" Mabel asked. "Nuts!" answered Homer, and hastily busied himself with his telephoto lens. The rebellious college-aged daughter pointed out that one mustn't anthropomorphize, and added that voyeurism was decadent; but she grew quiet when the bearded young man with shining eyes instructed her to "Just take it in!"

Another form of indigenous life the tourists found very interesting was the Maasai, the local tribespeople. They *actually lived* in houses of mud and straw, and were extraordinary in their person as well, very tall, the men in cloaks, all laden with beads, necklaces and bracelets, their earlobes weighted with heavy earrings. One young fellow even had a tomato can stuck through his earlobe. Homer made haste to get a shot of him, but was stopped: you had to pay extra for that privilege. One tourist who had tried to take pictures for nothing, warned the guide, had a spear thrown at him. Once the gratuity was paid, the villagers became much more accommodating. The women even bared their breasts, which they had only just recently covered, in order to charge for revealing them.

The Maasai also had souvenirs for sale: jewellery, spears, gourds, collapsible wooden camera tripods, plus, made of "smelly" cowhide, drums, shields, skirts, beaded shawls and flasks for a local drink of milk, blood and urine; also "smelly" tribal dolls. The guide, however, was very much against the tourists smelling up his van with these artefacts. Back in Nairobi, he promised, he could direct them to places selling much nicer stuff. The paintings and carvings he would show them would have been made to order for tourists, not for their original sacred function, and more to Western tastes: sometimes toned down and sometimes more obviously stylized, rather in the manner of Picasso, who had thought, all along, that it was the African primitives who were providing him with inspiration, not vice versa. At the Nairobi tourist shops, too, there would be a mark-up of up to 1000 per cent on what the producers of the souvenirs were paid; but Homer and Mabel tended to be trusting, and never suspected this.

Back at the camp in the evenings, the tourists enjoyed the best of both worlds with magnificent suppers prepared by the Kikuyu chefs: a sample menu consisted of hot fish savoury, followed by cream of avocado soup, a roast (gazelle, perhaps, or saddle of bush-buck), with three vegetables, and passion-fruit soufflé. The Japanese tourists were proud to deliver the day's animal-count: "Today I have seen 94 elephants, 42 giraffes, 12 buffalo, and 4 lions." A few of the party, though, were interested to get to know the Kikuyu. The guide, a white "old colonial", was horrified to see that the college-aged daughter was one of them. For their part, the Kikuyu found the tourists slightly absurd. Who would want to just *look* at animals and let good meat – and badly needed meat, for there was hunger among the Africans – get away? The Kikuyu did not find wild beasts "sweet", and chose to sleep locked inside the bus at night.

One night, there was special accommodation at the Ark Hotel. There the tourists could sit on the glassed-in observation deck, martini in hand, and watch the animals at the water hole. (One way that tourism benefited the animals, said its defenders, was by causing more water holes to be created.) Lest nothing be missed, rooms at the Ark were equipped with buzzers, which sounded in the night whenever there was an interesting sighting. Two buzzes signified an elephant herd. Three meant something really rare, like the striped, spiral-horned bongo. As they watched, the tourists remained silent, so as not to miss the special sounds of the night: the cries of birds, the howls of wild dogs – and most stirring of all, the growls and snarls of a lion as it tore into its prey.

Ultimately the most wonderful sight of all was the sight of the kill. Though the tourists would never be hunters themselves – perhaps because of that – they were riveted, and deeply gratified, to watch the animals doing it. Before the hyenas and jackals had made their approach, before the vultures appeared in the sky, the minibuses would be on the spot, watching the big cats stalk their prey. Lions had been known to starve to death because their prey were warned off by the minibuses. Sometimes, luckily for the cat, the tourists did not arrive until afterwards. Taking their place in the circle of scavengers, the tourists watched avidly as the hunter was bathed in the blood of the catch it was devouring. Nobody failed to appreciate the kill. Though Homer and Mabel might not have expected it of themselves, they felt no anthropomorphic revulsion: on the contrary. "The *pièce de résistance*," a lady correspondent on safari for *House Beautiful* wrote crisply, "was a cheetah making his dinner off a small antelope."

The transition back to modernity was perhaps made easier by a last night at the Nairobi Hilton. Outside it was like a slice of

Los Angeles, but inside, as the brochure said, the tourist found

a uniquely circular, seventeen-storey guest-room tower, inspired by tribal legends that life is a perpetual circle. . . . Dramatic murals of majestic Masai warriors . . . imaginative Afro-modern sculpture, ancient tribal symbols on wood, splashes of safari colours and zebra skins. Everywhere brilliant masses of exotic flowers accentuate the beauty.

And the Amboseli grill was "stunningly designed to represent the interior of a huge native hut". Homer and Mabel were no cynics: above all they wanted the real thing. But if the real thing should go – as indeed it might – the Hilton would surely still stand, a live-in museum with no tedious or smelly bits. And who could quarrel with American sanitation?

Next day, they flew again. Airports were always modern, if not always reliably so. Happily for them, Homer and Mabel did not know that, after twenty years' steady improvement in air safety, in 1971 the air accident rate suddenly began to soar, mostly because of insufficient instrumentation at the newer, i.e. Third World, airports. So, from the "peaceable kingdom" (or had it been "Hemingway country"?) Homer and Mabel entered the familiar capsule of metal, plastic and muzak – thus touching base with the familiar world of shopping malls, fast-food restaurants, and the universal modern setting they called home in general, so that they were never really far from home – to be transported to an even more exotically alien setting when the plane touched down at Denpasar airport on Bali.

They checked in at the Hilton – no shocks there – and enjoyed a guaranteed hygienic meal of local lobster with sliced papaya and pineapple for dessert: the fruits of paradise, if not its strange fruits. Mabel had read in a guidebook about the *durian*, reputedly the most delicious fruit of all, but with an odour like dirty feet, to put it politely. The idea of eating one sent her into hysterical giggles, but she never even caught a whiff of durian, because it was scrupulously kept away from her.

With the first bus trip round the island, a disorientingly magical world began to appear. Once past Denpasar, with its, albeit casually, paved streets and tourist shops, the tourists found themselves in a landscape that was everywhere artistically composed: tier upon tier of small rice paddies, like a geometric sculpture in green glass, set off with little fringed palm groves and sparingly patterned with bright multicoloured "god's eyes" of dyed string planted in the fields like scarecrows. At every cross-roads stood a stone god, dressed in a chequered wrapper, with flowers in its mouth. The elegant thatched roofs of the villages rose in cone-shaped tiers like a counterpoint to the rice paddies, and the carved temple gates were as intricate as filigree. Nothing disrupted the artistic composition: no bulldozers, no rubbish, no billboards, no empty lots. The people, too, seemed *all* to be beautiful, the women perfectly erect, wearing batiks patterned with leaves and long-tailed birds, balancing on their heads immense platters of fruit, arranged with symmetrical inventiveness, which they carried to the temples. Such beauty couldn't be *real*! But clearly it wasn't contrived for the tourists, because the women didn't even glance at the bus as they went gracefully about their business.

"Mother, isn't it *fantastic*!" cried the college-aged daughter.

"Very nice, dear," her mother replied.

Mabel had the window seat while Homer napped – she'd given up poking him. The bus went past a grove where young men were working, and one of them waved at Mabel. Friendly people, she registered: the guidebooks all said they would be. A second did a little series of intricate hand motions. She wrinkled her brow, wondering what it meant. Then a third did a kind of mock hula and, leering, pointed into the recesses of the grove; a fourth, grimacing, held his nose and made as if to wave her away. Mabel's jaw dropped. Was this *supposed* to happen? The bus rounded a curve, and the strange scene was gone.

Then they came upon two little boys performing acrobatics on the back of a water buffalo. Homer *had* to see that, and the bus had obligingly stopped as well for the photographers: Japanese, Germans, and Americans, all those from countries where the work ethic was strong, were not really happy unless they were *doing* something. Mabel, without knowing why, was a little sad when afterwards the boys came through the bus with their palms outstretched. Behind her in the bus, the college-aged daughter was saying, "You shouldn't give them money, mother, it disrupts their society."

"Give them something, Homer, they're so cute," urged Mabel. The boys stood before them, grinning angelically. One of them touched her hair (a shade of flame-red that must be new to them); Mabel beamed. Then, suddenly, the other one tweaked her nose and, giggling, the two scampered off the bus, which pulled away before Mabel could get her wits back. "Homer, did you see *that*?"

Mabel cried, in loud accents that made her British fellow travellers wince. It wasn't until several minutes later that she noticed that her newest charm, a miniature Big Ben from London, had come off her charm bracelet. She was distressed at the loss, but ultimately she smiled about it, having hit upon the epithet "little monkeys", which put the incident in a more tolerable perspective.

Later, there were more formal excursions. One was to the bat shrine, a cave by the sea. The Balinese, explained the guide, saw the prevailing spirits as mischievous children or animals who had to be placated. The tourists shook their heads wonderingly and smiled, in the prevailing spirit of liberalism. "Ugh," shuddered the women, because bats were so creepy. "Phew!" laughed the men, because the bat cave smelled so bad.

The tourists also visited the sacred monkey forest. They were discouraged from getting close: monkeys could be naughty, "cute" though they might appear with their long tails and silvery fur coats. Some hippie tourists were seen to ignore the warnings, going right up to them. Sure enough, a guy with a long beard was presently heard to yelp. "You see?" said the mother of the college-aged daughter.

There were many temples – lacy, pagodaed, whimsically lavish with offerings of fruit and flowers. The Balinese guide explained that it was forbidden for menstruating women to enter (a Western guide might have been more "discreet"), whereupon Mabel burst into noisy giggles and Homer wanted to disappear. The college-aged daughter frowned: she wasn't sure whether this taboo was beautifully traditional or sexist.

One evening, there was a *legong* dance, staged for the tourists at Denpasar but scrupulously beautiful nonetheless, for the tradition was very much alive, tourists or no tourists. The dancers were exquisite in their shimmering garments and tall gold-filigree head-dresses, performing the *mudras* (the language of hand gestures, each with a distinct significance), darting and swaying, against the background of chimelike *gamelan* music which rose and fell but never climaxed. The males in the party looked at the dancing girls with high appreciation; but though Bali was billed as the "island of love", among other touristic epithets, they were quite unapproachable. Among themselves, especially after marriage, they enjoyed sexual freedom, but its rules and connotations were bafflingly non-Western. Besides, they disliked large, hirsute men; there were few openings for Westerners in the role of *cisisbeo*. After the dance, the tourists watched longingly as one dancer, still in full costume, sped away on the back of a Honda with her boyfriend.

It was no problem at all, on the other hand, for a Western girl to make friends with a local young man. Bare-breasted blondes bathing in the sea had become a familiar sight by then at Kuta Beach, where the hippie travellers stayed. The Balinese were not priggish, but they found it funny (for their own part they would never bathe in the salty sea, another capricious presence to be placated in ritual but not deliberately engaged) – except for the young men, each with his Honda and tube of Brylcreem, longing for the freedoms of the West. No sooner had the college-aged daughter got away from her mother for a second than she found she had company. After respectfully introducing himself, her young companion asked if she had been to Kuta, and invited her to visit his family's hotel. "Last year," he said proudly, "John Lennon, the Beatle, stayed there! He gave me his picture"; producing his wallet, he showed her a snap of somebody with a guitar, but with a long red beard and bright red hair, nothing like the Beatle. "Of course, we let him stay for free," the young Balinese went on. Then, seeing his companion hiding a grin but moving away, he quickly came in with his stock question: "Please! Maybe you can tell me, what is meant 'free love'?" The young woman was beginning to think about it, when the tour bus showed signs of leaving. Saved by the bell, she went back to the safe precincts of the Hilton.

Among the various optional excursions out of Bali, there was one Los-Angeles-based company offering a trip to the island of Komodo, home of the world's only extant dragon. The five-day cruise in a cabin boat – there was nothing like a hotel on Komodo – also promised cobras, vipers and huge spiders. So far there had been no takers. Much more popular was an excursion to Toraja, freshly billed as the "land of heavenly kings", to attend a week-long funeral ceremony. Funerals were traditionally the most notable ritual on Toraja. Many water buffalo and razor-back hogs were sacrificed, and sometimes a corpse waited above ground for months until there was enough wealth to conduct the funeral properly. Christian missionaries had always been outraged at the practice, but they began viewing it differently when it started attracting tourists. The government too was pleased. The only ones perturbed by the tourists were the people of Toraja. For one thing, it was customary with them to offer free hospitality to the rare visitors to their island; now they found there was not enough meat to go round with all the guests at the funeral. There was outrage amongst the elders when one tribesman tried to sell tickets to the ceremony; and further outrage when a new, abbreviated, but more dramatic ceremony was devised for the tourists' benefit. However, the government supported the innovators, and by the mid-1970s two Chinese restaurants were in business on Toraja – though the locals never patronized them.

Homer and Mabel, however, contented themselves with attending a Balinese funeral. Word had got out that one would be taking place during their stay, and after a morning spent around the pool at the Hilton, followed by the usual tropically opulent lunch, they boarded their bus and set off for the field where the funeral procession would eventually arrive; several other tourist buses waited there too. Finally, amidst the hypnotic notes of the *gamelan*, the procession snaked into view. Every so often, it would disperse in a general flurry: this was done, explained the guide, to confuse the dead person's spirit, so it would not re-enter the body – another notion to make Homer and Mabel smile. Then the line formed up again and continued on its way, bearing aloft a great white sarcophagus, shaped something like a seated unicorn and trimmed in green glitter, in which the body would be cremated. Among the musicians the college-aged daughter caught sight of one with long black hair down to his waist, bare-chested and beating the drum, as magnetic as any rock star who ever played the Fillmore or the Roundhouse (and for essentially the same qualities – only more "authentically" so in the instance of the Balinese, intuitive man of the pagan spirits). Her glance was returned; and the meeting of eyes was also intercepted by her mother, who was glad the tour was moving on tomorrow – the speed of the tour made sure that the tourist was safe. However, she need not have worried, because the musician was an old-fashioned member of the brahmin caste (hence the long hair) and would have been unlikely to involve himself with a tourist girl he saw at an ancestor's funeral. Later in the cortège there appeared a few of the hippie travellers from Kuta, who had got in at the beginning somehow. They were in funeral finery too, of their own devising: batiks and tie-dyes and loose Chinese trousers and Indian costume jewellery and elephant-hair bracelets from Africa, hair variously hennaed and braided: all the accumulation of their wanderings. The self-contained Balinese mostly ignored them, though now and then they smiled, especially at a most remarkably wide-eyed girl who had devised her own dance step. Homer and Mabel, however, stiffened visibly. They would have taken many photographs had it not been forbidden.

Before the tour's departure, the group made a final visit to the Denpasar open market for souvenirs. Among the authentic *wayang* shadow puppets there was one representing Sophia Loren and another of Raquel Welch. But there were also many beautiful items crafted in the authentic traditions, living art forms that had continued to evolve so that the modern forms were as artful and "genuine" as the antiquities: batiks, embroideries, carvings, masks. The young man selling paintings – intricate patterns of foliage amongst which human and animal heads were hidden – was reading a copy of *The Moon and Sixpence*, Somerset Maugham's life of Gauguin, which somebody had left at *his* father's hotel. Trained since childhood in the traditional art of Balinese painting, the young man had never known before that colours could be mixed. Now he dreamed of nothing so much as a trip to Paris to study Western art: multivectored, tourism and its consequent effects pointed everybody's paradise in a different direction.

At that juncture, after forays into various versions of the unspoiled condition, the tourists were off to an idyll made expressly to *their* measure: the Moorea branch of the Club Méditerranée, near Tahiti in the South Pacific. The "peaceable kingdom" of Kenya could be watched only from a minibus. The "morning of the world" in Bali was beautiful but unknowable, and the "island of love" was off limits to Westerners. But Club Med, in the words of co-president Gilbert Trigano, was designed to "give back to urban vacationers the village of old in all its freedoms but without its hypocrisy": an instantly accessible tribe as per the desires of Western city people on short vacations.

By 1972, this exaltedly insouciant formula had generated over a hundred holiday villages around the world, and with 60,000 beds, Club Med was the third largest hotelier in the world. Four hundred thousand guests per year vacationed "under the sign of the Trident".

The Moorea village happened to be one of the earliest, established in 1955. It was also the first to epitomize the founders' ideal, which was inspired by Gauguin (though not in his capacity as one who mixed his colours when he painted): a hundred thatch-roofed grass huts in a coconut grove, where everybody unfastened their tight clothes, changed into a *pareo*, and otherwise just did what came naturally.

Telephones, radios, TVs, and newspapers were not allowed. Your wallet was kept in a safe, and instead of carrying money for the odd drink at the bar, you wore poppet beads and paid with those. There were no other expenses, for all the facilities were free, and the cost of room and board was just £8 per day (under £25 in 1980): another aspect of Club Med's democratic idealism. The only requirement was that each tourist be his "real self", and that he pronounce the words *gentil membre* and *gentil organisateur* ("nice member" and "nice organizer") with a reasonable French accent.

The GOs saw to it that Homer and Mabel lost no time in being their real selves and manifesting tribe spirit. Each was greeted with a big kiss, by a tanned and healthy young person of the opposite sex. Mabel giggled – she *did* like getting to know people – but Homer rather bristled. However, he might count himself lucky: elsewhere, GMs had been precipitated into the swim of things by being pulled, fresh off the plane and fully clothed, into the swimming pool by grinning GOs who pretended to be shaking hands with them.

When they were shown to their room, though, Mabel was the one to be dismayed. The floormats were frayed, the bed sagged and tropical bugs were in evidence: roughing it was supposed to be part of the regenerative process at Club Med. Homer was going to have to complain (though if he had read the small print in the tour contract, he would have known it wasn't going to be easy, for nobody – not the travel agent, not the tour operator, not the hotel – was precisely responsible: another aspect of the big package. It was even worse to discover that the showers and toilets were a distance from the hut, offered minimal privacy, and were not sexually segregated. What if you came down with "tourist tummy"? It wasn't the first time Homer and Mabel had shuddered over that possibility.

But it was part of Americans' reputation to be obsessed with comfort and hygiene. The French were known to be obsessed with food, and Club Med was French: it was at mealtimes that the luxury was laid on. A baroque fanfare sounded, and everyone headed for the dining area. There, they were seated as they arrived, eight to a table, so the company was always new. And the food! exclaimed the tourists. Arranged buffet style, an ordinary everyday lunch consisted of cold salmon, caviare, glazed cold veal, Russian eggs, dozens of salads, barbecued lamb chops, saffron rice, fried plantains, multitudinous cheeses, and local specialities like roast pig with mango and tropical fish steamed in a palm leaf with slices of banana, with chocolate mousse for dessert and unlimited helpings. The college-aged daughter objected categorically to such plenty when there were surely natives starving not far away. But Trigano expounded: "The microwave and the cauldron; super-sophistication and doing-it-yourself; the frozen food makers of the whole world and oneself." The metaphysics of food was an important part of the Club Med philosophy. "To hell with the diet," cried Mabel exuberantly, causing some consternation among her table-mates, who had come to Club Med because the atmosphere was supposed to be sexy.

After lunch, there was everything – or nothing, depending on your mood – to do. The village offered yoga, sailing, tennis, scuba diving, water polo, outrider canoeing, spear fishing, moped or horseback riding, or a jaunt through the jungle in "le truck", the communal vehicle. Another compelling activity at Club Med was "swinging": since the beginning, the place had a reputation for sexual freedom which it did everything to encourage. In Trigano's philosophy, "the solidarity of the village is such that it dispenses with conventional behavior. . . . One must have the effrontery to dress up this time given to us, this time of freedom." Women greatly outnumbered men at the Club Med, and the ones most likely to score were the male GOs, who had the darkest tans and wore their trunks tightest and lowest.

Returning to more reliable pleasures, supper was no less splendid than lunch. In the evening something jolly usually happened. There were home-made talent shows, and costume parties where everyone dressed in crêpe paper – though alone in the room with Mabel, Homer drew the line at that point. Another night, it was decreed that nobody could use the letter *r* in their speech. Most of the time, the ambience reached the necessary level of uninhibitedness. Trigano explained:

It is exceptional nowadays to pour a jug of water over the head of the next person at table, to the extent that we are sometimes forced to set an example ourselves – for it is necessary to create a diversion of that kind from time to time in order not to forget one's youth.

After getting as loose as that, many people found it hard to resume the harness of city life. Trigano reported complaints from department store managers that sales girls had rebelled against returning to their counters after a stint at Club Med (they often then applied for jobs as GOs). Nonetheless, Homer and Mabel stepped back into the enclosure of their package tour without resistance. Anyway, they had been a bit out of place at Club Med, whose modal guest was under forty and single.

Before they left the South Seas, the tourists had a final day's stop in Fiji. There they could walk along a harbour right out of Somerset Maugham; see a fire-walking display; or visit a "typical village" where people put on old-fashioned clothes that they hadn't worn normally for years and displayed the outmoded traditional crafts of weaving, basket-making, grinding nuts. The village represented the co-ordinated efforts of electricians, payroll clerks, mechanics, florists, PR men, and anthropologists; but Mabel couldn't get over how "real" it seemed, even "realer" than the *real* markets they had seen. She stared, fascinated, at the nut grinding. "It's really just like what I do for the almond cakes, Homer!" she marvelled, and, in fact, it was; but somehow the Fijian way seemed so much "realer". The main purpose of visiting Fiji, however – at least from the tour operator's point of view – was for shopping: the island was "duty free". The tourists stocked up on such exotic items as typewriters, electric razors, digital watches, radios, perfume, and fur coats; plus a grass skirt, for the memory. Then, it was back to the airport for the flight to Tokyo.

Mabel was especially looking forward to Japan. She had a "thing" about Japanese-y things. She and Homer strung paper lanterns over their patio in summer, and one of her most treasured possessions was a white-faced doll in red silk kimono and gold obi, kept in a lacquer-edged glass box. Her favourite food was Chinese (of course, you couldn't get Japanese anywhere near her town) and she had loved the movie *Sayonara*. Homer had warned her that it wouldn't be like that in Japan: air pollution in cities was denser than almost anywhere in the world, what they ate was stuff like raw octopus pickled in vinegar with giant radishes dyed purple, and don't forget they were almost up to the US in electronics and computers (it was because they worked like *ants*, Homer added; he couldn't forget about the kamikaze in the Second World War, who went on suicide missions in their planes – it was one thing to be a hero, but those guys, agreed

Homer and his buddies, were *nuts*). Mabel was sure she would find what she was looking for; it was one of the particular reasons they had chosen this tour, after all. Japanese music was piped through the flight cabin as their plane touched down, a little weird, but "fascinating"; and the mood was right.

They touched down into something that you'd hardly *travel* to see, thought Mabel. A bus carried them from the airport on a super-modern freeway past miles of dingy concrete buildings and industrial rubble: ugly! There were vast billboards and giant neon signs, towering skyscrapers – it seemed even more modern than LA, thought Homer incredulously. Mabel tried to have a little sleep; she wanted to save her energy for the *real* Japan.

They checked into a "first-class, Western-style" hotel, one of many, and it was really professional, the tourists agreed. The toilet seat was hygienically sealed with a paper streamer, and not only soap but toothpaste was provided, plus bedroom slippers, a complimentary sewing-kit you could keep, and, on the pillow, foil-wrapped chocolate: that was one of the details Mabel remembered best of the entire trip. That evening, they signed up for an "authentic Japanese-style meal" in the hotel dining room. The food was delicious: sukiyaki, which the Japanese ate rarely, though Homer and Mabel never knew that, and hot sake. The tourists were not expected to struggle with chopsticks, but Homer developed severe leg cramps from sitting on the floor. Never again, he told Mabel.

Next day, they had to be up early to "do" the city. Bus schedules were posted, precise to the minute; everyone knew how organized the Japanese were, "professional" in all things. The tourists were taken round to all the main attractions in brisk succession: the Imperial Palace, the Asakusa shrine, and then back to the famous Ginza district, where their hotel was, with its fancy nightclubs and monumental *depaatmento* stores, some eight storeys high (surpassing even Harrod's, even Macy's) and containing everything, including art galleries that showed serious modern and traditional work. Mabel had to admit it was very nice to find art galleries in department stores, though a bit funny; but Homer had never liked modern stuff, and couldn't figure out why there were so many Japanese guys, some of them obviously workmen, who seemed to be interested, even when their wives hadn't dragged them there. Bold Japanese characters alternated with English names like Kiss Me Hand Cream and Delicious Harmony Sale (over the door of a shoe shop), and in one of the many Western-style eating places there was "dlaft beer" on tap, to Homer's vast amusement. And every tourist's heart warmed when they came upon a familiar name like I. Magnin's, the famous San Francisco department store. You had to hand it to the Japanese for their gigantic office buildings, ultra-modern towering glass and steel constructions; and the stores really had everything. But so expensive! Homer shook his head in wonder: the prices were a marvel in themselves, another most vivid memory of the trip. Towards twilight there was a stop in Akasaka, where the tourists might catch sight of a geisha being carried to work in her sedan chair, as sumptuous and delicately lovely as Mabel's doll. Except weren't they some kind of prostitutes? Homer wanted to know. The guide explained that they were not: they danced, sang, did folding-paper tricks and provided conversation. Homer smirked; he doubted it. But that night they would be sampling a "Tokyo fascinating night" themselves, for their tour would be visiting the Nichigeki burlesque theatre.

They checked off steak and beer this time on the dinner application form – Homer was firm – and then re-boarded the bus, in all their finery: Homer in white jacket and his fanciest Hawaiian shirt, Mabel in her Courrèges-copy, modernistic hot pink, her favourite "young-looking" dress which she had been saving for such an occasion. Passing the various "clip joints", as Homer remarked knowledge-ably, called "Saron", "Crub", and "Crab" – ringing all the changes on the l–r discrepancy – where the girls made you buy them champagne at $25 a throw, they pulled up before the Nichigeki theatre in a state of high excitement. The lobby was filled with refined-looking Japanese couples of middle age (not many tourists, oddly) who eyed Homer and Mabel with discreet amusement, since in their opinion people of a certain age ought to dress accordingly.

The show started as per expectations, with a "professionally" Japanese Folies Bergère: troops of young women in elaborate head-dresses and little else high-kicking in chorus. But what came next beat all; for by a rare, unprofessional lapse, Homer and Mabel's group had been booked into the Nichigeki on a non-tourist night. First, two naked women came on stage and simulated a savage battle using teeth and nails. Then came a very realistically simulated coupling between a man and a woman, which culminated in the cutting of the woman's throat. And in the ultimate act, entitled "Harakiri", a young woman seemed to be disembowelling herself, with the use of pellets of fake blood secreted about her nude body.

"What the hell is this?" thundered Homer at the guide as they filed out of the theatre, amidst an otherwise genially orderly crowd. The guide winced painfully. "Japanese people are Buddhist," he offered, apparently by means of explanation. "Huh!" replied Homer, muttering to Mabel out of the side of his mouth, "Inscrutable, my foot!" Mabel hated a scene, and she felt the Japanese hated scenes too, so she murmured kindly to the guide, "*Shikata ya nai*" ("It couldn't be helped"), recommended in her phrase book for a range of awkward situations.

Still, this wasn't what Mabel had come to Japan for, either. Next day, a free day, Homer and Mabel wandered about the city – selectively, of course; they never saw the neighbourhoods where "ordinary life" took place, but stuck to the ones on the tourist agenda, the amusement and shopping quarters. Even then, things were not the way they were supposed to be. Women tottered along charmingly in their *geta*, dressed in exquisite kimono; and then the effect was wrecked by a gas mask. People bowed to each other in the dense throngs of the Ginza, then shoved past you rudely at a department store counter. In a bustling dry-cleaning shop, there was a lovely piece of *ikebana* (flower arrangement): sweet, but so inappropriate, thought Mabel – whoever heard of ikebana at a cleaner's? As to the dazzling modern abstractions of the Akibahara district, with bold Japanese characters and neon fantasias in every colour, which were in fact advertisements for discount goods, Homer and Mabel didn't have an eye for them. They just found them loud, and Homer got depressed when he saw he could have got a digital watch for less than he had paid in Fiji. Lunch was all right: eschewing the weird sea-creature-and-root-vegetable ensembles, they pointed to a plastic model of fried chicken and were well pleased; and Mabel thought the plastic models were cute and practical. But then there were all the boys with ducktail haircuts and white shoes playing pinball in the *pachinko* parlours – and the next minute, a "doll" of a young woman with small kids who beamed joyously when Mabel leaned over and tried another of the Japanese phrases she had memorized and was waiting to use: "Your children are very cute."

"They're nice when you get to know them," she observed to Homer afterwards. Homer admitted that you had to hand it to the Japanese, and took many photos of skyscrapers. But he and Mabel found two days were plenty in Tokyo because, as Mabel said, "We already have skyscrapers at home." The real Japan, they trusted, lay ahead.

If they boarded the tour bus on time early next morning, promised the brochure, the tourists would see the unique spectacle of millions of Tokyo workers hurrying to their jobs. Sure enough, there they were, looking even more purposeful than New Yorkers. The college-aged daughter couldn't see how these could be the people who invented Zen (it didn't occur to her that this ritual, too, had an aspect of concentration and loss of self). Homer and Mabel just shook their heads pityingly. Then they boarded the Bullet Train for Nikko, the Japan of their imagination, an exquisite gilded, enamelled and intricately sculpted shrine in a mountain setting of pine woods and waterfalls.

The Western tourist was a daily visitor to Nikko: over a low arch, a sign said in English, "Beware overhead, honey!" Though "different", its loveliness was not alien, and cameras clicked unceasingly. The Japanese tourists, better equipped and more practised, outdid their Western cousins, though, documenting everything in stills *and* movies.

The shrine tour was followed in short order with a French lunch, and after that a succession of visits to a pottery kiln, a painting studio, and a paper factory. The process transpired with professional speed and efficiency; but there were significant pauses in the shops.

Next day, it was off up the Chuo Expressway via de luxe motorcoach: first stop, Mount Fuji. *En route* the lady guide sang sweet snatches of Japanese folksongs over the public-address system, interspersed with facts and figures about the lovely landscape. "Wouldn't it be great if she read haiku instead?" suggested the college-aged daughter – rather aggressively, but not unreasonably: traditional Japanese tourism to beautiful places was in fact often accompanied by the reading and writing of poetry – for poetry writing among the Japanese was as universal as . . . taking photos, an expressive form by no means confined to adolescents and professionals as in the West.

It was from the coach that the ideal view of Mount Fuji presented itself. From Tokyo, where the carbon-monoxide level often reached 75 per cent (danger level was 20 per cent; but fresh air was on sale in many shops), Mount Fuji was almost never visible any more. From close up, the mountain was marred with commercialism and heaped with litter; for the fastidious Japanese were notorious litterbugs in public, especially when they were being tourists: a proverb had it, "Travellers away from home need feel no shame." So the best place to see, and to shoot, Fuji was from the expressway. Amidst clicks, the Japanese tourists hissed, sighed, and uttered the ritual clichés required by the occasion; while Homer and Mabel "spontaneously" came out with clichés in their language.

Lunch was at the Fuji View Hotel, where the tourists could see the mountain reflected in the waters of Lake Kawaguchi. Having had their fill, they boarded the coach once more and proceeded to the resort town of Hakone.

The rest of the afternoon was "free", but at the hotel there was an optional tea ceremony the tourists could attend. While Homer sorted and labelled rolls of film, Mabel went down to watch. At first she was enchanted by the gorgeous kimono and by the hairdos, but shortly the minimalism of the *chanoyu* ceremony caused it to elude her, and her mind wandered. She was startled back to attention by the noise of the delicately composed ladies loudly slurping their tea, the Japanese manner of showing appreciation – just what she was always on at Homer about when he drank his coffee too fast. Anyway, reasoned Mabel, who could "do" Japan without doing one tea ceremony? Tomorrow's attraction, though, would yield more palpable rewards, for they were sailing across Toba Bay to the Mikimoto Pearl Island, to see the women pearl-divers and to buy a string of tax-free pearls.

On the boat, they broadcast "It's a Long Way to Tipperary" in between bits of spiel. Then, arrived on the island, the college-aged daughter had a lot to say about the working conditions of the divers and of Japanese women in general; still, few passed up the once-in-a-lifetime purchase opportunity. After a tempura lunch at the Toba International, there was a professionally brisk visit to "Japan's most sacred Shinto shrine". Thereupon, the tourists boarded another super-fast train for Kyoto, their final destination in Japan.

The capsule that was the train made a good encapsulation of modern Japan, in all its paradox. Though Homer and Mabel didn't favour the paradoxical, they found plenty to exclaim over in the course of the journey. On the platform while they awaited their train, how delightful to hear the loudly broadcast strains of "Auld Lang Syne". But when it came time to board the train, the Japanese pushed past them in their usual "non-human" way; it was a good thing their seats were reserved, because no Japanese would have given up his seat to Mabel: grannies and even pregnant mothers were left standing while teenage boys sat. On the other hand, while the train roared up to its fantastic speed of 130 m.p.h., there was the stationmaster on the platform, ceremoniously bowing to the departing passengers; then the ticket-taker did the same when he left the car. Mabel was smiling, charmed, but the smile froze on her face when she saw the comic book that the gentle-looking, flower-faced young woman in the next place was reading: dismemberments, dripping leg-stumps, bodies shot through with arrows, bodies aflame. Most stops the train made were inhumanly brief, just fifteen seconds or so, but announced ahead of time with recorded music; so the disembarking passengers could queue at the door and be out in a trice before it snapped fiercely shut behind them. "Ants," muttered Homer. "Robots." At the single more lengthy stop, the flurry of activity was even more astonishing. Some raced over to the noodle stall and ingested an entire steaming bowlful in under five minutes; others ranged themselves along the platform to perform a complicated series of calisthenics, finished off by protracted gargling at the water fountain. That was very good, Mabel thought, remembering the exercise class she had failed to attend back home: so health-aware. Her admiration soured, though, as she made her way to the lavatory, for the corridor was strewn with tangerine peels, discarded sushi boxes, candy wrappers and whisky bottles. Yet in the tiny lavatory compartment itself she found an *ikebana* arrangement of chrysanthemums and daffodils. Homer and Mabel didn't "get it".

But they got it at last at Kyoto, Japan's most touristic city: *there* were the images they had imagined, and later, Mabel felt very smart and sophisticated when she could say, "Tokyo wasn't really for us, but we loved Kyoto" – after all, who were you if you loved everything?

After some debate, Homer and Mabel decided to spend their last two nights at a Western-style hotel as per the usual tour. To stay at the "optional *ryokan*" (Japanese-style inn) cost extra. "I'm not going to fork over fifty bucks a night to sleep on the floor," thundered Homer; and even Mabel had to admit she might not stomach the traditional breakfast of dried fish, bean paste soup, seaweed, pickles, and rice. However, neither of them knew that the normal price of a room at a *ryokan* was one-fifth the normal price of a Western-style room. Besides, Homer was convinced that the train seats were made for people with short legs, even though he had been assured that the ones he had been riding, built for the Tokyo Olympics, were roomier. So they checked into one of the soaring modern rectangles where at least they would be comfortable. And in the morning they were ready to see the great temples of the past.

Tokyo had teemed for centuries, but the impact of tourism on Kyoto was more drastic. From 1962 to 1972, the number of Western visitors there had doubled, up to 300,000 per year. The vaunted cherry blossoms were beginning to die of pollution, the venerable shrines were defaced by vandalism, and there was never an instant for silent contemplation of their beauty. But *those* contradictions were familiar ones to Homer and Mabel; they knew how to screen them out.

The first stop was the golden pavilion, Kinkakuji Temple, all covered in gold leaf, set amidst umbrella pines, the whole reflected in a lake. The guide tried vainly to persuade his charges not to walk up to the temple: little flag or no, he fretted, in such a crowd they'd be sure to get lost. He wanted them to remain in the parking lot instead, where there was a group of country girls willing to be photographed for a small fee; and indeed there was much photographic activity going on in the lot, with several solemn-faced Japanese tourists posing for group photos. But Homer and Mabel were not to be cheated of their money's worth: they pushed their way into the mob with the best of them, and while there was little chance to examine fine detail, at least they had been on the spot.

Then they went on to Kiyomizu Temple, a many-pagodaed, tiered shrine overlooking a deep gorge of cherry trees and evergreens, which was said to be the most beautiful view in all Japan. Next, there were the bright red and gold of the Heian shrine; the meditative perspectives of the Torii gates of Fushimi-Inari; the perfectly landscaped hillocks and tiny groves of Tofukuji, studded with boulders; all filled with admiring international tourists. But the tourists would have had to go a very long way to find a beautiful place in Japan that was untouched by tourism, for the millions of urban Japanese were as much in need of an escape to a beautiful place as their Western counterparts; places of beauty had long been cultivated in their country; and their characteristic "professionalism" provided them with an excellent infrastructure.

In the afternoon the tour went to Nara, the oldest capital, site of the giant Buddha of Todajji and of the deer park, where tame animals came up to eat out of the tourists' hands. Mabel bought some rice crackers, but the crowd was so thick that she couldn't get near enough to a deer to feed one.

Afterwards there was more buying of souvenirs. Nothing costly, now: the string of pearls had been enough, plus the lacquer vase for the coffee table. But the tourists acquired some small things: there was a variety of tea-towels; and then some of the cylindrical wooden *kokeshi* dolls, though unfortunately the ones on sale for the tourists tended to have round Occidental eyes; and for a favoured niece, a big, blonde, long-lashed Kewpie in a kimono. Among the milling crowd Mabel was delighted to fall into conversation with a well-spoken young man who had an excellent command of English. He absolutely insisted that she accept a stick of green tea chewing-gum. "*So* friendly," said Mabel afterwards; but what she didn't know was that the Japanese were particularly offended by Occidental breath, which always smelled to them of cheese and . . . garlic.

On their last evening in Japan, Homer and Mabel celebrated appropriately by attending the Miyako Odori geisha show. The performers were such dolls to look at, their hairdoes ornamented with flowers, stylized ribbons, and little hanging things of many colours like miniature wind chimes, and their strange *red* eye make-up – a great chorus line against a backdrop of painted screens showing cherry blossoms, pines, and blue skies, the ceilings hung with red lanterns. The show was somewhat lacking in a story line, the tourists felt (and Homer and Mabel were not close enough to the stage to see how bored the geishas looked). On the way back to the hotel, the group shared a laugh when one member told how he had read in an article that the geishas took American Express cards.

For Homer and Mabel, the circle was drawing to a close, though the tourist round kept going, encircling and covering the globe: the tour was bound next for the USA, with a stop in Los Angeles and one in New York, and now the British and Japanese tourists were getting excited. Leaving Japan, there was some apprehension: in this era of the hijacker the "selfless" Japanese would stop at nothing, and they had as many disaffected youth as any modern nation. But nothing worse befell them than jet lag, on that long leg of the journey. Jet lag, too, was ultra-modern: the result not of high speeds or long distances but of the pressurized cabin, an innovation of the 1950s. Homer and Mabel had heard the one about drinking a quart of water every hour, but they decided the cure might be worse than the malady; though they were aware that, as they got older, jet lag kept getting worse.

Tokyo might in many ways be futuristic, but LA was purely a city of the future, the great capital of American kitsch. The British tourists in the group felt a glow of satisfaction at how it conformed to their idea of America: all hamburger joints and freeways. The Japanese tourists were especially fascinated by a billboard they spotted on the way into town from the airport, a cigarette ad with a mouth blowing immense rings of real smoke. And French "alternative tourists", devoted modernists, loved LA, too. They carried a guidebook called *USA en Jeans*, which suggested that they hum to themselves the Jim Morrison song "Highway to the End of Night" to put them in the mood; and though they came from the land of gourmets, they couldn't wait to taste their first indigenous Macdonald's burger – or Macdo, as they called it.

First on the agenda was a tour of "Hollywood and the stars". It stopped at Graumann's Chinese Theatre, where the footprints of the famous were imprinted in cement, and the tourists could fit their own feet into them – a pilgrimage in both letter and spirit. Then it went down Sunset Strip, where there were more hippies to look at. It paused at Hollywood and Vine, so the tourists could shoot the famous street names. And at last it came to Beverly Hills, where the great resided. The guide quoted the price of every mansion, plus intimate tit-bits of movie gossip, calling the stars by their first names only, drawing the tourists into the charmed circle of acquaintance. The high moment came when one former film queen, in dark glasses and black picture hat, was actually seen pulling out of her driveway. She graciously smiled and waved at the tourists, who burst into applause; every camera clicked. Only the college-aged daughter grumbled. If she *had* to do something so *gross* as this, at least they might have shown Peter Fonda's house. Instead it was all *old* people, like Lucille Ball and Hopalong Cassidy.

The *pièce de résistance*, the perfect tourist attraction, was Disneyland. How could haphazard reality equal a pleasure dome created uniquely for tourists, where the past seemed sweet (on Main Street, USA, in Frontierland), the future looked hopeful (in Tomorrowland), and state-of-the-art technology assured that nothing could go wrong?

Disneyland derived from the mysteries and fantasies of childhood, but 80 per cent of the tourists there were adults. In 1970, Disneyland received approximately ten million guests, who stayed for an average of seven and a half hours and spent about $6.95 (£10 in 1980). Wandering about in a state of received innocence, safe from harm, Homer and Mabel and their fellow travellers found everything to their liking. For one thing, how *clean* it was; cleanliness was a sore point with Disney. Employees had to conform to a strict dress code: short hair for the boys, minimal make-up for the girls. Even guests were screened by their appearance. (Vigilance was redoubled after 6 August 1970, when a hundred Yippies threatened "destruction and violence" at Disneyland, including the staging of a radical circus in which a disrespectful version of the Mickey Mouse anthem was sung.) Disney charm was everywhere, and who could resist it? But what was really engaging was the *science* of the thing, Homer marvelled: the haunted house, with ghosts made of laser beams that melted before your eyes; the walking, talking replica of Abraham Lincoln, done with "audio-animatronics". Both the man and the boy within Homer were subtly gratified. And giggling guiltily, Homer and Mabel agreed that there were moments when Disney's jungle seemed better than the Kenyan safari, because in Kenya there'd been all those stretches where you saw nothing but grass, but here there was never a dull moment. Disney's animals could be *relied* upon to be cute: all was minutely scripted, from the flapping of the giant butterflies' wings, to the darting of the python's tongue, to the timely appearance of "Native Salesman Sam". As a Disney engineer told Anthony Haden-Guest, "It's a *concentrated* form of nature . . . we string together all the experiences you might see in a lifetime into one thing." "What it is," mused Mabel as she chewed her tuna sandwich aboard the Chicken-of-the-Sea Pirate Galleon, "is that here you're *participating* instead of just watching." Homer was in a good mood, and smiled his agreement. But he wondered for a moment why, if that were true, they'd spent all that good money going around the world.

The Japanese tourists were as happy as any, fortunately for the industry, since by 1973 they constituted the largest group of foreign tourists in the US. Though they did not speak much English (one of them only knew the words "Scotch and water"), Disneyland transcended language barriers. There was only one mishap, when, a guide having forgot to lower his flag, four kimonoed ladies conscientiously followed him into the men's room . . . or so the story went. Mickey Mouse was a familiar figure to them – they called him

Mik-kii Ma-u-su – and the all-time most popular souvenir from America for the Japanese, after a bust of President Kennedy, was a Mickey Mouse tee-shirt.

After that thoroughly satisfying interlude away from the world, it was time to return to *reality*: now for notorious New York City. Everybody had heard how bad it could be, and secretly hoped to catch a glimpse of the worst, from a safe distance.

A good place to look first at New York was from the top of the Empire State Building: because it was the city's emblem, because it gave a good view, and especially because, as one British lady visitor said, the city seemed so nice and *mild* from up there. The traffic noise was softened, and the megalopolis was reduced to a toy city with bridges and spires "like delicate lacework", she remarked with satisfaction. Thus given heart to plunge into the heart of the city, the tourists repaired to 42nd Street for a comprehensive bus tour.

They started out in Times Square, traditionally the focal point of the hotel and theatre district, now given over largely to hookers and porn cinemas. Discreetly omitting to point out these latter-day attractions, the guide told his charges instead how many light bulbs were in use in Times Square (just the facts, ma'am). But the Japanese men in the group noticed the hookers and porn theatres anyway and, giggling, promised each other to return that night, being far enough from home to feel quite without shame.

They passed the Cathedral of John the Divine, and the guide reeled off all its dates and dimensions, with no mention of its neo-Gothic architecture, to the British lady's annoyance. But America was not used to thinking of its architecture in terms of Old World aesthetics. As Americans saw it, nature was *beautiful*; buildings, except old "colonial" ones, were *useful* or *important*. It was the French alternative tourists, with *USA en Jeans* to hand, who succeeded in achieving a modernist aesthetic view of the big city, admiring it precisely for its uncompromising rectangular monoliths and geometric juxtapositions; the guide book also directed them to a certain seventeen-storey car park where they might stand and trip out on the whoosh of cars in spiralling descent. (Among its list of preparatory cultural material, the book listed the films of Andy Warhol.)

Next, the tour bus travelled past St Mark's Place. The guide did not mention that the poet W. H. Auden had lived there, though it would have pleased his British charges. But he did point a finger at the hippies: there they were again. On the sidewalk, American tourists from elsewhere in the country were looking at them too. Some had their cameras out; others, in freshly cut-off jeans or new white lipstick, were trying to make friends; it was hard to draw the line between spectator and spectacle.

There was no time for a cruise out of New York harbour to see one of the "Seven Wonders of the Polluted World", as per a *New York Times* article – though the tourists had already seen two, Tokyo's smog and London's Hilton Hotel. A dozen miles from shore, there was a twenty-mile sea of sewage and sludge, whose colours ranged throughout the greens and browns, with smells to match: it would have way outdone the odours of the Bali bat cave. But the tour did include a significant initiation into the modern condition with its visit to the Stock Exchange on Wall Street.

The Stock Exchange was all fitted out for the tourist; there were visitors' hours, a visitors' entrance, even jazzy music to accompany a prepared spiel on how it all worked. (An alternative musical accompaniment, suggested *USA en Jeans*, might be Pink Floyd's "Money", to be hummed to oneself several thousand times.) Sure enough, there were the apocryphal men in grey flannel suits, gesturing and calling to each other in capitalistic abandonment. It quite tickled Homer to find himself, literally, "looking down" on stockbrokers. The British lady found it vulgar: only the Americans, she said, would go so far as to make a show out of making money, putting the marketplace above all, as usual. She was missing the point, anthropologically speaking. It was only in post-industrial society, when one's own work, mechanical and repetitive, had lost its cultural significance, that people were driven to make a "museumized" display of *other* people's work. As their own everyday lives grew more colourless, they felt a greater and greater need to exoticize other people's ordinary lives. The sober Stock Exchange, all digits and percentages and conservatively dressed "white supremacist males" – not much unlike the banks and offices and dealerships where the tour members themselves spent their days – was in many ways the ultimate tourist attraction.

With that, the tour had come full circle. Now was the time for Homer and Mabel to get off and go back home. Their children were naturally glad to see them, and greeted them with cries of "What did you bring me?" – as befitted the children of two cartoon characters. Otherwise, their return was unremarked; *everybody* travelled nowadays. Nobody was eager to see Homer's slides of Bali, when they were so far surpassed by the pictures in *National Geographic*. Nobody wanted to hear about the safari when there was *Wild Kingdom* on TV. In fact, why, in the McLuhanesque technological "global village" that the world had become, would anybody need to travel at all? You could stay home, read and watch TV; save the money and avoid the crowds.

Homer and Mabel's nephew, a long-haired and bearded young man taking time off from college, stopped in for a visit. He took a dim view of tourists, who violated hitherto undisturbed cultures. He and some friends were going on a trek in the Sherpa country of Nepal, to a hidden valley where there had never been any tourists. . . .

"So," asked the nephew laconically, "how was the world, Aunt Mabel?"

"Very nice," Mabel answered, "except for some plumbing problems."

Was there anything left to say?

CHAPTER NINE

The Post-Tourist

The year is 1984, the year when Orwell promised the worst would be upon us, the worst consequence of mass society. The month is August and the city is Paris. It is the month when all the Parisians leave town and when, by recent tradition, only the least knowing foreign tourists come to visit. The place is the Eiffel Tower. The one in the tourist's shoes is me.

It was in 1974 that the great tourist "boom", which began in the 1950s and detonated with increasing force yearly, suffered a setback. That was the year of the Middle Eastern oil crisis and an abrupt shortage of fuel. Economic depression was general, and the price of travel rose in particular. Under those pressures, several travel agencies went bankrupt in that year..Some were major ones: most notably in England, Horizon Holidays, who had inaugurated the first air-inclusive package tour.

Newspapers proclaimed that the "tourist boom" was finished. In the years that immediately followed, a somewhat disillusioned society turned more sharply in on itself, especially questioning its most "modern" productions. One of those productions was the tourist: profligate, pollutant, voyeur. His bad name came into wide circulation, and radical critiques were published against him (a few titles are given at the back of this book).

Yet, as it turned out, the setback was just an interruption: through the depression, through to this writing, tourism has remained a major growth industry – by some reckonings, still the biggest growth industry – unequalled in the steadiness of its growth. The tourist has not gone away – where could he go, if not all over the world, to get away from his 49-weeks-per-year job?

The quest for romantic exotica is still alive, too, with all its attendant illusions and well-meaning blunders – disruption of the unique and fragile scene that is its object being the major one. *Time Out*, London's "alternative" weekly, lately published a selection of holidays "without any agent to help them" including a Tunisian camel festival; the monastic peninsula of Mount Athos in Greece, where no women are allowed ("you'll need to prove a genuine and serious interest in the orthodox religion, or, in a pinch, in Byzantine architecture"); and best of all, to Mai Hong Song in the golden triangle – opium country – of Thailand, where you can meet both sides in the guerrilla war on "a trip down the By river, which will make you think you've just changed places with a character from *Apocalypse Now*" (and must surely – though the article does not say so – make *him* feel he's just changed places with *you*, at the very least).

Yet, the trend in tourism has changed its direction. Now that he has been around for thirty years, the modern tourist is more self-confident. While travel agents sell just as many air tickets, they now sell fewer all-in packages. The tourist is more ready to go around on his own; and he has also developed a taste for foreign foods. With the recent resurgence of the dollar, Americans are back in Europe in great numbers; but now they come "quietly and assuredly, like friends of the family", as a recent article in *Time* expressed it; and along with camera and phrasebook, they now carry the indispensable pocket calculator to reckon with the fluctuating exchange rate. But the British are in force, too: despite their smaller population, there are as many British tourists on the Continent as American ones. What are they looking for, apart from *everything*?

In art, that great image-bank from which "pleasure and culture" are largely drawn, there has been a dominant concern with the contemporary and the quotidian, full frontal: an appropriately blatant emblem is the Andy Warhol soup can. The most recent round-the-world trip I read about was Clive James's "Around the World in One Pair of Shoes" (*Sunday Times*, 29 July 1984): he did it by air in sixty-eight hours. He was never far from an airport – so what could he expect? – yet he wrote that his purpose was to "rediscover the old strangeness in the new normality". And while few would choose to go to such extremes of encapsulation, we are all in the same boat, or rather, on the same plane: modernity is irrevocably upon us.

Via the mass media, one knows a little bit about a lot of things. But a characteristic of our time is the absence of a universally held and *conscious* world view – though there have been many proposals. A context is missing. At the same time, the notion of "objectivity" has been greatly discredited: one cannot responsibly speak for anyone but oneself, by current ethics; one knows that one's point of view can be only one's own. So, having got myself into that position, I'm setting out, in my own shoes, into the thick of things, to see if I can put something together about the tourist now.

A Canadian friend of mine made her third trip to Europe recently. She travelled at an unhurried pace, and there were just a few specific things she wanted to see: the maritime museum at Greenwich in England, the Norwegian fjords, and the Greek islands of Santorini; but she was looking forward, in a nonspecific way, to whatever might lie in the way between them. It did not really matter what – it was a kind of random sample; not-seeking was a good way to find things of interest. I thought of her as I made my way by night train from my home in southern France to Paris, *just* to visit the Eiffel Tower.

Boarding the Paris train with me is a man in his mid-forties, being seen off by a woman of about the same age with whom he had been vacationing: obviously, they were new lovers, quite delighted with each other but not naïvely so. It was a nice beginning to my trip.

On arrival next morning, after coffee and croissants (though I live in France, croissants are only for special treats; I rarely eat them), I look for a bus to the Eiffel Tower. The 87 bus goes straight from the Gare de Lyon to the Champs de Mars, I discover, delighted with myself for figuring out how to operate the city. But I don't know the fare system, and get that wrong. The bus driver, contrary to the stereotype of the rude Parisian, politely calls me back to pay properly, and I recognize in myself that dazed, slightly stumbling comportment that I have noticed in tourists who come to see the village where I live.

Through the bus window, here is my random sample of Paris, unfolding like a triptych. First comes a series of shabby shopfronts, presenting varied surfaces of worn wood, old stone, and broken cement: a nice visual variety. These are decorated, though, with high-gloss posters illustrating newly released "soft porn" movies: one is all soft gold tones and stockinged legs in gilt mirrors; the other, sinister but also "pretty", shows white-gloved hands reaching out to embrace a naked woman in dark transports. There's

plenty to do with tourism, already: high contrast; the history of Paris
érotique, always a strong tourist attraction; the notion of escape (from
the grim shopfronts) to a fantasy of pleasure; and are the spectators of
these movies sexual adventurers too, or do they just look? Anyway,
enough of that – I'm in another kind of neighbourhood, now: the
gracious quotidian Paris, a broad, accommodating boulevard of
cafés, florists, *fromageries*, *patisseries*, *parfumeries* – all the elements
that gave the French their reputation for good living.

Modernity, I notice, starts at the bottom: the street level is all new
shopfronts, but if I raise my eyes, there's the old Paris of elegant pale
stone apartments with wrought-iron balconies and clustering
geranium pots. Then we come to a particularly lovely crossing of the
Seine, with a view of a medieval elbow bridge guarded by a single,
sparely executed statue of a madonna, and behind that, Notre Dame
– and the water all freshly silver in the early morning light. And now
it's the Latin Quarter: esoteric bookshops, Oriental restaurants,
narrow streets, a little green square presided over by Montaigne; and
now, St Germain, with beauty shops, boutiques, and, at a café table,
a young man of the *jolie-laid* type, with a *very* becoming red scarf
round his neck, posing for the passers-by as he lingers over coffee.

Always, in the distance, there's the Eiffel Tower. It is said to be
visible from any point in Paris, the tallest building in the world in
1889 when it was first erected (to an original height of 300 metres).
Like the obelisks that the ancient Romans admired in Egypt and the
cathedrals that the pilgrims marvelled over, the Tower is another
expression of man's desire to penetrate the sky. It stands present to
all Paris, and then it stands *for* all Paris, the consummate touristic
emblem of a place,

it belongs to the universal language of travel. Further: beyond its
strictly Parisian statement it touches the most general human-image
repertoire . . . the symbol of Paris, of modernity, of science or of
the nineteenth century, rocket, stem, derrick, phallus, lightning rod
or insect, confronting the great itineraries of our dreams . . . that
simple line whose sole mythic function is to join . . . *earth and
heaven.*

So I read in Roland Barthes, the structuralist critic whose essay "The
Eiffel Tower" serves as my guide on this post-modernist excursion.

Romantic purists wanted the Tower out of their sight: when
Eiffel's plans were proposed, there was an artist's petition circulated

to try and stop him. After the fact, the author Guy de Maupassant used to eat there regularly, even though he didn't like the food, because he said the Eiffel Tower was the only place in Paris where you didn't have to be looking at the Eiffel Tower all the time. (Later, in accordance with perennial touristic transformation, the remark was attributed by the English to Oscar Wilde.) But to the modernist eye, from Cocteau and Utrillo through to Barthes, the Tower is welcome; and it welcomes in turn. Wherever I am in Paris, says Barthes, I know all my friends can see it: "The Tower is *friendly.*"

The bus has arrived at its terminus, the Champs de Mars, and suddenly I'm right at the foot of the Tower, which looms up enormously. Sure enough, it's like a friendly giant: it makes me think for a minute of those early cartoon dinosaurs appearing over the treetops that I loved on Saturday morning TV as a kid. There is also, in my first close-up glance, an inevitable element of *déjà vu,* since I've seen the Tower represented so often. Most famous sights that you have seen in pictures before seeing them in "person", though, seem less than their image, I've noticed. It is really instructive to stand before the "Mona Lisa" in the Louvre and hear the embarrassed confession of tourists surprised by how sombre and diminutive it turns out to be. But that couldn't possibly happen with the Eiffel Tower: it looms, when you stand right next to it – a very distinct sensation.

It turns out to be a bad day for seeing the Tower: the sky is overcast; on the other hand, the clouds have tempered the usual sweltering August weather. Still, at nine-thirty there are already at least 200 people on line, and many more arriving. They adapt to waiting easily. But the line moves briskly, for, unlike most tourist attractions, the Eiffel Tower was *made* to accommodate masses. One way and another, people keep coming: in 1967, seventy-eight years after the Tower first opened, its fifty millionth visitor arrived; but only fifteen years after that, in 1982, the hundred millionth visit was recorded; now they come at a rate of about three and a half million a year. The tourists are all races and colours, part of the vast mobile middle class. Most are wearing the "new mufti": soft, pliant cotton-blend synthetics, loose trousers and loose shirts, brush-cut hair – easy.

I overhear the man on line behind me talking to his lady: "Twenty years ago," he says, "I was here and I couldn't even afford to go to the first floor. Now, I can take you to the top." It costs 34 francs:

almost tripled since 1976, I calculate from my Michelin guide. He puts his arms around her in a cheerful embrace.

We have come to the Eiffel Tower to ascend it, but the inside is interesting, too: lots to think about. From a distance, the Tower expresses pure verticality; so it is startling, as one stands waiting for the elevator, to see how this

very verticality absorbs its departure in slanting forms . . . a kind of agreeable challenge for the visitor; then come the elevators, quite surprising by their obliquity, for the ordinary imagination requires that what rises mechanically slide along a vertical axis . . .

And then "the enlarged spectacle of all the details, plates, beams, bolts . . . an operation of reducing an appearance (the straight line) to its contrary reality (a lacework of broken substances), a kind of demystification", as Barthes puts it elegantly. Among others of the spectators here today, the original 1889 aesthetic controversy persists. A couple is disagreeing: he says, "Amazing!" She says, "I don't know . . . it's just a big, horrible bit of scaffolding." I notice him stiffen slightly, and he withdraws his arm from her shoulder to scratch his nose. At any rate, looking inside the Tower is lively. It is even "thrilling", for the sight itself creates an impression of motion quite different from the motion of ascending in the elevator.

As we wait for our lift, tourists strike up acquaintance quickly, to trade survival tactics: the price of bread in Rome ("Not $1 per basket, but $1 per *slice*! We died when we got the bill."); the best buys in Florence; and are Italians *friendly*? (This sounds like a really naïve question – unless its purpose is functional – meaning, are they helpful?) But when we board the elevator, we are all impelled into the present moment. As the car's ascent begins, a collective sigh of delight rises. And when we emerge at the top, everyone comes out of the car smiling. The sweep and dimension of my first high view of Paris are perfectly euphoric.

Then we begin looking down and around. "Habitually," writes Barthes,

belvederes are outlooks upon Nature, whose elements – waters, valleys, forests – they assemble beneath them, so that the tourism of the "fine view" infallibly implies a naturist mythology. Whereas the Tower overlooks not Nature but the city; and yet, by its very position of a visited outlook the Tower makes the city into a kind of

Nature; it constitutes the swarming of men into a landscape, it adds to the frequently grim urban myth a romantic dimension, a harmony, a mitigation . . . a new Nature, that of human space.

Sure enough, I hear the people around me seeing Paris as a sensuous mass. One woman says, "I like the colour scheme of the buildings": delicate beiges, cooled reds, ice greens. Her companion adds, "And the roofs are neat, all together from up here", a varied geometry of points and polygons.

But Barthes goes on, "the bliss of sensation does not succeed to elude the questioning nature of the mind". The most absorbing pleasure of the Eiffel Tower – the one I can see absorbing all the people around me, who spend quite a while up here – is the pleasure of *reading* Paris, recognizing familiar landmarks and seeing how they fit together. From wherever you're standing, a keyed photograph of the segment of the view that's facing you identifies the important places. You look out, try to recognize something you know is there, then check yourself with the key. Everyone finds the domes of Sacre Coeur, and the dark swathe of the Bois de Boulogne, and the action off the top of the heliport. Then comes the pleasure of identifying smaller monuments, testing your knowledge of history and current events a bit. And the big challenge is finding your hotel.

A twelve-year-old boy is having a most interesting time by tracing his own passage through Paris. He takes me round to show me where he's been: from the Louvre (look along the river to find it), to the Arc de Triomphe (what a traffic jam!) to his hotel (it's right near a high green steeple). The trick, he explains, is to notice the big places; then you can find the little ones. Meantime, his father is counting the parks and green squares, noticing their relative position: from that, he explains, you can tell a lot about how a city is *used*. I read from Barthes, "the panoramic vision adds an incomparable power of *intellection*: the bird's-eye view, which each visitor to the Tower can assume in an instant for his own, gives us the world to *read* and not only to perceive".

"It gives you a great *feel* for Paris," the boy's father says. For a minute I'm puzzled: feel? But then I see what he's getting at: you can get a feel for it if you know how to read it. The more you knew, the more you could feel, I think; and I experience one of those swoons of exhaustion common to the tourist, thinking of all I'm not getting.

But then, the Tower is a big toy, too. Since it went up, birdmen have used it as a launching pad; acrobats have swung off the top; Alpinists have scaled the sides; and trick cyclists have wheeled down them. It's the perfect setting for a movie chase scene, especially if the pursued one drops his hat. The Tower has been decked out in fairy lights, and was even draped to look like a cathedral to celebrate the end of the Second World War. Artists have depicted it wearing shoes, dancing a jig, standing on its head, made out of playing cards, reduced to its Cubist essence or covered with snow in a Parisian pastorale. The Tower is *available*: there are a minimum of barriers inside it. The only thing you can't do is jump off and commit suicide, because there are railings and light fences to stop you, as the tourist with vertigo gratefully discovers.

Then, as a final act comes the purchase of a souvenir. Now, with new wave fashions, the clothes and knick-knacks suddenly look witty and chic. There's a tee-shirt showing Tweety and Sylvester flying over the Tower, with the ubiquitous legend "J'♥ Paris"; another with Mickey Mouse in a track suit by the Arc de Triomphe, and one with a frog in a beret drinking a bottle of Beaujolais and eating a labelled Camembert with a knife and fork: suffice it to say that, if the ensemble were right, these could be worn to the most expensive discothèque in any capital. Among the crowd at the souvenir boutique is a young man wearing a sweatshirt with the legend "Marc O' Polo" on it: this form of wit, displayed on clothing and signifying a participation in world culture – i.e. tourism – is everywhere now. More handsomely hi-tech, there's a scarf with slender, arrowlike Eiffel Towers crossing it diagonally like slanting rain; and a pink shirt with the letters p, a, r, i, s scattered about, along with reduced, iconographic representations of the Tower. Then there are all the little perfume flasks, thermometers, paperweights replicating the Tower. One heavy paperweight shows a kind of schematic Paris: Sacre Coeur, the Arc de Triomphe, and the Tower of course, with the Seine winding amongst them, calling to mind the flasks the ancient Romans bought at Baiae.

In the end, I buy myself a pair of earrings: one of them will go well with one of another pair I bought lately – hot-pink triangles bought at a craft market near my home in the south, where I was told they had been brought back from Bali. . . . And, of course, there are the postcards: always popular, more popular than ever since the recent advent of "art" postcards. From my researches, I know that the picture postcard industry was a French innovation; it began in 1889, and the very first issue bore a picture of the Eiffel Tower.

Before I leave, I must ask the dreaded question: Why do people come to see the Eiffel Tower – though in these days of wry hyper-self-awareness, what kind of "truth" can be hoped for? Yet, so modernistically, in the demystified mode of having nothing to hide, the answer turns out to be as obvious as Andy Warhol's soup can. "It's a tourist thing to do," says the man who admired the rooftop ensemble, eyeing me suspiciously for asking such a question; "I've been to Paris dozens of times and I always come."

"Are you kidding?" answers a woman cheerfully. "Because we're *tourists*. We've seen all the out-of-the-way places on other trips. This trip, we're just doing touristy things."

Another lady says, first off, "When you think of Paris, you think of the Eiffel Tower." *Then*, they go on to praise the view.

I leave the Tower with a feeling of affection. In the near-century it's been standing here, it has generously offered itself to so many uses, and now I have used it, too: hunted and found the post-modern tourist. I am standing now regarding it from the Champs de Mars, which unfurl before the Tower like a green, flower-bordered carpet, its triangularly sculpted yew trees echoing (deliberately?) the Tower's form; while, on the grass, tourists and lovers loll about. Paris is still a gracious city, I think magnanimously; no wonder people buy little Eiffel Tower effigies to remember it by.

But my trip goes on a little longer. I decide to take myself out to a well-known and expensive restaurant; I have five hours until my train leaves. The lunch is good, but overpriced: I've paid for the "ambience" of Gay Nineties gilding and frescoes and over-solicitous waiters like a . . . stupid tourist.

To sober myself, I go for a walk near the Gare de Lyon, down the busy Rue St Antoine. This time, there's no ambience at all, because the ensemble is dominated by a deafening pneumatic drill: *that's* urban life really. Mostly to escape the noise, I duck into the Hôtel de Sully, a handsome old building with a Renaissance maze of low hedges in the courtyard and, this day, an exhibition of medieval religious art from the Morvan region of Burgundy. Resolutely, I try to make myself equal to this chance discovery of something little-known and beautiful out of the past. Of course, it *is* beautiful. Or is it? Is it just more images of fear and suffering, designed to enslave? Worse, is it second rate? I haven't the power at this moment to "decipher" the exhibition, to use Barthes's favoured verb. Still, dutifully, I take a short stroll through.

A handsomely dressed couple appears in the entranceway. They glance in and frown, "C'est trop petit." I think indignantly: Such spoiled people! What has being small got to do with it? But I still don't get much out of the exhibition myself.

Outside, at least, the drill has let go of the city for the moment. Gratefully, I stop for a last coffee, and then board the train for home. I doze in my place for about an hour, and when I wake up the light is just turning golden – and we're going through the Morvan. It's beautiful, a landscape of steep hills with small copses and silvery white cows and hamlets of rosy-stoned, slate-roofed houses. *Now* it is interesting to remember the painted madonnas and carved stone crosses from the exhibition.

I get home – as all tourists eventually must – by midnight. Exhilarated by motion, I am looking around my house with new eyes for the moment: Southeast Asian batik covering one wall, juxtaposed with a framed page from an eighteenth-century herbal; a collage of postcards; a local straw basket for shopping hung from the doorknob. The little Eiffel Tower earrings suspended from a tiny nail like a pair of miniature bells will add a barely discernible high note, a little joke – but I should stop, I'm home now.

Postscript

As epochs rise and fall, the tourist goes around in cycles, too. It's the same world, but his view of it changes. Now he wants to behold something sacred; now something informative, to broaden him; now something beautiful, to lift him up and make him finer; and now something just different, because he's bored.

He travels also for the possibility of living differently, in his small time away from "real life": to cut loose from the restraints of routine, or of city living, or of living with people who know him; to prove himself, by scaling an Alp or by deciphering a Paris Métro plan; to take life in instead of putting out a product; and, simply, to perform the ritual of covering ground.

As the McLuhanesque global village of communications media gets bigger and more elaborate, the passive functions of tourism (i.e. *seeing*) can be performed right at home, with video, books, records, TV. Now there is even the Sony Walkman, the portable tapedeck· with headphones to enable the anti-tourist to remain in a place of his choice mentally while he is physically travelling around. The ultimate anti-tourist was surely Huysman's protagonist Des Esseintes in *Against Nature*, who virtually locked himself in his own house, its décor culled from all the world's culture and arranged according to the dictates of his personal fantasy, where he went around and around in the universe of his own imagination: a kind of *dernier cri* of the simulated environment. With all the cries against tourist blight, it might be argued that we should all use our leisure in emulation of Des Esseintes instead of in being tourists and going around despoiling other people's places.

Still, the outward-bound tourist persists in going around, if only because "man was created to move, as birds to fly". As Homer and Mabel had much in common with the ancient Roman tourist, and as the Romantic was a kind of pilgrim who travelled to immerse himself in an irreducible essence that was closer to the sacred, so it might be proposed that the post-tourist is, or has the possibility to be, a cousin of the Elizabethan: a bright-eyed modernist who wants to see "reality" (Homer's favourite word – though the post-modern tourist might use the word more . . . stylishly) in context.

His eye, as he traverses a landscape or a cityscape, can pick up the classic beauty and Romantic uniqueness of natural forms, and on the geometric complexities and even the jazzlike discordances of industrial forms and decompositions: there is a variety of aesthetic contexts available. He has a humorous eye for "kitsch", as well: when he buys his miniature replica of the Eiffel Tower, he can enjoy it as a piece of geometric formalism, as a socially revealing artefact, in the old-fashioned way – or as all three. Yet, unlike the reader of *USA en Jeans*, he need not make a fetish out of it. It's playful.

Freed from the Romantic straining after high moments, he can enjoy the connective tissue between "attractions" as much as the vaunted attractions themselves. The 87 bus ride across Paris makes an excellent tour of the city; and the elevator ride up the Eiffel Tower has a naturally dramatic sequence which Thomas Cook himself would have been proud to contrive. The world's a stage, and the post-modern tourist is less dependent on the tourist industry to stage events for him. But his consummate view, perhaps, whether examining an ensemble of old walls and new movie posters or overlooking *tout Paris*, is the bird's-eye-view of the intellect, the overview, connections in context. If, on holiday, the tourist can relax enough to take pleasure in that exercise, it should make a particularly restful escape from the bombardment of fragments that makes up ordinary work-life. These techniques could make nice souvenirs to take home, too.

Unlike his predecessors Homer and Mabel, the post-tourist does not imagine a tour wherein he will not be waiting in line or puzzling over schedules or exchange rates: the glossy tourist brochure full of colourful promises is an interesting piece of pop culture, maybe, but not "reality". By the same token, the post-tourist knows all about the ethos of "little places" to eat or stay or explore. He must be aware of the social implications of tourism to *really* little places like the By

River in the golden triangle of Thailand; and conversely of what it means to blow a day's wages on lunch in Paris.

Above all, though, the post-tourist knows that he is a tourist: not a time traveller when he goes somewhere historic; not an instant noble savage when he stays on a tropical beach; not an invisible observer when he visits a native compound. Resolutely "realistic", he cannot evade his condition of outsider. But, having embraced that condition, he can stop struggling against it and, in the Japanese mode of paradox, which gave Homer and Mabel such a headache, then he can turn it around.

Sources

Addison, Joseph, *Letters*, ed. Walter Graham (Oxford: Clarendon Press, 1941)
   Remarks on Italy (London: J. Tonson, 1726)
Amfitheatrov, Eric, *The Enchanted Ground* (Boston: Little, Brown, 1980)
Andrieux, Maurice, *Daily Life in Venice in the Time of Casanova*, trans. Mary Fitton (London: Allen & Unwin, 1972)
Armstrong, Martin, *Lady Hester Stanhope* (London: Gerald Howe, 1927)
Auget, Roland, *Cruelty and Civilization: The Roman Games* (London: Allen & Unwin, 1952)
Bacon, Francis, "Of Travel", in *The Essays* (London: Dent, 1972)
Balsdon, J. P. V. D., *Life and Leisure in Ancient Rome* (London: Bodley Head, 1969)
Barthes, Roland, "The Eiffel Tower", in *A Barthes Reader*, ed. Susan Sontag (London: Fontana, 1983)
Bates, E. S., *Touring in 1600* (London: Constable, 1911)
Bathe, Basil W., *Seven Centuries of Sea Travel* (London: Barrie & Jenkins, 1972)
Baumgarten, Martin, *The Travels of Martin Baumgarten* (London: Churchill, 1732)
Beckford, William, *Italy, Spain, and Portugal* (London: Richard Bentley, 1840)
Beebe, Lucius, *The Big Spenders* (London: Hutchinson, 1966)
Beyle, Henri, *Rome, Naples, and Florence in 1817* (London: Henry Colburn, 1818)
Blanch, Lesley, *Under a Lilac-Bleeding Star* (London: John Murray, 1963)

Blessington, Countess Marguerite, *The Idler in France* (London: Henry Colburn, 1841)

    The Idler in Italy (London: Henry Colburn, 1839)

    Journal of a Tour through the Netherlands (London: Longman, Hurst, Rees, Orme, & Brown, 1842)

Bocca, Geoffrey, *Bikini Beach* (London: W. H. Allen, 1963)

Boorstein, Daniel, *The Image* (Harmondsworth: Penguin Books, 1961)

Borde, Andrew, *The First Boke of the Introduction of Knowledge* (London: N. Trubner, 1870)

Boswell, James, *Boswell in Holland*, ed. Frederick Pottle (London: Heinemann, 1952)

    Boswell on the Grand Tour: Germany and Switzerland, ed. Frederick Pottle (London: Heinemann, 1953)

    Boswell on the Grand Tour: Italy, France, and Corsica, ed. Frederick Pottle (London: Heinemann, 1955)

Bowle, John E., *John Evelyn and His World* (London: Routledge & Kegan Paul, 1981)

Braudel, Fernand, *The Structures of Everyday Life*, trans. Sian Reynolds (London: Collins, 1981)

Brinnin, John Malcolm, *The Sway of the Grand Saloon* (London: Macmillan, 1972)

Burgess, Anthony, and Francis Haskell, *The Age of the Grand Tour* (London: Paul Elek, 1967)

Burkhardt, A. J., and Medlik, S. A., *Tourism Past, Present, and Future* (London: Heinemann, 1974)

Byron, Lord George Gordon, *Byron, a Self Portrait*, ed. Peter Quennel (London: John Murray, 1950)

Campbell, Harriet Charlotte Beaujolais, *A Journey to Florence in 1817* (London: Geoffrey Bles, 1951)

Casson, Lionel, *Travel in the Ancient World* (London: Allen & Unwin, 1974)

Chesterfield, Earl of, *Letters to His Son* (London: Dent, 1929)

Collis, Louise, *The Apprentice Saint* (London: Michael Joseph, 1964)

Collison-Morley, Lacey, *Italy after the Renaissance* (London: Routledge, 1930)

Cook, Thomas & Son, *ABC Programmes: Short, Cheap, and Easy Tours* (London: Thomas Cook & Son, 1973)

    The Excursionist, various editions

Coryate, Thomas, *Coryate's Crudities* (Glasgow: James Maclehose, 1905)

Cowell, Frank R., *Everyday Life in Ancient Rome* (London: Batsford, 1961)

Craven, Countess Elizabeth, *The Beautiful Lady Craven*, ed. A. M. Broadley and L. Melville (London: John Lane, 1914)

Croall, Thomas, *A Book about Travelling* (London: William P. Nimmo, 1877)

Dangerfield, Elma, *Byron and the Romantics in Switzerland* (London: Ascent Books, 1978)

D'Arms, John, *Romans on the Bay of Naples* (Cambridge, Mass.: Harvard Press, 1970)

Davidson, Lilias Campbell, *Hints to Lady Travellers* (London: Iliffe, 1889)

Dickens, Charles, *Pictures from Italy* (London: Chapman & Hall, 1846)

Dodwell, Edward, *A Tour through Greece* (London: Rodwell & Martin, 1819)

Doran, J., *Mann and Manners in the Court of Florence* (London: Bentley, 1876)

Durant, Will, *The Renaissance* (New York: Simon & Schuster, 1951)

Edwards, Amelia, *A Thousand Miles up the Nile* (London: Longmans Green, 1877)

Evelyn, John, *Diary*, ed. E. S. de Beer (London: Oxford University Press, 1959)

Fabri, Felix, *Wanderings in the Holy Land* (London: Palestine Pilgrim's Text Society, 1897)

Fagan, Brian M., *The Rape of the Nile* (New York: Scribner's, 1975)

Finucane, Roland C., *Miracles and Pilgrims* (London: Dent, 1977)

Fitzgerald, F. Scott, *Tender is the Night* (Harmondsworth: Penguin Books, 1955)

Flaubert, Gustave, *Letters*, ed. Francis Steegmuller (Cambridge, Mass.: Harvard Press, 1980)

Fleming, George, *A Nile Novel* (London: Macmillan, 1877)

Forney, John, *Letters from Europe* (Philadelphia: T. B. Peterson, 1867)

Fothergill, Brian, *Beckford of Fonthill* (London: Faber, 1979)

Franco, Victor, *The Club Mediterannée* (London: Shepheard Walwyn, 1972)

Frazer, Sir James G., *Pausanias* (London: Macmillan, 1900)

Friedlander, Ludwig, *Roman Life and Manners under the Early Empire* (London: Routledge & Kegan Paul, 1965)

Fuller, Ronald, *Hellfire Francis* (London: Chatto & Windus, 1939)

Gailhard, J., *Directions for the Education of Youth Travelling Abroad* (London: Savoy, 1678)

Geikie, Sir Archibald, *The Love of Nature among the Romans* (London: John Murray, 1912)

Gell, Sir William, *Sir William Gell in Italy*, ed. Edith Clay (London: Hamish Hamilton, 1976)

Gentleman, A, *Pocket Companion for Travelling into Foreign Parts* (London: 1722)

Goethe, Johann W., *Italian Journey*, trans. W. H. Auden and Elizabeth Meyer (Harmondsworth: Penguin Books, 1970)

Graves, Charles, *Royal Riviera* (London: Heinemann, 1957)

Gray, Francine du Plessix, "On Safari", in *New York Review of Books*, 28 June 1973

Grylls, R. Glynn, *Claire Clairmont* (London: John Murray, 1939)

Guest, Anthony Haden-, *Down the Programmed Rabbit Hole* (London: Hart-Davis, MacGibbon, 1972)

Guide des U.S.A. en Jeans (Paris: Hachette, 1976)

Harff, Arnold von, *The Pilgrimage of Arnold von Harff* (Glasgow: University Press, 1946)

Henderson, Bernard, *The Life and Principate of the Emperor Hadrian* (London: Methuen, 1923)

    The Life and Principate of the Emperor Nero (London: Methuen, 1903)

Hibbert, Christopher, *The Grand Tour* (London: Spring Books, 1974)

Hobhouse, John C., *A Journey through Albania* (London: James Cawthorne, 1813)

Howard, Clare, *English Travellers of the Renaissance* (London: John Lane, 1914)

Howard, Donald R., *Writers and Pilgrims* (Berkeley, Calif.: University of California Press, 1980)

Howarth, Patrick, *When the Riviera Was Ours* (London: Routledge & Kegan Paul, 1977)

Howell, James, *Instructions for Forraine Travel* (London: Humphrey Mosley, 1642)

Hudson, Kenneth, *Air Travel, a Social History* (Somerset: Adams & Dart, 1972)

Hughes, Charles, *Shakespeare's Europe* (London: Sherratt & Hughes, 1903)

Jenkins, Alan, *The Twenties* (London: Heinemann, 1974)

Josephson, Matthew, *Stendhal* (Garden City, NY: Doubleday, 1946)

Jusserand, J. A., *English Wayfaring Life in the Middle Ages*, trans. Lucie T. Smith (London: Benn, 1950)

Kemble, Fanny, *Further Records* (London: Richard Bentley, 1890)

Kirkup, James, *These Horned Islands* (London: Collins, 1962)

    Tokyo (London: Phoenix House, 1966)

Lassells, Richard, *An Italian Voyage* (London: Richard Wellington, 1698)

Lauder, John, *Journals*, ed. Donald Crawford, volume 6 Scottish History Society (Edinburgh: University Press, 1900)

Laver, James, *The Age of Illusion* (London: Weidenfeld & Nicolson, 1972)

Lees-Milne, James, *Earls of Creation* (London: Hamish Hamilton, 1962)

Lenoir, Paul, *The Fayoum* (London: Henry S. King, 1873)

Lever, Charles, *The Dodd Family Abroad* (London: Chapman & Hall, 1872)

    Upon Men, Women, and Things in General (London: Chapman & Hall, 1872)

Lindsay, Jack, *Men and Gods on the Roman Nile* (London: Frederick Muller, 1968)

Lithgow, William, *Rare Adventures and Painful Peregrinations* (London: Jonathan Cape, 1928)

Lochsberg, Winifred, *History of Travel* (Leipzig: Edition Leipzig, 1979)

Loftie, W. J., *A Ride in Egypt* (London: Macmillan, 1879)

MacCannell, Earle Dean, *The Tourist, a New Theory of the Leisure Class* (London: Macmillan, 1976)

Madden, R. R., *Literary Life and Correspondence of the Countess of Blessington* (London: T. C. Newby, 1855)

Mandeville, Sir John, *The Travels of Sir John Mandeville* (London: Dent, 1928)

Marlowe, John, *The Golden Age of Alexandria* (London: Gollancz, 1971)

Massingham, Hugh and Pauline, *The Englishman Abroad* (London: Phoenix House, 1962)

Michell, H., *Sparta* (Cambridge: University Press, 1952)

Middleton, Dorothy, *Victorian Lady Travellers* (London: Routledge & Kegan Paul, 1965)

Miller, Helen Hill, *Greece through the Ages* (London: Dent, 1972)

Mirsky, Jeanette, *The Great Chinese Travellers* (London: Allen & Unwin, 1965)

Montagu, Lady Mary Wortley, *Letters* (London: Dent, 1906)

Montaigne, Michel de, *The Diary of Montaigne's Journey to Italy*, trans. E. J. Trenchman (London: Hogarth Press, 1929)

    Travels, trans. and ed. W. G. Waters (London: John Murray, 1903)

Morrell, Jemima, *Miss Jemima's Swiss Journal* (London: Putnam & Sons, 1963)

Moryson, Fynes, *Itinerary* (Glasgow: James Maclehose, 1907)

Moynahan, Brian, *Airport International* (London: Macmillan, 1978)

Mullins, Edwin, *Pilgrimage to Santiago* (London: Secker & Warburg, 1974)

Murray, John, *Egypt*, seventh edition (London: John Murray, 1888)
   Handbook for Travellers in Northern Italy, eleventh edition (London: John Murray, 1869)
   Handbook for Visitors to Paris (London: John Murray, 1862)

Nash, Thomas, *The Unfortunate Traveller* (London: T. Burby, 1594)

Newett, Margaret M., *Canon Pietro Casola's Pilgrimage to Jerusalem* (Manchester: University Press, 1907)

Newton, Arthur P., *Travel and Travellers in the Middle Ages* (London: Kegan Paul, 1926)

Nugent, Thomas, *The Grand Tour* (London: 1778)

Osborn, James M., *Young Philip Sidney* (New Haven, Conn.: Yale University Press, 1972)

Owen, Charles, *The Grand Days of Travel* (Exeter: Webb & Bower, 1979)

Page, Martin, *The Lost Pleasures of the Great Trains* (London: Weidenfeld & Nicolson, 1975)

Palestine Pilgrim's Text Society, *The Library of the Palestine Pilgrim's Text Society* (London: 1894)

Pan American Airways, *Total Travel Planners* (New York: Bantam, 1973)

Parks, George B., *The English Traveller in Italy* (Rome: Edizioni di Storia e Litteratura, 1954)

Paston, George, *Lady Mary Wortley Montagu and Her Times* (London: Methuen, 1907)

Pausanias, *Guide to Greece* (Harmondsworth: Penguin Books, 1971)

Pfeiffer, Ida, *A Lady's Voyage Round the World* (London: Longman, Brown, Green, & Longmans, 1851)

Plimlott, J. A. R., *The Englishman's Holiday* (London: Faber, 1947)

Pliny the Younger, *Letters of the Younger Pliny* (Harmondsworth: Penguin Books, 1963)

Plumb, J. H., *The Renaissance* (London: Collins, 1961)

Polnay, Peter de, *A Door Ajar* (London: Robert Hale, 1959)

Prescott, H. F. M., *Jerusalem Journey* (London: Eyre & Spottiswoode, 1954)

Pudney, John, *The Thomas Cook Story* (London: Michael Joseph, 1953)

Quennel, Peter, *Byron in Italy* (London: Collins, 1941)
   John Ruskin (London: Collins, 1949)

Rowling, Marjorie, *Everyday Life of Medieval Travellers* (London: Batsford, 1971)

Ruskin, John, *The Stones of Venice* (Orpington: George Allen, 1881)

Sadler, Michael, *Blessington-d'Orsay, a Masquerade* (London: Constable, 1933)

Schivelbusch, Wolfgang, *The Railway Journey*, trans. Anselm Hollo (Oxford: Blackwell, 1977)

Sells, A. Lytton, *A Paradise of Travellers* (London: Allen & Unwin, 1964)

Seneca, *Letters from a Stoic*, trans. Robin Campbell (Harmondsworth: Penguin Books, 1969)

Sharp, Samuel, *Letters from Italy* (London: Henry & Cave, 1767)

Shelley, Mary W., *History of a Six-Weeks' Tour* (London: Hookham & Ollier, 1817)

   Letters of Mary W. Shelley (Norman, Okla.: University of Oklahoma Press, 1944)

Shelley, Percy B., *Letters*, ed. Frederick L. Jones (Oxford: Clarendon Press, 1964)

Sigaux, Gilbert, *History of Tourism*, trans. Joan White (London: Leisure Arts, 1966)

Sketchley, Arthur, *Mrs Brown on the Grand Tour* (London: Routledge, 1870)

   Out for a Holiday with Cook's Excursion through Switzerland and Italy (London: Routledge, 1870)

Smith, Logan Pearsall, *The Life and Letters of Sir Henry Wotton* (Oxford: Clarendon Press, 1907)

Smith, Valene, *Hosts and Guests* (Oxford: Blackwell, 1978)

Smithers, Peter, *The Life of Joseph Addison* (Oxford: Clarendon Press, 1954)

Smollett, Tobias, *Travels through France and Italy* (London: Oxford Press, 1907)

Sontag, Susan, *On Photography* (London: Allen Lane, 1978)

Stephen, Sir Leslie, *The Playground of Europe* (London: Longmans Green 1899)

Sterne, Laurence, *A Sentimental Journey* (Harmondsworth: Penguin Books, 1967)

Stowe, Harriet Beecher, *Sunny Memories* (London: Samson & Low, 1854)

Strachan, Michael, *The Life and Adventures of Thomas Coryate* (London: Oxford University Press, 1962)

Suetonius, *The Twelve Caesars*, trans. H. M. Bird (Chicago: Argus Books, 1930)

Sumption, Jonathan, *Pilgrimage* (London: Faber, 1975)

Swinglehurst, Edmund, *The Romantic Journey* (London: Pica Editions, 1974)

Theroux, Paul, *The Great Railway Bazaar* (London: Hamish Hamilton, 1975)

Thompson, J. W., *The Frankfurt Book Fair* (Chicago: The Caxton Club, 1911)

Titmarsh, M. A. (William Makepeace Thackeray), *The Kickleburys on the Rhine* (London: Smith Elder, 1866)

Tomkins, Calvin, *Living Well Is the Best Revenge* (London: André Deutsch, 1972)

Torkington, Richard, *Ye Oldest Diarie of Englysshe Travel* (London: Field & Tuer, 1884)

Trease, Robert G., *The Grand Tour* (London: Heinemann, 1967)

Treatise Concerning the Education of Youth (London: J. Starkey, 1678)

Tregaskis, Hugh, *Beyond the Grand Tour* (London: Ascent Books, 1979)

Trollope, Frances, *The Robertses on Their Travels* (London: 1846)

Turner, Louis, and John Ashe, *The Golden Hordes* (London: Constable, 1975)

Twain, Mark, *Innocents Abroad* (New York: Harper & Brothers, 1869)

    A Tramp Abroad (London: Chatto & Windus, 1925)

Vaussard, Maurice, *Daily Life in Eighteenth-Century Italy*, trans. Michael Heron (London: Allen & Unwin, 1962)

Verax, Viator, *Cautions for the First Tour* (London: J. Ridgeway, 1863)

Walpole, Horace, *Letters* (Oxford: Clarendon Press, 1903)

Waugh, Evelyn, *Labels* (London: Duckworth, 1930)

Wethered, H. Newton, *The Four Paths of Pilgrimage* (London: Frederick Muller, 1947)

Wey, William, *The Itineraries of William Wey* (London: J. B. Nichols, 1842)

Woon, Basil, *The Frantic Atlantic* (New York: Knopf, 1927)

Young, Arthur, *Travels in France and Italy* (London: Dent, 1927)

Young, Sir George, *Tourism, Blessing or Blight?* (Harmondsworth: Penguin Books, 1973)

Numerous articles from *The Daily Telegraph*, *The Economist*, *Fortune*, the *Guardian*, *The New York Times*, *Nova*, *The Observer*, the *Spectator*, *The Sunday Times*, *The Times*, *Vogue*, the *Wall Street Journal*, and other publications.

Index